The Philosophy of
Sri Chinmoy

Explorations in Indic Traditions:
Theological, Ethical, and Philosophical

Series Editor: Jeffery D. Long, Elizabethtown College

Advisory Board

Purushottama Bilimoria, Christopher Key Chapple, Jonathan Gold, Pankaj Jain, Nathan Katz, Kusumita P. Pedersen, and Rita D. Sherma

The region historically known as the Indian subcontinent (and more recently as South Asia) is rich with ancient and sophisticated traditions of intellectual and contemplative investigation. This includes both indigenous traditions (Hindu, Buddhist, Jain, and Sikh) and traditions that have found a home in this region (Islamic, Christian, Jewish, and Zoroastrian). This series is devoted to studies rooted in critical and constructive methodologies (such as ethics, philosophy, and theology) that show how these traditions can illuminate universal human questions: questions about the meaning of life, the nature of knowledge, good and evil, and the broader metaphysical context of human existence. A particular focus of this series is the relevance of these traditions to urgent issues that face humanity today—such as the ecological crisis, gender relations, poverty and social inequality, and religiously motivated violence—on the assumption that these traditions, far from being of merely historical interest, have the potential to enrich contemporary conversations and advance human understanding.

Recent Titles in Series

The Philosophy of Sri Chinmoy: Love and Transformation, by Kusumita P. Pedersen
Gandhi and Rajchandra: The Making of the Mahatma, by Uma Majmudar
Swami Vivekananda: His Life, Legacy, and Liberative Ethics, edited by Rita D. Sherma
Beacons of Dharma, edited by Jeffery D. Long, Michael Reading, Christopher Miller
Thinking with the Yogasutra of Patanjali: Translation and Interpretation, edited by
    Christopher Key Chapple and Ana Funes Maderey
The Metaphysics of Paradox: Jainism, Absolute Relativity, and Religious Pluralism, by
    Wm. Andrew Schwartz
Digital Hinduism: Dharma and Discourse in the Age of New Media, edited by Murali Balaji
Sri Chaitanya's Life and Teachings: The Golden Avatara of Divine Love, by Steven Rosen
Shakti's New Voice: Guru Devotion in a Woman-Led Spiritual Movement, by Angela Rudert
The Vedantic Relationality of Rabindranath Tagore: Harmonizing the One and its Many,
    by Ankur Barua

The Philosophy of Sri Chinmoy

Love and Transformation

Kusumita P. Pedersen

LEXINGTON BOOKS
Lanham • Boulder • New York • London

Published by Lexington Books
An imprint of The Rowman & Littlefield Publishing Group, Inc.
4501 Forbes Boulevard, Suite 200, Lanham, Maryland 20706
www.rowman.com

86-90 Paul Street, London EC2A 4NE

British Library Cataloguing in Publication Information Available

Library of Congress Cataloging-in-Publication Data

Names: Pedersen, Kusumita Priscilla, 1946- author.
Title: The philosophy of Sri Chinmoy : love and transformation / Kusumita P. Pedersen.
Description: Lanham : Lexington Books, [2021] | Series: Explorations in Indic traditions : theological, ethical, and philosophical | Includes bibliographical references and index.
Identifiers: LCCN 2021020618 (print) | LCCN 2021020619 (ebook) | ISBN 9781793618986 (cloth) | ISBN 9781793618993 (epub) | ISBN 9781793619006 (pbk)
Subjects: LCSH: Chinmoy, Sri, 1931-2007. | Spiritual life. | Yoga. | Meditation. | Religious leaders—India—Biography.
Classification: LCC BP610.C552 P43 2021 (print) | LCC BP610.C552 (ebook) | DDC 294.5092—dc23
LC record available at https://lccn.loc.gov/2021020618
LC ebook record available at https://lccn.loc.gov/2021020619

For Sri Chinmoy
with deepest Gratitude

Contents

Preface

My first and greatest expression of gratitude is to Sri Chinmoy, the subject of this study and my spiritual teacher since 1971. He affirmed my undertaking to write about his philosophy and through the years I was able to ask him questions; on occasion he read what I had written and commented on it. In countless other ways his guidance and example has deepened my understanding. What I owe to him can never be adequately stated.

I offer deep thanks to friends and colleagues Purushottama Bilimoria, Christopher Key Chapple, Rajinder and Jyoti Gandhi, Veena Howard, Kazi Nurul Islam, Gerald James Larson, Jeffery D. Long, Christopher Patrick Miller, Rama Rao Pappu, Joseph Prabhu, Michael Reading, Rita D. Sherma, Mary Evelyn Tucker, and Franz Wöhrer, all of whom have given support and useful comments. Many of my fellow students of Sri Chinmoy have offered encouragement and at times have read parts of this work, providing important input. These include Kakali Atkin, Paree Atkin, Chandini Bachman, Vidagdha Bennett, Chidananda Burke, Devakripa Cohen, Nemi Fredner, Bhitihara Fulton, Ashrita Furman, Ranjana Ghose, Nayana Hein, Radha Honig, Prema Jackson, Paramita Jarvis, Adhiratha Keefe, Rupantar LaRusso, Shatapatri Mahar, Pragati Pascale, Swarnodaya Plumbly, Brahmacharini Michelle Rebidoux, Satyajit Saha, Nilima Silver, Ranjit Swanson, Sahishnu Szczesiul, Bhikshuni Weisbrot, Salil Wilson, and Tahereh Ziaian.

The Sri Chinmoy Library website has been indispensable. I am immensely indebted to those who have created it and maintain it with great expertise and dedication. Without this essential resource, this work could not possibly have reached its present form.

The purpose of this book is to offer a straightforward, accurate, and unembroidered account of Sri Chinmoy's philosophy, with much of the exposition given in his own words. This being said, there can be no finally definitive account as his works are vast, rich and profound, multi-dimensional and created over a span of some sixty years. This study brings together and seeks to integrate discipleship and scholarship, and thus can be called a work of theology. I offer it hoping to be of service to those who seek insight into the subjects Sri Chinmoy treats in his philosophy—in the primary and ancient sense of "the love of wisdom"—and to learn about his unique vision and understanding of these subjects: God, creation, evolution, the soul, knowledge through yoga, love of God, love for the world, and transformation.

Chapter 1

From Shakpura to the World

A CHILD IN CHITTAGONG

In East Bengal the Karnaphuli River flows southwest down from the Chittagong Hill Tracts, becoming broad and swift before it enters the Bay of Bengal forming a wide and deep harbor. For twenty centuries the port city of Chittagong, at the easternmost point of the Ganges-Brahmaputra Delta, has been a center of trade and a crossroads between the West, India, and Southeast Asia. The larger region of the Bay of Bengal has been for millennia a site of cultural, economic, and ecological interchange.[1] Like many maritime hubs, Chittagong, also called Chattogram, has long been home to a diversity of ethnicities and religions including Hinduism, Buddhism, Islam, the Sikh religion, and Christianity.[2] Natives of the area speak the Chittagonian dialect or Catgāla Buli,[3] while using standard Bengali in writing and education. In the first half of the twentieth century Chittagong was a thriving multi-cultural city of 200,000.[4]

The village of Shakpura lies on the southern bank of the Karnaphuli in a fertile agricultural area. Here Chinmoy Kumar Ghosh was born in 1931,[5] the youngest of seven children in a prosperous and well-educated Hindu family.[6] His father, Shashi Kumar, was born in 1882, and went to work as a young man for the Assam Bengal Railway. Beginning as an ordinary officer, he rose to become the Chief Inspector of the entire line at a time when the British did not normally promote Indians to such high positions. In his late twenties he married Yogamaya Bishwas, twelve years younger, from the village of Kelishahar five and a half miles away from Shakpura. In the mid-1930s he retired from the railway and opened a bank, the Griha Lakshmi, in the city of Chittagong. During the week he would stay in town and spend weekends back in the village, commuting across the river by ferryboat. Shashi Kumar

1

was a leading citizen, head of the Shakpura village council, and an honorary judge in a district court, the benefactor of friends as well as relatives and an advisor to many. Over twenty years, he and Yogamaya had four sons and three daughters. Their youngest child had been given the name Ganapati at birth based on his horoscope, but was called "Madal" by everyone. A *madal* is an Indian drum[7] and the child received this nickname because he was lively and mischievous. He was given the name Chinmoy Kumar in 1936 by Chitta, his second oldest brother.

The family home in East Shakpura, not far from a ferry across the Karnaphuli, was an ample two-story house on spacious grounds. In front there was a grove of many mango, guava, and other fruit trees and in the rear several ponds. A guest house, servants' quarters and other buildings included a temple dedicated to Lakshmi. Madal attended the village school, where both teachers and students included Muslims, Hindus, and Buddhists;[8] he and his brother Manoranjan, or "Mantu," only three years older, were also taught at home by a tutor. He spent his childhood in an unspoiled rural setting of great natural beauty. He could easily visit relatives in the neighboring villages and roamed freely in nearby fields and woods, and in the wild forested mountains further off. Images from his communion with nature permeate the poetry he later wrote prolifically: the sky, sun, moon and stars; dawn and evening; rainbows; the flight of birds; the flow of rivers and boats that travel on them; trees and the germination of a seed which grows into a plant, then a tree bearing blossoms and fruit. He was a skilled tree climber and would go up to collect mangos or other fruits to eat himself and also to bring down and give to others— an image he often used in later years as a simile for God-realization and God-manifestation.[9]

When he became older, he would at times prevail on his father to let him go with him into the city of Chittagong, and while Shashi Kumar and Chitta were at work the bank messenger would take him around the city on the back of his bicycle. His favorite pastimes were to go down to the harbor to see the boats and ships and to visit the majestic Chittagong High Court where he observed the accused criminals and listened to the trial proceedings with fascination. During these years Madal was the much-loved youngest child in a large extended family, embedded in its thick fabric of relationships with all of its joys, sorrows, human dramas, and ties of intense affection.

His childhood was deeply nourishing and fulfilling. A poem written four decades later says, "Every day I water Heaven / With the tears of my heart / So that I can live / My beautiful, soulful / And powerful childhood / Once again."[10] He also writes,

I remember …
My mother loved me, her world.

My father loved me, his dream.
My home loved me, its 'supreme.'

I remember …
I prayed with the blooming dawn,
I played with the glowing sun.
My life, the nectar-fun.

I remember …
I sang with the twinkling stars,
I danced with the floating moon,
All lost, alas, too soon.

 I remember, I remember, I remember.[11]

He also reflects on how a love that is all-embracing can begin with our earliest and most intimate relationships and our identification with what is closest to us—and then grow larger and larger, becoming universal yet not losing the particular. He says,

> When I was born, my whole world was my father and mother. Then, when I grew a little older, my tiny village of East Shakpura was my whole world. Then my city, Chittagong, my province, East Bengal, and my country, India, became my whole world. Each time I became more awakened or developed, my consciousness expanded. … From our home, we expand to claim the entire world. … I cannot say I have lost my love for India or East Bengal or Chittagong or Shakpura. … I am only expanding, expanding my heart. … Until we can claim the whole world as our own, very own, with our love-power, we will have no peace. … It is love that unites us, and that love is inside the heart. … Only in the expansion of love do we find peace.[12]

As a child he not only knew deep particular affections but also experienced great bereavement and the violence of war. As he grew older and consciously entered the spiritual life, he aspired to go beyond loss and destruction to transformation of the world through the expansion of love and the achievement of peace. This would become his life's work.

He had been born under British rule and between two World Wars which created immense carnage and upheaval. Chittagong was within two concentric historical processes: the conflict of nations and the Indian Independence Movement. The Partition of Bengal in 1905 galvanized popular support for revolutionary organization and East Bengal became a stronghold of the struggle for Indian sovereignty. Peter Heehs notes that the Dhaka Anushilan was "the region's pre-eminent revolutionary *samiti*" or assembly, the headquarters of some 500 groups.[13] A surge of activity in the area culminated in the Chittagong Armory Raid on April 18, 1930, an unsuccessful uprising against the British led by Surya Sen. Sen fled and was later captured, tried, and hanged in 1934, after which the movement in East Bengal was suppressed while Sen became a national hero, revered to this day.[14] The young Chinmoy thus grew up among fresh and dramatic memories of local martyrs to the cause of Indian freedom and was even more connected to these events because Surya Sen was a distant relation, who while in hiding had been harbored by the child's relatives, some of whom were directly involved in the independence struggle.

Under British rule Bengal had also become the center of a new self-definition of religion, an evolving development of thought and practice that critiqued, defended and reconstructed the understanding of Hinduism. It drew on the study of Vedic texts and other early sources, historical methods introduced by British Orientalists, Western philosophy, native culture, and personal spiritual experience.[15] This decades-long process was marked by the emergence of a number of new movements with reform elements, including the Brahmo Samāj,[16] the Ārya Samāj,[17] and the Ramakrishna Mission.[18] A modern universalist Vedānta was stated in the teachings of the great mystic Sri Ramakrishna (1836–1886), his best known disciple, Swami Vivekananda (1862–1902), and Sri Aurobindo (1872–1950), an England-educated revolutionary, poet, yogi, and one of the most prominent Indian philosophers of the twentieth century. All three were originally from Kolkata and became known throughout Bengal and all over India.

The Ghosh family were devout orthodox Hindus, observing religious festivals and other practices in a traditional manner and engaging the services of a family priest. On many evenings two local Brahmins came to the house to sing the names of Krishna for protection. Wandering Baul musicians would also sometimes appear. In additional to major annual festivals such as Durga Puja and Kali Puja, the visits of traveling theatrical troupes performing *jatra*, the traditional folk theater of Bengal often on religious themes, were a highlight of life in the village. A first cousin of Shashi Kumar became a Vaiṣṇava *sannyāsin* in Navadwip with the name Saradānanada, while a maternal uncle, Ambika Charan Bishwas, was reputed to have supranormal powers bestowed on him by Kali; he was relieved when at times the Goddess withdrew these powers, as then people did not ask him to solve their problems. The whole family venerated Sri Ramakrishna, Sarada Devi and Swami Vivekananda, referring to Sri Ramakrishna as "Thakur," or "the Master." While Shashi Kumar was devoted to Kali, his family's presiding deity, Yogamaya had an affinity for Durga and Krishna. She spent long hours in prayer and meditation and Madal would awake in the morning hearing her chanting the names of Durga. She read to him daily from the Mahābhārata in the melodious poetry of the seventeenth century Bengali rendition of Kashiram Das, and by the time he was six he was sharing stories from the epic with his family and friends. When at age three he had a severe case of smallpox and was not expected to live or, if he survived, to be deaf and blind, Yogamaya bathed him in coconut water and prayed unceasingly and fervently. She attributed his recovery to the power of her prayers, and ever after he fully agreed with her: "I was cured only because of my mother's prayer to God and her concern and affection for me. She saved my life."[19]

Madal, like his siblings, learned to pray at the age of five or six. Each member of the family pursued an inner life of contemplative practice and in this setting the child's spirituality was formed and grew. Many years later he said, when asked when he began his spiritual life, "I have known intuitively, since my early childhood, that there is a deeper Self within me."[20]

THE SRI AUROBINDO ASHRAM

Hriday Ranjan, the oldest child in the family, was a brilliant student with a deep interest in philosophy. After his graduation from Chittagong College, he took a decisive action that would eventually determine the destiny of the entire family. After some years of spiritual search he had concluded that his spiritual teacher was Sri Aurobindo. In 1918 a Sri Aurobindo Center named the Matri Mandir, or Temple of the Mother, had been founded by Mohini Mohan Dutta in his home near Shakpura.[21] Possibly around the same time Manodhar Dasgupta from Comilla was asked by Shashi Kumar to tutor his two oldest sons in English, and according to Mantu it was from him that Hriday and Chitta may first have heard of Sri Aurobindo; Manodhar later became a resident of the Sri Aurobindo Ashram.[22] At the end of 1932, traveling to Pondicherry alone and without his parents' permission, Hriday became a permanent member of the Ashram, having been accepted by the Mother, Mirra Alfassa. He was at this time twenty-one and his youngest brother an infant of only one year and three months. In the summer of 1933 Shashi Kumar brought the entire family to Pondicherry. Although Yogamaya had intended to bring her oldest son back home, when she came to speak with the Mother instead she was moved to ask her to accept all of her children as disciples. To this the Mother assented, and so eventually it came to pass. The family visited again in 1936, 1939, and 1941. On their second visit the Ashram General Secretary, Nolini Kanta Gupta, asked about the youngest child, "What is his real name?" since "Madal" is a nickname. It was then that

Chitta gave him the name "Chinmoy" or "full of consciousness" when, as he later recalled, he heard the name "echoing and re-echoing in my heart."

On September 3, 1939 Britain and France declared war against Germany and on December 7–8, 1941 Japan entered the war, attacking Pearl Harbor and landing on the east coast of Malaysia prepared for assault on Southeast Asia and then on India. Japanese forces advanced rapidly and took Rangoon, Burma in March of 1942.[23] In the next month they began to bomb the city of Chittagong itself. Sri Chinmoy later recalled hiding in caves during air raids and a hole "the size of a swimming pool" made by Japanese bombs in front of his father's bank.[24] Refugees flooded into eastern India and Chittagong became a center of British military operations. A complex set of factors resulted in calamitous food shortages in all of Bengal including Chittagong. Historians estimate that a minimum of two million Indians died in the Bengal Famine of 1943.[25]

Late in 1942 after several months of declining health, Shashi Kumar died. Yogamaya had become gravely ill with goiter and passed away in March 1944. Under the extraordinary circumstances of wartime, at the end of 1943 the Mother gave permission for children to live at the Ashram and the Ashram School was established. In the summer of 1944, Chinmoy, with his brothers and sisters not already there and a few other family members, made the journey from Shakpura to Pondicherry for the last time. They arrived at the Ashram on July 23, about one month before Chinmoy's thirteenth birthday. Chinmoy's six brothers and sisters—Hriday, Chitta, Arpita, Lily, Ahana, and Mantu—remained on the Ashram for the rest of their lives. None ever married; they were a close-knit family of spiritual practitioners.

Here a very brief account may be offered of Sri Aurobindo, the Mother, and the Integral Yoga, although in its brevity it cannot even begin to be adequate to the subject.[26] Aurobindo Ghose was born in 1872, educated in England from the age of seven and completed a First Class degree in Classics at Cambridge University. He returned to India in 1893, the same year that Swami Vivekananda went to America to attend the World Parliament of Religions in Chicago. A scholar of literature knowing several languages and also a poet, Sri Aurobindo soon became a leader of the Independence Movement. He was reunited with the culture of his homeland, learned Bengali and Sanskrit, and plunged into Hindu tradition through study and the practice of yoga. In 1908, he was arrested and imprisoned by the British authorities on charges of terrorism; after one year he was acquitted. He then left British India for French-controlled Pondicherry, where he devoted himself to the spiritual quest on which he was already well advanced, and wrote his major works including *The Life Divine*, *The Synthesis of Yoga*, *Essays on the Gita*, and *Savitri*, a retelling in verse of a story from the Mahābhārata. His spiritual collaborator was Mirra Alfassa of France, a mystic of Sephardic Jewish background, who had first met him in 1914 and resided permanently in Pondicherry from 1920 on. The Integral Yoga is integral as it includes all powers of the human person as the means of spiritual development and realization.[27] Sri Aurobindo states that it is new because it aims "not at a departure out of the world and life into Heaven or Nirvana, but a change of life and existence . . . here the object is the divine fulfillment of life," and moreover not "an individual achievement of divine realization for the sake of the individual, but something to be gained for the earth-consciousness here, a cosmic, not solely a supra-cosmic achievement."[28] The next phase of human evolution is to be the divine fulfillment of life here in this world. Sri Aurobindo wrote his major works in English and draws on Western conceptual language as well as Indian sources and his own spiritual experience as he develops his account of the worldview, norms, and practices of the Integral Yoga.[29]

As soon as he arrived at the Ashram, Chinmoy immersed himself in spiritual practice, meditating intensely for many hours a day. He was now entering his teens. At once there took place, by his own account, a great opening of his inner life with a flood of experiences increasing in height and depth. These led swiftly to samādhi and awareness of union with God. He has described some of these experiences in his autobiographical writings and poems such as "The Absolute," the first lines of which are:

No mind, no form, I only exist;
Now ceased all will and thought,
The final end of Nature's dance,
I am It whom I have sought.[30]

In the following years he would expand and solidify these realizations. He has explained this awakening and attainment as a recovery of what had already been achieved in previous births, saying, "It was like turning the pages of a book that I had already devoured."[31] His profound inner experience and comprehensive spiritual knowledge is the main source of the philosophy later articulated in his large body of writings. He prioritizes spiritual experience epistemologically and his expression is formed accordingly, seeking to describe and affirm rather than to demonstrate formally or argue the points he wishes to make.[32]

In his writings he draws from the works of Sri Aurobindo and also from Sri Ramakrishna and Swami Vivekananda, with whom his family felt a strong connection as mentioned, and whose influence also permeated the life of the Ashram.[33] Sri Chinmoy powerfully affirms the worldview of these immediate forebears, and like them he looks to the Upaniṣads and the Bhagavad Gītā as fountainheads of Indian tradition. Allowing for differences of style and vocabulary, as well as areas of special focus, we may say that this shared worldview includes the following features: a concept of the Divine as a plenitude of being with many aspects—with form and formless, personal and impersonal, and both within and beyond the world;[34] pluralism of the yogas or spiritual paths, each of which is a valid approach to realization; acceptance of evolution as a cosmic progress which unfolds aspiring consciousness from within matter, taking yoga to be part of this progress; and acceptance of the manifested world and the necessity of service to others, working to transform not only the individual but society at large.

At the same time that he was pursuing his deep and intense spiritual practice, Chinmoy attended the Ashram School, wrote poems, essays and music, and excelled in athletics. The Sri Aurobindo Ashram, then as now, was a center of cultural and intellectual life. During his twenty years on the Ashram, Chinmoy was surrounded by aspirants devoted to literary and artistic pursuits as part of their yoga. He began to write poetry in his early teens and continued without pause for the rest of his life. Beginning in 1955, for eight years he was the assistant of the eminent Bengali man of letters Nolini Kanta Gupta, who was one of Sri Aurobindo's first disciples, his revolutionary compatriot and fellow prisoner on trial, and later the General Secretary of the Ashram.[35] In his years with Nolini, Chinmoy acquired an extensive knowledge of Bengali literature and more generally of Indian, English, and American writers. He translated dozens of Nolini's essays into English from Bengali and assisted K. D. Sethna (also known as Amal Kiran), who was Editor of *Mother India*, the Ashram's monthly cultural journal. He flowered as a writer in both Bengali and English, and his poetry, essays, and plays were published in *Mother India* and elsewhere. His other mentors included Sisirkumar Ghose, an associate of Rabindranath Tagore and professor of English at Shantiniketan's Vishwa Bharati University, and also the renowned singer Dilip Kumar Roy.[36]

The perfection of the body is one aim of the Integral Yoga of Sri Aurobindo and the Mother, and accordingly the Ashram became a venue of physical cultivation as well as contemplative practice and culture. The Mother was a dedicated sportswoman, and when the Ashram School was founded in 1943 she established what would become an elaborate sports program with Pranab Kumar Bhattacharya as its first director. The newly arrived Chinmoy, then thirteen, was one of Pranab's first students. He became an outstanding track and field athlete, winning the Ashram's "Fastest Sprinter" prize in the consecutive years 1946–1960 and the decathlon trophy in 1958 and 1959. He retired from competition in 1962 but continued sports for general fitness and inspiration, still enjoying soccer, volleyball, and table tennis and also coaching. He would later integrate physical fitness and sports, especially running, into his spiritual teaching and as himself a lifelong dedicated sportsman, set an example of the role of sports in spirituality.[37]

JOURNEY TO AMERICA

As Chinmoy entered his early thirties, his life took a previously unforeseen turn in which it changed enormously. In 1962, the American painter Sam Spanier visited the Ashram and was accepted by the Mother as a disciple. He and Chinmoy became friends, and in 1963 he and another disciple, Ann Harrison, invited Chinmoy to come to New York, where they lived, offering to serve as his sponsors. This was the outer form taken by what Sri Chinmoy always referred to as an inner call from the Supreme to leave India and come to the West. In April 1964, responding to this call, he journeyed to New York to begin his lifework of teaching and inspiring spiritual seekers first in America and eventually all over the world. New York City became his permanent home. Soon after his arrival, he was urged by a fellow disciple to seek a job at the Indian Consulate. Although he did not have a college degree or even a high school diploma, on the strength of his published writings and work with Nolini on the Ashram, he was hired and began employment in June 1964.[38] He was a junior clerk in the passport and visa section and in his spare time gave talks on spirituality and continued to write, living in a series of apartments in Manhattan and Brooklyn. There was a strong sense of community among the staff members of the Consulate, and a number of them strongly encouraged him in spiritual and literary activities. On weekends he would often go to the Woodstock area, where Sam Spanier and Eric Hughes were establishing the spiritual center Matagiri or "Mother's Mountain."[39]

As he continued to give talks and hold meditation meetings in the homes of spiritual seekers, some wished him to become their teacher. He now became known as Sri Chinmoy. In July 1966 the Aum Centre in San Juan, Puerto Rico was the first to be formally registered; less than a month later the Centre was also officially founded in New York (the name was later changed to the Sri Chinmoy Centre). The inaugural issue of *Aum* monthly magazine publishing his writings came out in August 1965. In the spring of 1967 he received the permanent residency visa that would allow him to teach full time and in June resigned from the Indian Consulate, remaining always deeply grateful to the friends and mentors there who had offered him great kindness and support for three years. In the summer of 1968 he moved to a house on a quiet street in the Jamaica Hills neighborhood of the New York City borough of Queens, where he lived until his passing on October 11, 2007 at age seventy-six. As he began to offer lectures at universities, many young seekers became his disciples and Centre activities began to increase. Sri Chinmoy Centres grew in number, first in the 1970s and 1980s in the Americas and Western Europe, and in the 1990s and thereafter in the former Soviet Union, Australia and New Zealand, Asia, and Africa. Today about 300 Sri Chinmoy Centres and meditation groups are found worldwide in over fifty countries, their members dedicated to meditation and to service through a wide range of programs.[40]

We turn now to a summary of the many-faceted activities and programs that Sri Chinmoy and his students created and carried forward, placing them in roughly chronological order of their development. The indispensable basis of all these activities is the regular daily practice of meditation and prayer, on which Sri Chinmoy spoke and wrote extensively. He offered a simple and powerful message which remained the foundation of all that he did: that God is real and that God-realization—conscious union with God—is possible through meditation. This realization is the birthright of every human being and its attainment is the purpose of life. He affirmed that the time has now come for people everywhere to take up the practice of spirituality in the fullest sense, known in India since ancient times as yoga. He declares, "Who is fit for Yoga? All human beings without exception are fit for Yoga."[41] All human beings are capable of meditation, without limitation of religious tradition, culture, or station in life. Sri Chinmoy states that "The art of meditation is something inherent in each individual."[42] He described the spiritual path which he taught and set forth in his writings as the path of "love, devotion, and surrender."

WORK IN DIVERSE AREAS: AN INTEGRAL MANIFESTATION

We have already seen that on the Ashram Sri Chinmoy was a writer living among writers, and that one of the very first projects that he undertook in the West was the publication of *Aum* magazine. Writing, like speaking, is a primary means of communication to the world and is also a form of art. Sri Chinmoy gave writing priority and is the author of over 1,500 published works of poetry, aphorisms, essays, stories, plays, talks, and answers to questions.[43] His earliest poetry, written in India, is in formal meter and rhyme. After he settled in New York he began to develop other and freer styles. *The Dance of Life*, a 1000-poem series written in 1973, marks the beginning of a characteristic style of short poems based on the single stanzaic unit and compressed lyrical utterance. This was followed by a number of other lengthy series eventually totaling all together over 100,000 poems, written in English.[44] In his later years, from the 1990s on, he increasingly wrote briefer poems of just a few lines, constantly seeking to distill his meaning. In his poetry he reiterates and expands the philosophical content of his prose writings, which include his hundreds of lectures at universities, the United Nations, and elsewhere.[45] Most of his works have been published by Agni Press and Aum Publications, founded in the 1970s and both located in the Jamaica Hills neighborhood of New York. More recently volumes of his collected works are being brought out nonsequentially by Ganapati Press, based in Oxford, England and Lyon, France.

Sri Chinmoy loved music all his life and musical training had been part of his education in India. After coming to New York he began to compose regularly, beginning with melodies for Sanskrit verses and his own poems. In March 1966, he gave a recital at the Indian Cultural Centre in New York of Sanskrit chants and devotional songs, singing and accompanying himself on harmonium.[46] The "Invocation to the Supreme," which his disciples sing daily, was written in August 1967. In the early 1970s he began to write Bengali songs in large numbers and formed singing groups in the Centres, giving great importance to music as a part of spiritual practice. In his lifetime he composed over 23,000 songs in Bengali and English (and a small number in other languages), homophonic melodies of "meditative music" which evoke the many different moods and colors of human experience.[47] He offered over 750 Peace Concerts throughout the world, always without charge, singing and performing on esraj (an Indian bowed instrument), flute, cello, and many other instruments from different cultures, on occasion with audiences of more than 5 or even 10,000, or more.[48] Sri Chinmoy held that music has great ontological significance. The divine Music is God's "transcendental Self-communion" and "The Universal Consciousness is fed constantly by the immortal, divine, and supreme Music of the Absolute."[49] Music can bridge inner and outer realities. It is a global language understandable across cultures and thus can play a key role in fostering world-oneness. Sri Chinmoy's disciples, many of whom are accomplished musicians, continue the tradition and offer free "Songs of the Soul" concerts of his music regularly in many countries.

In 1970, at the invitation of Secretary-General U Thant, Sri Chinmoy began leading twice-weekly meditations for peace at United Nations headquarters in New York. Sri Chinmoy: The Peace Meditation at the United Nations, as the nondenominational meditation group is known, is comprised of United Nations staff members, delegates, and other personnel of the missions of Member States, and representatives of Non-governmental Organizations (NGOs). Over the years the group has offered an array of programs to promote the values articulated in the Charter of the United Nations. During Sri Chinmoy's lifetime the Peace Meditation presented the U Thant Peace Award to individuals who exemplified the ideals of U Thant; recipients included Nelson Mandela, Mother Teresa, Mikhail Gorbachev, Pope John Paul II, and The Dalai Lama. In the early 1970s the Peace Meditation held some of the first interfaith programs at the United Nations, including an observance of the National Day of Prayer in 1975 and an annual Interfaith Prayer Breakfast (1986–2001). These efforts along with others by many UN staff and NGOs have over several decades developed into a broad commitment within the United Nations context to integrate a spiritual, values-centered and interfaith perspective into work on critical global issues and partnership-building.[50]

Sri Chinmoy was a lifelong supporter of the interfaith movement, first inspired in his childhood by the example of Swami Vivekananda, who was a major figure at the first World Parliament of Religions in Chicago in 1893. He regarded interreligious harmony as indispensable for world-oneness.[51] For decades he met with spiritual leaders and members of different religious communities in many countries for dialogue emphasizing what is best in every religion. Firmly upholding each religious tradition in its full integrity and particularity, in his writings he also recognizes that all religions are impelled by the cry for union with an Ultimate Reality or God, and by the universal values of love and peace that can transform humanity. True interfaith harmony must be founded in the deepest oneness. He says:

> Spirituality is not merely tolerance. It is not even acceptance. It is the feeling of a universal oneness. In our spiritual life, we look upon the Divine not only in terms of our own God, but in terms of everybody else's God. Our spiritual life firmly and securely establishes the basis of unity in diversity. Spirituality is not hospitality to the other's faith in God. It is the absolute recognition of the other's faith in God as one's own.[52]

This oneness can be palpably experienced when we meet without using words, and over the years Sri Chinmoy was personally committed to interfaith encounter through silent contemplation and music. He often offered a powerful silent meditation at such events as the annual Interfaith Service in New York observing the opening of the UN General Assembly (1997–2005) or the Parliament of the World's Religions, where he gave the opening meditation at the Convenings in 1993 in Chicago and in 2004 in Barcelona.[53]

Jharna-Kala in Bengali, or "Fountain-Art" is the name Sri Chinmoy gave to his paintings and drawings. This was an entirely new undertaking, as neither he nor anyone in his family had been an artist and on the Ashram he had done only a few art works. In November 1974, without formal training, he began to paint for many hours each day.[54] In a year he had done 120,000 nonrepresentational abstractions, usually in acrylics, of intense color and movement. The total number of his paintings today is about 200,000 while the subsequent series of "Soul-Bird" drawings, begun in 1991, numbers more than fifteen million.[55] Both have been exhibited internationally over the years; venues have included L'espace Miro at UNESCO and the Carrousel du

Louvre, both in Paris, the Nehru Center in London, the Agung Rai Museum in Bali, the Reinisches Landesmuseum in Bonn, the National Arts Center in Ottawa, and the United Nations Secretariat in New York, as well as many universities.[56]

Concerning the large numbers of Sri Chinmoy's poems, songs, paintings, and drawings, stated simply there have been two reasons for his prodigious creativity. The first is that it was spontaneous, the outer expression of a flood of inner spiritual dynamism; he often said that he never had to wait for inspiration but that it was a constant flow. The second reason is that a great number of varied works has the capacity to communicate broadly to a diverse audience. Sri Chinmoy would say that revision or selection was not his concern; his task was just to keep creating. The reader, hearer or viewer is free to focus on the works he or she likes or responds to and to ignore the others, as well as enjoying the overall variety of the multitude.[57]

Sri Chinmoy says that art of any kind that expresses aspiration for a better and higher life is a primary means of human transformation and also a form of service. He was once asked whether art actually adds something to already existing reality. He answered that it does, saying, "When we create a piece of art, immediately it adds to reality in terms of inspiration, in terms of capacity, in terms of beauty. Each time we create we are offering new life."[58] He also says, "We came into the world to make others happy. If we can bring joy to others, touch their hearts even for a moment, our spiritual life will be worthwhile."[59] In this spirit his students offer to the public not only concerts but also other cultural programs, always free of charge, and involve themselves in the arts both as part of their individual spiritual practice and their life together as a community.

Sri Chinmoy was an athlete all his life and taught that physical fitness expedites spiritual practice and that athletics itself can be a yoga, developing concentration, discipline, and determination.[60] Building on his experience as a sprinter and track and field athlete at the Sri Aurobindo Ashram, he continued these sports later in life and also became an avid tennis player and a distance runner, completing twenty-two marathons and five ultra-marathons. When a knee injury put an end to his running and tennis, he took up weightlifting in 1985 at age fifty-three. This became the arena for dramatic feats of self-transcendence and manifestation of the spiritual in the physical. Sri Chinmoy's weightlifting was comprehensively recorded on film, analyzed by weightlifting experts and witnessed by large audiences. Always seeking to transcend his previous achievements, he lifted as much as 1,300 pounds with two arms using an apparatus that suspended weights overhead in two U-shaped brackets. In the standing calf raise he lifted on a platform not only groups of people but airplanes and elephants. He never described what he was able to do as miraculous or the result of superior physique, but attributed it to "God's unconditional Grace." Its purpose, he always said, was to inspire others to transcend themselves.[61]

In 1988 he inaugurated the Lifting Up the World with a Oneness-Heart Award, in which he lifted the honoree overhead on a specially designed platform. For their service to humanity over 8,000 persons in different fields received this award, including many world figures such as Nelson Mandela, Muhammad Ali, and Ravi Shankar as well as thousands of ordinary citizens serving their communities. The award was a vivid expression of Sri Chinmoy's commitment to honor all areas of human endeavor.

Running has a special place in the practice of Sri Chinmoy's philosophy as a lived metaphor of the spiritual journey. Distance running became an integral part of the life of Sri Chinmoy and his students beginning in the mid-1970s. The Sri Chinmoy Marathon Team was founded in 1977 and has grown to organize each year some 500 sporting events internationally with branches in over 35 countries.[62] The Sri Chinmoy Marathon Team has pioneered in the field of ultra-distance running and today is the world's largest organizer of these events, with a reputation for expert care and support of the runners. The ultras include six and ten-day races, and the world's longest certified foot race, the 3,100-Mile Self-Transcendence Race held each summer in New York. In all of these events many world and national records have been set.[63] Sri Chinmoy's disciples also aspire to self-transcendence through other sports including cycling, triathlons, mountain climbing and open water swimming.

Since 1987 the Marathon Team has organized the Peace Run (also called the World Harmony Run), a global biennial torch relay for world friendship. The Peace Run takes place in full form every other year, with relays lasting several months each in several different regions of the world. There are many additional events at other times. With this format, in over thirty years of its existence with thousands of participants annually, the global program has involved hundreds of thousands of people, the majority of them school children and youth, in over 150 countries. The Peace Torch is a powerful symbol of our aspiration for peace, as can be seen from the spontaneous response of people everywhere along the running route and at Peace Run programs. The expansion of the spirit of peace is facilitated by the runners' outer journey from one location to another, but it also travels inwardly as an aspiration that spreads in the consciousness of an ever-increasing number of people.[64]

Another very important feature of life in the Sri Chinmoy Centres all over the world is "Divine Enterprises," small businesses (each individually owned) which root the Centre in the local community and provide a liveli-hood for some of its members while serving the community's needs in a peaceful, friendly and inspiring atmosphere. The first of these date back to the early 1970s. About half of the enterprises are restaurants and cafes, but they also include health food stores, gift shops, printing presses, flower shops, laundromats, clothing stores, yoga studios, professional consultancies and more, exemplifying the principle of service through vocation.

All of these undertakings have a single purpose: the increase of fulfillment and perfection in the world. The world is the manifest aspect of God. The practice of Sri Chinmoy's philosophy and spirituality calls for both God-realization through contemplative practice and also for an embrace of the world with self-offering in service. This is in reality a single process, as dedicated service leads to "a vast expansion / Of our conscious oneness / With God the creation;"[65] indeed, he says throughout his writings, "Self-giving is God-becoming." The essence of self-offering is love: "The very nature of the heart/ Is to love God the Creator/ And to serve God the creation."[66] Love for the world means acceptance. Once, when asked to state his philosophy in a single line, Sri Chinmoy said: "Our philosophy is the acceptance of life for the transformation of life and also for the manifestation of God's Light here on earth at God's choice Hour in God's own Way."[67]

THE APPROACH OF THIS BOOK

The following chapters of this book offer an exposition of this philosophy based mainly on Sri Chinmoy's writings, as these are his main statement. The word "philosophy" is understood in its ancient sense of the love of wisdom and search for the ultimate—a way of life and path of transformation. It is the term he himself uses. As historian Pierre Hadot has said concerning the ancient Greeks and Romans, "philosophy was a mode of existing-in-the-world, which had to be practiced at each instant, and the goal of which was to transform the whole of the individual's life. For the ancients, the mere word *philo-sophia*—the love of wisdom—was enough to express this conception of philosophy . . . Wisdom . . . was a way of life which brought peace of mind (*ataraxia*), inner freedom (*autarkeia*), and a cosmic consciousness."[68]

The aim of this work is to give to the reader a straightforward, unembroidered, and accurate account of Sri Chinmoy's philosophy. It makes every attempt to allow him to speak for himself in his own words and thus provides very ample quotation. As he preferred poetry to prose as a form of expression, the book draws on his poetic works as much as on his other writings. Sri Chinmoy regards philosophy and poetry as allied endeavors, and has said, "The philosopher is a poet in the mind. The poet is a philosopher in the heart."[69] He was never inclined to write a single formal exposition of his thought and the main points of his philosophy are found reiterated throughout his many writings in different genres. In his prose as in his poetry, his style is highly condensed and pithy, so that he often makes a series of important statements in a few paragraphs, and in lectures may do this in a structure that resembles a prose poem or a series of aphorisms. In his prose he sets forth a more discursive account, and also answered a great many questions. He does not write in a scholastic mode, nor does he engage in point-by-point formal presentation, almost always adopting an affirmative and poetic expression. In his poetry he supplements the statements and explanations made in his prose writings, making many other points often not found in his essays and talks. He articulates these additional points in a compressed and intuitive manner in his own distinctive poetic-philosophical idiom.

The book presents the philosophy's main themes in chapters on the nature of God, the creation and evolution of the universe, the soul's journey and the human person, the epistemologies of knowledge and of love, and the acceptance of the world and the transformation of life. As I am myself an adherent of this philosophy, this account is also informed by my experience of practice under Sri Chinmoy's guidance since 1971. In those places where I offer thoughts on the meaning of a statement or its implications and on the definition and interconnections of key ideas, this is signaled by appropriate wording. The historical context has been outlined in this first chapter and hereafter is indicated only briefly. This is also the case with points of philosophical comparison. A detailed treatment of history or comparative philosophy would easily double the book's length and that is not its intention, nor is this a work of argumentation. Instead it is my hope that as a basic introduction, this study will not only make Sri Chinmoy's philosophy known to those who wish to learn about it but also can serve as a resource for more thematic, specialized, and comparative studies in the future.

NOTES

1. See Sunil S. Amrith, *Crossing the Bay of Bengal: The Furies of Nature and the Fortunes of Migrants* (Cambridge, MA: Harvard University Press, 2013).

2. See Willem Van Schendel, *A History of Bangladesh* (Cambridge: Cambridge University Press, 2009), esp. ch. 4, "The delta as crossroads."

3. See Ethnologue: Languages of the World, https://www.ethnologue.com/language/crg, and Norihiko Učida, *Der Bengali-Dialekt von Chittagong: Grammatik, Texte, Wörterbuch* (Wiesbade, Germany: Otto Harrassowitz Verlag, 1970).

4. Suniti Bushan Qanungo, *A History of Chittagong,* vol. 2 (Chittagong: Dipankar Qanungo, 2010), 86.

5. The following account of Sri Chinmoy's early life is based on his autobiographical writings, including *My Father Shashi Kumar Ghosh: Affection-Life, Compassion-Heart, Illumination-Mind, by Madal* (New York: Agni Press, 1992); *To the Streaming Tears of My Mother's Heart and to the Brimming Smiles of My Mother's Soul, by Madal* (New York: Agni Press, 1994); and *My Brother Chitta,*

by Madal (New York: Agni Press, 1998). Autobiographical passages are also found in many of his other works. I draw as well on Vidagdha Bennett, *Madal the Child* (Mandurah, West Australia: Equilibrium Books, 2010) and *A Shakpura Village Boy* (Mandurah, West Australia: Equilibrium Books, 2011).

6. Ghosh or Ghose is a common surname among Bengali Kāyasthas, a high-ranking caste of writers, record-keepers and administrators. See Ronald B. Inden, *Marriage and Rank in Bengali Culture* (Berkeley: University of California Press, 1976). Sri Chinmoy later adopted the English spelling "Ghose;" in Bengali letters the spelling is the same for either transliteration.

7. The *madal*, often rendered as "kettledrum," is a two-headed drum said to be played by the gods in heaven.

8. The Buddhists of East Bengal are an ancient community, most of whom in the Chittagong area belong to the Barua ethnic group. In the 19th century Theravāda monks came to Chittagong from today's Myanmar and Sri Lanka with the mission of restoring true Buddhism from a perceived condition of syncretism and decline; as a result the dominant form of Buddhism today in Chittagong is Theravāda. See Sukomal Chaudhuri, *Contemporary Buddhism in Bangladesh*, 2nd ed. (Calcutta: Atisha Memorial Publishing Society, 1987), esp. Appendix No. 1, "The Buddhists of Chittagong."

9. Sri Chinmoy uses British spellings which are retained in all quotations from his writings, while American spellings are kept in the body of this book's text; thus both "realisation" and "realization" are used.

10. "Every day I water Heaven," in *Ten Thousand Flower-Flames*, Part 27 (New York: Agni Press, 1982), No. 2,654.

11. In *My Flute* (New York: Aum Publications, 1996 [1972]), 86.

12. *Sri Chinmoy Answers*, vol. 2, 2nd ed. (Oxford and Lyon: Ganapati Press, 2015), 857–858.

13. Peter Heehs, *The Bomb in Bengal: The Rise of Revolutionary Terrorism in India 1900-1910* (Oxford: Oxford University Press, 1993), 82–83.

14. Leonard A. Gordon, *Bengal: The Nationalist Movement 1876-1940* (New York: Columbia University Press, 1974), 247–248, and *Brothers against the Raj: A Biography of Indian Nationalists Sarat and Subhas Chandra Bose* (New York: Columbia University Press, 1990), 228–229.

15. See David Kopf, *British Orientalism and the Bengal Renaissance: The Dynamics of Indian Modernization 1773-1835* (Berkeley: University of California Press, 1969) and Kusumita P. Pedersen, "The Hindu Renaissance in Bengal," *World Faiths Insight* New Series 21 (February 1989): 35–46.

16. See David Kopf, *The Brahmo Samaj and the Shaping of the Modern Indian Mind* (Princeton: Princeton University Press, 1979).

17. On the Ārya Samāj, see the biography of its founder by J. T. F. Jordens, *Dayananda Saraswati: His Life and Ideas* (Delhi: Oxford University Press, 1997).

18. See Gwilym Beckerlegge, *The Ramakrishna Mission: The Making of a Modern Hindu Movement* (Delhi: Oxford University Press, 2006).

19. *To the Streaming Tears of My Mother's Heart*, 19.

20. *Yoga and the Spiritual Life* (New York: Aum Publications, 1996 [1970]), 91.

21. He subsequently founded the Sri Aurobindo Girls' High School School in West Shakpura on January 1, 1943. Ratan Kanti Bhattacharjee, personal communication to the author, 2009.

22. Mantu Ghosh, *Mantu's Heart-Songs* (New York: Agni Press, 2000), 196.

23. Amrith, *Bay of Bengal*, 196–197.

24. *My Brother Chitta*, 40.

25. Paul R. Greenough, *Prosperity and Misery in Modern Bengal: The Famine of 1943-1944* (Oxford: Oxford University Press, 1982), Appendix C, "Famine Mortality, 1943-46," 299–315.

26. See the biography of Sri Aurobindo, Peter Heehs, *The Lives of Sri Aurobindo* (New York: Columbia University Press, 2008). Most of Sri Aurobindo's works are published in the *Sri Aurobindo Birth Centenary Library*, 30 vols. (Pondicherry: Sri Aurobindo Ashram Publications Department, 1971–1973). More recently the Ashram has been bringing out the *Collected Works of Sri Aurobindo*, http://www.collected worksofsriaurobindo.com.

27. See for example, *The Synthesis of Yoga*, Part IV, The Yoga of Self-Perfection, Ch. 1, "The Principle of the Integral Yoga" (Twin Lakes, WI: Lotus Press, 1996), 609 ff., as quoted in Robert McDermott, ed. *The Essential Aurobindo* (Great Barrington, MA: Lindisfarne Press, 1987), 157–163.

28. *Birth Centenary Library*, Vol. 22, 100–110.

29. There has been much discussion by scholars of Sri Aurobindo's sources, roots, influences, and resemblances. Debashish Banerji aptly observes, "Schooled in London and at the University of Cambridge, he understood the constitution and boundaries of the modern knowledge academy originating in the European Enlightenment. Aurobindo's texts thus need to be viewed, both discursively and conceptually, as hybrid sites for the politics of translation and/or the possibilities of global translatability;" he also comments that Sri Aurobindo "understood well the braided vectors of knowledge and power making up the fabric of modernity." Debashish Banerji, ed. *Integral Yoga Psychology: Metaphysics and Transformation as Taught by Sri Aurobindo* (Twin Lakes, WI: Lotus Press, 2020), 5, 215. In his essay "Traditional Roots of Sri Aurobindo's Integral Yoga," Banerji traces as "roots" multiple streams of Indian tradition and culture, including not only the texts of Vedānta and the Bhagavad Gītā, along with the works of Swami Vivekananda and the teachings of Sri Ramakrishna, but also Tantra, "Pāñcarātra Vaiṣṇavism, and the Śākta and Vaiṣṇava traditions strong in Sri Aurobindo's native Bengal, with devotion to Kali and Krishna," *Integral Review* 9, no. 3 (2013): 94–106.

For comparative philosophical studies, see S. K. Maitra, *The Meeting of the East and the West in Sri Aurobindo's Philosophy* (Pondicherry: Sri Aurobindo Ashram Trust, 1968 [1956], Wilfried Huchzermeyer, *Sri Aurobindo and European Philosophy* (Auroville: Prisma, 2016) and on a range of topics, the volume edited by Peter Heehs, *Situating Sri Aurobindo: A Reader* (Oxford: Oxford University Press, 2013), which collects fifteen essays published in recent decades, and also McDermott, Robert A. McDermott, ed. *Six Pillars: Introductions to the Major Works of Sri Aurobindo* (Chambersburg, PA: Wilson Books, 1974). It should be noted as well that when Sri Aurobindo was in England, Britain had become the epicenter of debate and public awareness of evolution after the 1859 publication of Charles Darwin's *The Origin of Species*. Evolution was soon known in India; for a detailed account of its reception by Hindus, see C. MacKenzie Brown, *Hindu Perspectives on Evolution: Darwin, Dharma and Design* (London: Routledge, 2013), including a chapter on Sri Aurobindo.

30. *My Flute*, 55.

31. *Sri Chinmoy Answers,* vol. 2, 2nd ed. (Oxford and Lyon: Ganapati Press, 2015), 786.

32. Epistemological questions will be taken up in detail in the chapter below on "Knowledge." On the priority of spiritual experience in the stream of thought to which Sri Chinmoy belongs, see Jeffery D. Long, "Religious Experience, Hindu Pluralism, and Hope: *Anubhava* in the Tradition of Sri Ramakrishna," *Religions* (2019) 10/3, 210; doi:10:10.3390/rel10030210.

33. On Sri Chinmoy's lifelong connection with Sri Ramakrishna, Sarada Devi and Swami Vivekānanda, see Kusumita P. Pedersen, "Sri Ramakrishna and Sri Chinmoy," *Prabuddha Bharata or Awakened India* 116, no. 1 (January 2011): 109–114.

34. Sri Chinmoy's vision of the Divine can be characterized as panentheistic. For succinct statements of the panentheistic perspective see Loriliai Biernacki, "Introduction: Panentheism Outside the Box," in *Panentheism across the World's Traditions,* ed. Loriliai Biernacki and Philip Clayton (New York: Oxford University Press, 2014), 3, and Philip Clayton, "Panentheisms East and West," *Sophia* 49, no. 2 (2010): 183–191; both refer to the "classic definition" of Charles Hartshorne. See Charles Hartshorne and William L. Reese, eds., *Philosophers Speak of God*, 2nd ed. (Amherst, MA: Humanity Books, 2000 [1953]), 16–18.

35. He published excerpts of his journal of his years with Nolini as *A Service-Sun, a service-flame, by Chinmoy*, 3rd printing (New York: Agni Press, 2003 [1974]).

36. Vidagdha Bennett, *Reverie* (Mandurah, West Australia: Equilibrium Books, 2013), 156–188.

37. See Kusumita P. Pedersen, "Uniting Sports and Spirituality," *Hinduism Today* April /May 2018, 56–63, and Vidagdha Bennett, *Under a Blue Pondicherry Sky* (Mandurah, West Australia: Equilibrium Books, 2012).

38. *My Consulate Years* (New York: Agni Press, 1996).

39. See www.matagiri.org.

40. For information on the Sri Chinmoy Centres, see www.srichinmoy.org including the website's links to different aspects of the Centre's programs and activities.

41. *Yoga*, 17.

42. *United Nations Works,* Vol. 1 (Oxford and Lyon: Ganapati Press, 2020), 177.

43. The on-line Sri Chinmoy Library makes available most of these works, including song lyrics, and is searchable. www.srichinmoylibrary.com.

44. The major poetry series in English are: *The Dance of Life*, 1973 (1,000 poems); *Europe-Blossoms*, 1973 (1,000 poems); *The Goal Is Won*, 1974 (360 poems written in 24 hours); *The Wings of Light*, 1974 (1,000 poems); *The Golden Boat*, 1974 (1,000 poems); *Transcendence-Perfection*, 1975 (843 poems written in 24 hours); *Ten Thousand Flower-Flames*, 1979-1983 (10,000 poems); *Twenty-Seven Thousand*

Aspiration-Plants, 1983-1998 (27,000 poems); and *Seventy-Seven Thousand Service-Trees,* 1998-2009 (50,000 poems). There are numerous shorter collections. His Bengali songs, many of which he translated into English poetry, number over 13,000 and form another distinct part of his body of poetic works.

45. Studies of Sri Chinmoy's poetry include Vidagdha Bennett, *Simplicity and Power: The Poetry of Sri Chinmoy 1971-1981* (New York: Aum Publications, 1991); Kusumita P. Pedersen, "The Poetry of Sri Chinmoy: A Philosopher in the Heart," in *Antonio T. de Nicolás: Poet of Eternal Return*, ed. Christopher Key Chapple (Ahmedabad: Sriyogi Publications & Nalanda International, 2014), 299–307; Saudamini Siegrist, "The Writing of Devotion: Teresa of Avila, Richard Crashaw, Julian of Norwich, 'Cloud of Unknowing', John Donne, Thérèse of Lisieux, Emily Dickinson, Sri Chinmoy Kumar Ghose." PhD. diss. New York University 1999. *Dissertation Abstracts International,* Section A: The Humanities and Social Sciences 60, no. 5 (1999): 1545; and Mrinali C. Clarke, with a Foreword by Purushottama Bilimoria, *The Ever-Transcending Quest: A Literary Analysis of the Poetry of Sri Chinmoy* (New Delhi: D. K. Printworld, 2015).

46. This program, including excerpted texts of the songs performed and Sri Chinmoy's introduction of each one, is published as "Indian Devotional Songs" in *Eternity's Breath: Aphorisms and Essays* (New York: Agni Press, 1975), 88–95.

47. The words for most of these songs, and music notation for over 9,000 of them, are available at https://www.srichinmoysongs.com.

48. A detailed list of the largest concerts can be found at: https://us.srichinmoy centre.org/sri_chinmoy/largest-concerts.

49. *God the Supreme Musician,* rev. 2nd ed. (New York: Agni Press, 1976), 9, 35.

50. Kusumita P. Pedersen, "Sri Chinmoy's Work at the United Nations: Spirituality and the Power of Silence," *CrossCurrents* 60, no. 3 (September 2010): 339–351. Special Issue on Religion and the United Nations edited by Azza Karam and Matthew Weiner.

51. Kusumita P. Pedersen, "Sri Chinmoy's Contributions to Interreligious Harmony," in *Unity in Diversity,* ed. Tapan Camillus de Rozario, Eva Sadia Saad and M. Tazuddin, publication of the 2nd International Conference on Interreligious and Intercultural Dialogue, Department of World Religions and Culture, University of Dhaka, November 2010, 53–63.

52. *Yoga*, 53.

53. The author was present for all of the Opening Meditations mentioned.

54. See https://www.srichinmoyart.com; https://www.srichinmoybio.co.uk/art/index.html; https://www.srichinmoy-reflections.com/artworks. At these websites, the viewer can see many images of Sri Chinmoy's art in including both paintings and Soul-Bird drawings, as well as videos of exhibits giving an impression of the scale of display.

55. The exact number of paintings is not known, as many are in private hands. It should be noted here that when Sri Chinmoy painted, he did so very rapidly without revising and, as mentioned, especially in his first year of painting would paint for many hours a day, doing thousands of works. These were counted on the same day, so that a running total was maintained. As almost all works are on paper, a large

number can be stored in files. The Soul-Bird drawings, numbering over fifteen million, were also counted as they were being created. After Sri Chinmoy's passing, the total number was reviewed; records are held at the Jharna-Kala Foundation in New York (I am indebted to Paree Atkin, who was part of this process at each stage, for this information). A video of the "One Million" exhibit in Ottawa of the first million (see previous note) shows the great numbers of drawings on display in the gallery space and gives an impression of the bird-drawings. In some cases a great many small birds make up a larger work in a pointillist manner.

56. A list of Jharna-Kala exhibitions is available at: https://www.srichinmoyart .com/jharna-kala-art-exhibitions/.

57. See Kusumita P. Pedersen, "The Creativity of Sri Chinmoy," paper given at the Convening of the Parliament of the World's Religions, Barcelona, July 2004. An appreciative reflection on Sri Chinmoy's creative works by Shrinivas Tilak is found in his book *Understanding Karma: In Light of Paul Ricoeur's Philosophical Anthropology and Hermeneutics* (Nagpur: International Centre for Cultural Studies India, 2006), 444–453.

58. *Art's Life and the Soul's Light* (New York: Agni Press, 1974), 45.

59. Talk at Public School 86, New York, on the occasion of the visit of sitarist Ravi Shankar, November 16, 2003 (the author's notes).

60. See Pedersen, "Uniting Sports and Spirituality."

61. See the award-winning film by Natabara Rollosson, Sanjay Rawal et al on Sri Chinmoy's weightlifting, "Challenging Impossibility" (New York: Illumine: Social Change through Media, 2011) can be seen at: http://www.challengingimpossibility .com A detailed history with abundant illustration and comments by a number of well-known figures in the fields of weightlifting and body-building is also available at www.inspiration-lifts.org.

62. See https://www.srichinmoyraces.org/sri_chinmoy.

63. See the 2018 film: "3100: Run and Become" by Sanjay Rawal (New York: Illumine: Social Change through Media, 2018). https://3100film.com.

64. See www.peacerun.org and Pedersen, "Uniting Sports and Spirituality."

65. *Aspiration-Plants,* Part 16 (1981), No. 1, 576.

66. *Seventy-Seven Thousand Service-Trees*, Part 27 (New York: Agni Press, 2002), No. 26,291.

67. *A Peace-collecting Pilgrim-Soul* (New York: Agni Press, 1980), 23.

68. *Philosophy as a Way of Life: Spiritual Exercises from Socrates to Foucault,* edited with an introduction by Arnold I. Davidson, trans. Michael Chase (Malden, MA: Blackwell Publishing, 1995), 265.

69. *Commentaries on the Vedas, Upanishads and Bhagavad Gita* (New York: Aum Publications, 1996 [1971–72]), 16. This collection brings together lectures given at universities and colleges in 1970–1972.

Chapter 2

God

THE CENTRALITY OF RELATIONSHIP

God is the constant theme of all Sri Chinmoy's writings. He holds that God is the Source of all that is. Conscious oneness with God and the manifestation of God's qualities in the world are the goals of our evolving personal and cosmic existence. God is the true self or soul of each being, which shares the divine Nature.[1] Sri Chinmoy calls God "The Supreme" and names God as Father, Mother, Friend, and beloved Lord as well as the infinite Absolute beyond all form. He uses the Sanskrit "Brahman" only when referring directly to texts in that language such as the Upaniṣads. The following words may offer a condensed expression of his vision of the nature of God and serve as a prelude to the more extended account given in this chapter.

He is eternal and immortal.
He is within this world and beyond it.
He is the Creator,
    Both universal and transcendental.[2]

Personal and impersonal,
    With form and without,
God the Supreme
    Encompasses all.[3]

Who is God? God is an infinite Consciousness. He is also the self-illumining Light. There is no human being who does not own within this infinite Consciousness and this self-illumining Light.[4]

God is Delight.[5] Delight is the source of existence. Delight is the meaning of existence. Delight is the language of Infinity, Eternity and Immortality.[6]

God is all Love.[7] Love is God's Life-Breath in us.[8]

In his poetry Sri Chinmoy addresses God directly and intimately with intense devotion, as in this Bengali song.

In secrecy supreme I see You.	*Nayane nayane gopane gopane*
You live in my eyes, in my sleep,	*Shayane swapane*
In my dreams, in my sweet wakefulness.	*Madhu-jāgarane*
In the stupendous mirth of life,	*Jibaner dole*
In the abysmal lap of death,	*Maraner kole*
You I behold.	*Taba prema-līlā*
Your Love-Play is my world.	*Āmār bhubane*[9]

Although he speaks of God constantly, it is difficult to find in Sri Chinmoy's works statements only about God in God's own Self and transcendent Being, apart from God's creation of the universe, God's Love for creation, or the relation of human beings to God. Most often he speaks of God in relationship to the individual human person or of the relationship of God and humanity. His central concern for relationship is found even in the very few passages that come close to speaking of "God alone." God's Self is mentioned along with God's Self-revelation, God's creativity and the dynamic interplay of God's different aspects or attributes.

GOD AS SILENCE AND DELIGHT

Before anything exists, within God's own Being[10] there is still relation and process in the unfathomable depths of the supreme Mystery:

Before God created the universe, He created Himself.[11]
God originated Himself out of His own Silence.[12]
God's secret is a beginningless Silence.[13]

At the very beginning of the creative action of God, there is Silence. Silence is the source of the Source. It is the Ineffable, of which nothing can be said in words and which cannot be thought of by the mind.[14]

From the transcendent Source there then emerges divine Reality in its universal and interior dimension. "The universal Heart originated in God's Silence," Sri Chinmoy says. "When God was absolute Silence, inside this Silence something was growing . . . . The universal Heart came into existence before God's sound-life came into existence. And where is the universal Heart? It is deep inside us, where reality constantly grows."[15] "Silence" is the predicate of God in Sri Chinmoy's philosophy that is perhaps closest in meaning to the traditional Sanskrit term *nirguṇa* or "without qualities."[16] "Silence" is often paired with "Sound," the dyad indicating the unmanifest Transcendent and the manifest existent. And "What is silence? Silence is that which alone bears the teeming vast. It upholds activity and inactivity in its own supreme delight."[17] Silence not only generates but also sustains both unmanifested and manifested existence through God's aspect of "Delight" which is both self-contained and outwardly expressive.

Delight or Bliss (*Ānanda*) occupies a key place in the divine ontology. It is the third term of the traditional Vedāntic formulation for Brahman or the Absolute—*Sat-Cit-Ānanda* or Existence-Consciousness-Bliss. "Delight" is present at all "levels" of existence and in all "worlds" as the mode of divine dynamism and creativity. More will be said below about ontological "levels" and the spatial language that refers to them. Sri Chinmoy says, "Delight is the divine bridge between Peace and Power, between Light and Truth, between God's unmanifested Dream and His manifested Reality," adding that only in the experience of Delight can God be fully understood.[18] In this poem he clarifies the complementary roles of "Delight" and "Silence."

What is the fount of my life?
  Delight.

What is the fount of my love?
  Delight.

What is the fount of my perfection?
  Delight.

What is the fount of my God?
  Silence.[19]

Delight here is said to be the origin of "life." In Sri Chinmoy's poetic-philosophical vocabulary the word "life" most often means an integral reality encompassing several or all of the levels of existence. Delight here is also the origin of "love," or the affective and self-giving experience of relationship, and of "perfection," which is the actual achievement of integral transformation. While God-as-Delight is the Source of all these, Its own "fount" or Source can only be described as "Silence."

"God expresses Himself through Silence. God expands Himself through Light. God unites Himself with His Creation through Delight."[20] This is a summary of the process of divine Self-revelation and creation. Since "Silence" is ontologically the "first" thing we can speak of when we speak of God, before God "expresses Himself through Silence" God is not yet even "Silence"—but is something "before Silence" which we do not know, cannot conceive of and about which we cannot speak at all. "Silence" may anticipate the imminent appearance of Reality or *sat*, since after God's very first Self-expression as Silence, God continues the process of revealing God's Self, as God "expands Himself through Light," a synonym for Consciousness or *cit*, by envisioning and then bringing forth the universe. When creation has come into actual existence, God's relation with it is that of "Delight." Each of God's core attributes, it seems, could be said to have an unmanifested "silence" dimension and also a manifested or "sound" dimension in the unfolding process of creation. When we break the silence, so to speak, to describe the Supreme as well as positive language can, in what follows we will refer to God's qualities as "attributes." The word "essence" is used only to speak of God as Love, mentioned below.

GOD'S ATTRIBUTES

God is a plenitude of Being comprising countless divine qualities. Sri Chinmoy states that "God is infinite, and His attributes are infinite,"[21] and often calls the Supreme "the Infinite," recalling the Upaniṣadic *Pūrṇam* or "fullness" to which he at times refers.[22] Language for God's limitless attributes saliently includes the three of *Sat-Cit-Ānanda: Sat*, rendered as Existence, Reality, or Truth, *Cit* or Consciousness, for which Light is an equivalent, and *Ānanda*, Delight or Bliss.

Like Delight, Consciousness is present at all levels of existence, and even more completely since it reaches down even to the lowest planes. Consciousness is able to hold a full range of different qualities, and is also dynamic.

> [I]t is the divine consciousness that connects earth with Heaven. . . . Consciousness is only one. It houses silence and it houses power. When it houses silence, at that time it houses its true form. When it houses power, at that time it [outwardly] manifests its inner reality. . . . Its nature is to expand constantly. . . . In the divine consciousness there is always a goal, and this goal is always transcending itself.[23]

Three divine attributes or aspects of the divine Nature also often mentioned are "Infinity," "Eternity," and "Immortality," generally found as a triad standing for the entirety of God's Being and corresponding to Consciousness-Existence-Bliss. Almost always in Sri Chinmoy's writings this correspondence is expressed implicitly, but in the following passage it is explicit:

> The Secret Supreme is the Supreme Himself. He can be seen. He can be felt. He can be realised. When He is seen, He is Existence. When He is felt, He is Consciousness. When He is realised, He is Delight. In His embodiment of Existence, He is Eternal. In His revelation of Consciousness, He is Infinite. In His manifestation of Delight, He is Immortal.[24]

We notice again the constant concern for relationship, as these three aspects of the Supreme are introduced in terms of how they are known. The verbs "seen," "felt" and "realised" are a progressive sequence indicating that initially the human person "sees" God as eternal Existence or Reality, subsequently "feels" God as infinite Consciousness, a more intimate experience, and finally "realises" God as immortal Delight. "Realisation" is a culminating knowledge attained through contemplative practice or yoga and is a permanent state of conscious oneness with God, the Reality that is realized. In God's own Being God "embodies" or realizes Existence, reveals Consciousness, and manifests Delight in a sequence corresponding to the phases of knowledge attained by the human person—but in reverse, moving not "inward" but "outward."

In another passage pairing each of these three nouns with a key verb, the sequence is different from the one in the passage just cited. Here Sri Chinmoy says, "Infinity means the realising, and the realised, and the eternally realising God. Eternity means the revealing, and the revealed, and the eternally revealing God. Immortality means the fulfilling, and the fulfilled, and the eternally fulfilling God."[25] Since "realisation" is knowing through identification or "embodiment" (a term Sri Chinmoy uses almost invariably in this specific sense) here he seems to be saying that God realizes, is identified with or "embodies" God's own Self. Following this, "revealing" takes place as a kind of coming-forth, appearing or being shown, and finally "fulfilling" takes place not only as God's enjoyment of Delight in God's own Being, but also as God's fulfillment in God's own creation as it evolves towards its perfection—"God unites Himself with His Creation through Delight." A schematized summation of this passage might suggest that for Sri Chinmoy the "Infinite Consciousness" (*Cit*) is ontologically prior to "Eternal Existence" (*Sat*), so the position of the first two terms of *Sat-Cit-Ānanda* is reversed. "Immortality" and "Delight," together or as one entity, are linked to Love, which "fulfills," and continue to occupy the third position.

But as the three summit attributes of God are inseparable, any attempt to prioritize them must in the end be artificial. There may well be no settled before or after, but rather an interplay of aspects of God which are plural yet one or nondifferent. And we must be cautious about seizing upon the notion that all of the infinite attributes of God might somehow be subsumed under these three, as there are other and alternate "models" and locutions, as we shall see.

The following poem meditates on the interrelation of some of the meaning-laden nouns standing for God's qualities and their totality, using "ecstasy" as the experiential mediator that establishes their relationships.

What is Peace?
Fulfilment-ecstasy.

What is Light?
Truth-ecstasy.

What is Delight?
Love-ecstasy.

What is Perfection?
God-ecstasy.[26]

The poem can be read to mean: when one attains fulfillment, the ecstasy one experiences is Peace, when one attains Truth and Love, one experiences the ecstasies which are Light and Delight. As frequently happens in Sri Chinmoy's poetry, the final stanza gives an unexpected twist which challenges the reader: when one attains God, one will then also attain the ecstasy which is Perfection.

GOD IS LOVE

While the divine plenitude has countless qualities or aspects, its very nature is Love. Love, or *Prema*, is not an "attribute" of God, but rather God is Love itself. Sri Chinmoy states that "Love is the essence of God's Divinity"[27] and that "no definition of God can be as adequate as the definition of God as all Love."[28] If there is a moment when divine ineffability is most challenged, it is when this affirmation is made. In a poem written in the last years of his life Sri Chinmoy says, "God means / God-Love-Ocean."[29] He refers in his Bengali songs to *Prema Sāgar* or the Ocean of divine Love, a phrase also used by Swami Vivekānanda, who like Sri Chinmoy affirms that the very nature of God is Love itself.[30]

In an early prose poem he says: "I prayed to God for Power. He said, 'Take it and use it.' I prayed to God for Light. He said, 'Take it and spread it.' I prayed to God for Bliss. He said, 'Take it and stay in your Source.' I prayed to God for Love. He said, 'Take Me; I am yours.'"[31] The following poem personifies aspects of God, who converse with one another:

One truth speaks to another truth:
God is proud of us.

One life speaks to another life:
God is fond of us.

One love speaks to another love:
God is made of us.[32]

God is "made of Love" and "Truth is in all, but Love is all."[33] Yet Truth, or Reality, and Love are dimensions of one another; he also says, "In the life of aspiration we come to realize that Love is Truth embodied, and that Truth is Love revealed,"[34] and "Love in the process of its manifestation is conscious Truth enjoying itself."[35] In both aphorisms, Love is the interior and transcendent dimension and Truth as the more externalized and manifest. Truth is described as "conscious" and "enjoying," that is, in terms of its two companion attributes, Consciousness and Delight—so that it might be said that the three aspects of *Sat-Cit-Ānanda* are united with one another as Love. Sri Chinmoy frequently describes God as "all Love" and as just mentioned, declares that "no definition of God can be as adequate as the definition of God as all Love."[36] Divine Love in its different aspects is the subject of this book's chapter 6.

GOD'S SELF-TRANSCENDENCE

A distinctive feature of Sri Chinmoy's vision of God is his affirmation that God is always transcending God's own Being. The process of expansion in the created world has its source in the transcendent plane. Sri Chinmoy often refers to God as "the ever-transcending Beyond"[37] and declares that "God the Infinite constantly transcends His own Infinity, God the Eternal constantly transcends His own Eternity and God the Immortal constantly transcends His own Immortality."[38] Using the traditional Vedāntic term for the Absolute, he says, "Brahman, the infinite Consciousness, is always in the process of transcending the limitless expanse of the Beyond. Brahman's Infinity, Eternity and Immortality are ever-evolving."[39] The apparent illogic of saying that Infinity can increase is perceived only by the mind, while the heart is able to embrace the divine paradox of the increase of Infinity: "[T]he mind goes on trying to bind that which cannot be bound. But when you use the heart, you realise that something can be infinite, and at the same time, it can transcend itself."[40]

It is thus possible to say that God in God's full Being can go beyond God's nature as Truth (Reality or *Sat*) or more precisely, that God's Truth can go beyond itself to become a new Truth.

> Truth has no existence without God. God is the very breath of Truth. Truth and God are one, indivisible. On the one hand, Truth is another name for God. On the other hand, Truth cannot exist without God, whereas God can at each moment transcend Truth—earthly truth and heavenly truth, earthbound truth and heavenward truth. Even His own Transcendental Truth God can transcend at His own sweet Will. Although we can safely say that God and Truth are one, God alone has the power to transcend all truths, even The Truth itself.[41]

It is God's unlimited freedom that makes this perpetual divine transcendence possible, just as God's omnipotence makes possible the manifestation of the Infinite in the finite.

> God has learned from Self-transcendence that His own Light and Delight are constantly increasing. ... God has learned from Self-transcendence the message of His own Freedom. Each time He transcends Himself, God increases His Freedom-Power. When He uses His Freedom-Power in Heaven, it is His Vision-Power. . . . And when He uses His Freedom-Power here on earth, it is His Compassion-Power.[42]

God's unbounded freedom sustains the evolving expression of God's Goodness and Compassion. In the following passage, the ceaseless divine change is a movement of progress and transformation, as the different aspects of the Divine not only expand in their own transcendental realm but also are increasingly "manifested" in the phenomenal world. Sri Chinmoy stressed this aspect of divine creativity in its universal cosmic dimension in answering the question of a scholar with a deep interest in process theology, who asked him, "Does God change?"[43]

> God is constantly changing, sleeplessly changing. From the finite He is going to the Infinite. Again at His sweet Will, from the Infinite He is coming into the Finite. . . . On the one hand, God is changeless and deathless. On the other hand, He is in the process of constant change, constant self-creation and self-immolation. . . . When we ordinary human beings change something, we are not sure that the change is going to be an improvement. Change in and of itself does not necessarily mean improvement. But when God changes something,

He changes Himself in and through that thing, always for progress and true satisfaction.[44]

God's Self-transcendence thus takes place in two ways. God's own transcendent Reality can go beyond Itself, God's Infinity can "increase," God's Truth can become a new Truth. As well, God evolves in and through the creation: He becomes the finite and then, by evolutionary change that is always positive, He progresses in and through the infinite forms He has assumed in the created world.

GOD AS "FORMLESS"/"IMPERSONAL"
AND "WITH FORM"/"PERSONAL"

Sri Chinmoy uses the terms "formless" and "form" as equivalent to "impersonal" and "personal" and not to mean "without" and "with" qualities or attributes. The "formless" can be spoken of as having "attributes" which, to be precise, are "impersonal attributes."[45] He consistently states that God is both with form and formless, both personal and impersonal, saying "The Highest is beyond personal and impersonal but, at the same time, He embodies both. The Highest is formless, and at the same time He is with form. If we have to state what He is, we have to say that He is both, and again, that He is beyond both."[46] Moreover, "A true lover of God is he who believes in God's existence as both personal and impersonal"[47] so that neither aspect is to be excluded from recognition. Sri Chinmoy almost always discusses these two aspects of God as they pertain to the individual aspirant's own experience, or sought-for experience, of the Supreme: "God can be seen with form, with personal attributes, and He can be seen without form, with impersonal attributes."[48] Each individual can and should "define" God as he or she wishes, and will also seek to realize God according to his or her disposition—the aspect of God she or he receives "joy" from or "is fond of." Indeed, God will appear to the devotee in the particular form that he or she longs for.[49] At the same time, Sri Chinmoy stresses that although it is easier to begin by approaching God as personal and "with form," every aspirant will ultimately realize both aspects.

God can be seen, felt and realised as a personal being, more luminous, infinitely more beautiful than a human being. And again, we can experience God as an infinite expanse of Light, Bliss, Power or any divine quality. Each individual will realise God in both the personal and the impersonal aspect. But if we think of God in His personal aspect first it is easier, because right now we are in the finite. If we can imagine God as a person, then from the form we can go to the formless aspect.[50]

Two of his more recent poems underscore the point: "Without becoming one / With the Form of the Supreme, / We cannot enter into / The formless Supreme." And "The Supreme with Form / Has to be seen, felt / And realized / Before we discover / The formless Supreme."[51]

This sequence might make it appear that since knowledge of the formless aspect of God comes later and thus seems to be more difficult or "advanced," it is also "higher" and more true, a more authentic experience of God. But Sri Chinmoy emphasizes that the truest realization of God is not when the "formless" aspect supersedes the aspect "with form," but rather holds that it is the most complete or "integral" realization that is the most "true." It is attained when one has a free access to *both* aspects of the Divine. He also says, "should our Beloved Supreme / Come to us without form, / We must cultivate the same kind of / Faith, love and devotion / For His formless aspect / As we have for His physical form."[52] In another poem he declares, "The formless is as true / As the form, / As beautiful, / If not infinitely more beautiful, / As the form."[53]

On one occasion Sri Chinmoy responded with special intensity to the suggestion that the formless is "higher" and said that, if anything, God "with form" is more important for a particular reason that is at the heart of his understanding of God and the world. He was asked, "It seems to me that at the start of the spiritual path we see God with form, and that as we grow into oneness He starts to lose His Form. Is this true?" His answer is crucially important for understanding his vision of God taken in its entirety.

> It is our own mental conception that the formless is something superior to the form. We feel that before the creation, the Supreme was formless and only later he took a form to come to us ...We feel that something beyond the body or form is vaster. True, it is vaster, but it is a mistake if we say that the formless is more meaningful than the form. The idea that the higher we go, the more we are in touch with the formless is not true. When we go higher it need not be towards the formless. It can be toward the supremely divine [personal] God with form, who possesses boundless Affection, boundless Love, boundless Concern— everything in infinite measure. We can go beyond the form of the mind, but not beyond the supreme Form.

He continues,

> You can touch any part of the form to enter the formless. If in that way you can feel the form and the formless as equally important, then you will realise God sooner. . . . Again, I wish to tell you that it is a mistake to feel that the formless is superior to the form. They are equally important. . . . At times if one wants to get joy from the formless, he can. If one wants to get joy from the form, he can.

But I wish to say that *even after you have realised the Highest Absolute you will get more joy from the form because you care for manifestation. The spiritual seekers who cry for the manifestation of the Divine on earth will get abundant joy, much more joy, from the Absolute with form than from the Absolute without form* [emphasis added].[54]

The importance of this passage is not only in Sri Chinmoy's repeated emphasis on the equal value for us as human persons of God "with form" and God "without form," but also and even more in the explicit connection he makes between valuing God's personal aspect and the mission of "God-manifestation" or "the manifestation of the divine on earth."

What is "God-manifestation"? We have already seen and employed the terms "manifest" and "unmanifest" as meaning something like "appearing," "created," "with form" and their opposites. It is now necessary to say that for Sri Chinmoy "manifestation"—a word of immense ethical importance for him—is different from "revelation" because it is a further stage of concreteness in the process of transformation. In this transformation, "divine qualities" are not only revealed to, but also are assimilated by, the outer world in an evolutionary process of which conscious human aspiration, the "inner cry" or hunger for a higher and better life, is the most recent outcome. Sri Chinmoy compares "realisation" of God to possessing a mango, "revelation" to taking out the mango and showing it to someone, and "manifestation" to sharing it with others so that they eat it and digest it.[55] The purpose of God's creation, as he states constantly, is this very God-manifestation. For human beings, it is a God-ordained task calling for acceptance of the world and work in the world for the benefit of all. Because God-manifestation is so central to his entire philosophy, Sri Chinmoy's strong affirmation that those who care for God's manifestation in the world must also care for God's personal aspect casts abundant light on why throughout his writings he always emphasizes the personal as well as the relational nature of God and our approach to God through love, devotion, and surrender.

GOD AS INFINITE AND AS FINITE

The same overall point concerning formlessness and form is taken up in slightly different language when Sri Chinmoy discusses the nature of God as both infinite and as finite:

When God created Himself, He created Himself in two aspects: the Infinite and the finite. When you think of the finite, you think of form, and when you think of the infinite, you think there is no form. Yet inside the finite is the message of the Infinite; in the finite is first the revelation and then the manifestation of the Infinite. The finite is necessary because it is through the finite that the Infinite plays its role in the cosmic game here on earth. At the same time, the Infinite is necessary because it is in the Infinite that the finite has its eternal shelter. There it finds protection and perfection.

The Formless is necessary to realise the Highest, the Ultimate, the Infinite, and *the form is necessary to reveal and manifest the Highest and the Inmost in an intimate way*. That which is infinite in consciousness can be seen only in the formless form. Again, it can house itself in form. That is why the heart can hold Infinity inside itself [emphasis added].[56]

The interiority of the heart is found at a mysterious boundary between the infinite and the finite. The Chāndogya Upanisad says, "As vast as the space here around us is this space within the heart (*antar hrdaya ākāśah*), and within it are contained both earth and sky, both fire and wind, both the sun and the moon, both lightning and stars. What belongs here to this space around us, as well as what does not—all that is contained within it" (8.1.3).[57] A recurring statement in the Upanisads is that the soul or *ātman* is located within the heart.[58] The soul, in some way a presence or emanation of the limitless Divine, is at once infinitesimally small, infinitely vast and all-pervading.

Sri Chinmoy explicitly connects God's Omnipotence with God's Omnipresence, God's Power with God's capacity to become immanent in creation, saying, "God, being infinite, can also be finite. Otherwise, He is not infinite. He is omnipotent because He can be in the atom and at the same time in the vast universe."[59] Elaborating on this point, he says,

God is infinite Consciousness, infinite Bliss, yet He can also assume a finite form. He is infinite, He is finite, and at the same time He transcends both the Infinite and the finite. He is life, He is death, yet again, He is beyond both life and death. ... God is boundless and in the field of manifestation He takes all forms. ... He is as vast as the universe but because He is in everything, God can also be finite. God is omnipotent. Where is His omnipotence if He cannot become a small child, a tiny insect or an atom? ... Just because God is omnipotent, He can do anything He wants to do ... He can be vast, He can be infinitesimal.

Finite and Infinite, according to our outer understanding, are opposites of each other. But in God's Eye they are one, one complements the other . . . . The finite wants to reach the Absolute, the Highest, which is the Infinite. The Infinite wants to manifest itself in and through the finite. Then the [cosmic] game is Complete. Otherwise it will be only a one-sided game. There will be no true Joy, no achievement or fulfilment. In and through the finite, the Infinite is singing its song of unity. In and through the Infinite, the finite is singing its song of multiplicity.[60]

The One is the boundless Infinite and becomes the Many, which are finite—and both are aspects of God's Fullness. Sri Chinmoy says, "The Supreme is infinite Consciousness, infinite Bliss, yet He can also assume a finite form. He is infinite, He is finite, and at the same time He transcends both the Infinite and the finite."[61]

Ultimately there is no opposition or contradiction between these two aspects of the Divine, and although for finite beings like ourselves form is at first easier to apprehend, in due time our full comprehension of reality must embrace both God with form and also the formless, as just mentioned. The ontological continuity of Creator and creation is of the greatest epistemological and ethical importance for Sri Chinmoy. It is true that we cannot know the world as it really is without knowing God, its Source, but it is equally true that because God is not apart from or other than God's creation, we cannot attain complete knowledge of God by rejecting the world or disregarding how the Highest and the Inmost are manifested "in an intimate way" in particularity and multiplicity. Moreover, we cannot truly love God the Creator without loving and serving God the creation; this is the subject of our final chapter. The very purpose of creation and of the world's existence is the increase of joy and perfection: God-manifestation through the ongoing cosmic Game, the divine Līlā. Sri Chinmoy at all times stresses acceptance of the world and love for the world. Spiritual practice or yoga thus necessarily includes service in the form of work that will expedite the world process of God-manifestation and growth of greater and greater perfection and fulfillment.

The divine Plenitude becomes apprehensible in a new manner as it assumes countless finite forms; "God is boundless, and in the field of manifestation He takes all forms."[62] The fact that God the Infinite can become each and every finite being, however small, weak, or unillumined, is a demonstration of God's Omnipotence. "God, being Infinite, can also be finite. Otherwise, He would not be Infinite. He is Omnipotent because He can live in the tiny atom and in the vast universe at the same time."[63] A poem says: "Eternity's atom / And Eternity's Infinity / Have the same source: / God's Vision-Eye."[64]

The formless Infinite paradoxically contracts Itself to manifest Itself, to become the world of finite forms and fulfill Itself through the Līlā. "In form the cosmic Consciousness manifests itself by circumscribing itself. In the formless the cosmic Consciousness transcends itself by expanding and enlarging itself."[65] The description of divine Consciousness as "circumscribing itself" brings to mind the divine Self-contraction by which God the Limitless creates the world according to the Jewish mystical tradition of Lurianic Kabbalah. Arthur Green explains, "The God who is all can have no other. Hence the divine light has to hide itself so that it might be revealed. It withdraws itself from being in order that it might be seen, in order to allow for us to exist as 'other,' so that we might see and bear witness to it. This paradox of divine self-withdrawal is what the Jewish sages call *tsimtsum*."[66] Gershom G. Scholem says, "According to Luria, God was compelled to make room for the world by, as it were, abandoning a region within Himself, a kind of mystical primordial space from which He withdrew in order to return to it in the act of creation and revelation. The first act of *En-Sof*, the Infinite Being, is therefore not a step outside but a step inside."[67] There is here a similarity to Sri Chinmoy's view that God, being all in all, comprehends both the Infinite and the finite—and that therefore there is nothing "outside" the limitless Being of the Supreme.[68]

NAMES, ASPECTS, AND IMAGES OF THE DIVINE

Sri Chinmoy speaks of God as "The Supreme." He values this term as one expressing special intimacy with God as personal, "Our Beloved Supreme," but also prefers it because for him it conveys the sense of God's Self-transcendence which is central to his vision of God. He says,

> [A]lthough God and the Supreme are one, there is a subtle distinction between the two. The highest Supreme is different from what we call "God." When we speak of God-realisation, here "God" is synonymous with the Supreme. But usually when we say "God," we feel that He embodies a height which is static. . . . He has reached His height and stopped. He does not have a constantly evolving Consciousness. . . . But when we say "Supreme," we are speaking of the Supreme Lord who not only reaches the absolute Highest, but always goes beyond, beyond and transcends the Beyond. There is a constant upward movement.[69]

On very rare occasions he has used the term "emptiness" or "void" to refer to the Supreme. In one of his earliest collections of talks, we find this brief mention: "We can expect Him to make us understand everything, everything in nothing and nothing in everything, the Full in the Void and the Void in the Full,"[70] suggesting that the *śūnya* and the *pūrṇam* are aspects of one another. This is confirmed in two Bengali songs, one of which says "O emptiness, vast emptiness, / Inside you is the satisfaction of completeness" (*Śūnya tumi mahā śūnya / pūrṇa tomar antare*)[71] and the other, "Inside emptiness / Fullness abides" (*Śūnya bakke birāje pūrṇa*).[72] A more recent poem makes the same statement: "In Eternity's emptiness /Abides / Infinity's fulness."[73]

Concerning the gender of God, Sri Chinmoy is consistently clear that God is unlimited in this respect as in all others. God is "He" and equally "She." In a Bengali song he says to the Supreme, "In one form, You are my Father and Mother eternal" (*Ekadhare tumi janaka janāni*).[74] God is also, as "impersonal" and infinite, beyond gender. One may feel more affinity to one or another "aspect" of God, but all are real. Indeed, there is no need to confine oneself to a single way of imaging and experiencing God, and one is free to name God in any way and in all the ways one wishes. In ordinary human life, "We have to express our emotion to an individual in a particular way. But when we deal with God it is totally different. God is our father, mother, sister, brother, friend; He is everything. We can have all relationships with God. With Him there is no bondage."[75]

It is significant that in Bengali, the third personal pronoun *se* can mean either "he" or "she" and when writing in Bengali Sri Chinmoy just as often speaks of God as "Mother" as "Father." He uses the masculine pronoun when writing in English. Altogether it may be said that Sri Chinmoy's use of "He" for God is neither strong nor exclusive. Indeed, he states unequivocally: "It is a deplorable mistake when we take God only as a male figure. The Eternal Supreme is everything. God is not bound by our ideas of masculine and feminine. He transcends everything. He transcends all our human concepts. That is why He Is God."[76] He adds,

God is at once our father and our mother, our divine Father and our divine Mother. In the West, God the Father is prominent, while in the East, in India especially, God the Mother comes first. ...Both East and West are perfectly right. When we realise God the Father, we are bound to see God the Mother within Him. When we realise God the Mother, we will unmistakably see God the Father within Her.[77]

While saying that, "God is at once our Father and our Mother. As Father He observes, as Mother, He creates,"[78] only in early lectures does he make reference to the traditional Indian philosophical terms *puruṣa* and *prakṛti*.[79] He accepts the various names for the Supreme of the theistic traditions of India, saying that "The gods are the divinely individualised branches of the all-sheltering and all-protecting Tree, the Supreme,"[80] but rarely uses their names except in his Bengali songs, where they are frequent. He affirms *Avatāra* or the direct descent of God into the world to defend *dharma* or the good and to expedite world progress,[81] and construes this as the highest degree of God-realization as attained by world-historical spiritual figures. These include Krishna, the Buddha and Jesus, who possess not only total and complete God-oneness but also the capacity to manifest this oneness here in the world in fully global measure.

GOD'S EYE, GOD'S HEART, AND GOD'S FEET

In his later poetry[82] Sri Chinmoy makes extensive use of three images for God's "aspects": God's Eye, God's Heart and God's Feet. While these terms have been present in his work from the beginning, especially in poems written in his last ten years they are used more than other terms, though references to God's Face, God's Smile, God's Breath and God's Arms and Hands also occur. Here only a brief reflection on their meaning can be offered, giving some sense of how they are employed to disclose the divine Being to the reader's intuitive apprehension.

The ontology of God's Eye and God's Heart is stated explicitly in two poems: "When I look at God's Eye, / I clearly see / That His Eye is transcendental," and "When I feel God's Heart, / I unmistakably feel / That His heart is universal."[83] "God's Eye" is the power of Vision or seeing, and corresponds to the transcendent Source of existence: "Eternity's Silence-Eye / Gives birth / To Infinity's sound-life."[84] The poet says, "From God's Eye / We awake. / Into God's Heart / We retire."[85] As mentioned above, the dimensions of "God's Heart," preceding the world of "sound-multiplicity," are universality and interiority. What of "God's Feet"? In an early lecture, Sri Chinmoy says, "In Heaven we see God's Eye. On earth we see God's Feet. With God's Eye we enter into His world of silence. With His feet we follow Him into the world of sound. In the world of silence we see God as the many in the One. In the world of sound we see God as the One in the many."[86] "God's Feet" represent the concrete particularity of the Divine; the poems show the divine Feet preeminently to be the place of personal encounter and relationship, one that is ever accessible to all. All three images are linked to the divine Compassion.

As we seek to discern the meanings of the three images, we find that "God's Eye" is spoken of in the language of agency. It is transcendent yet omnipresent, travelling everywhere and seeing all. "I know not where / My Lord's Compassion-Eye / Is unavailable,"[87] Sri Chinmoy says. "I clearly see / That my Lord's Compassion-Eye / Is closer than my own breath."[88] God's Eye constantly acts: It beckons, blesses, claims, teaches, guides, employs, scolds, cradles, intervenes, and protects. It would seem to stand not only for God's power of Vision, but to be connected to "God's Will" which is also referred to simply as such. For "God's Heart," in contrast, Sri Chinmoy uses spatial language. It is a place into which we can go and remain: most often God's "Heart-Garden," but also God's Heart-Home, Heart-Nest, Heart-Palace, Heart-Guesthouse, Heart-Cottage, Heart-Ocean, even Heart-School. Having entered into this space, within it we sing, play, dance and are spontaneously transformed. While God's Eye is more closely associated with divine Justice, God's Heart offers unconditional forgiveness. "Nobody can ever close/ The door / Of God's Heart-Home."[89] References to God's "Justice-Eye" can be found, but there is no such phrase as "God's Justice-Heart." God's Feet are also spoken of as a place, but rather than "entering into" their reality, a person goes to them and forms a relationship with the Supreme by placing at God's Feet one's "very existence." God's Feet are the place of surrender. In placing oneself at God's Feet, the poems say, one has reached a crucial moment of transformation through self-offering: "My Lord, / Now that I have embraced Your Feet / With all the devotion / That You have bestowed upon me / Over the years, / I feel that I am completely liberated / From the snare of earthly desires."[90] One arrives and sits at God's Feet, then remains and lives there. One looks at, touches, embraces, shed tears over, and eventually "devours the Dust" of God's Feet in a culminating and continuing realization of intimacy and oneness. And in sum, "God's Eye / Cannot live / Without caring," "God's Heart / Cannot live / Without loving," and "God's Feet / Cannot live / Without giving."[91]

THE INFINITE PLENITUDE

For Sri Chinmoy God is the one Supreme Reality of infinite plenitude and limitless self-transcendence. This God is a Mystery, the unknowable God who originates God's own Being out of God's Silence and in boundless freedom and dynamism is unceasingly transcending God's Self to attain a new Reality. The Supreme is without form, is with form, and is beyond both form and formlessness; the Supreme is "He" and is "She," is also both, and is beyond gender. While certain attributes of God such as Delight, Light, Consciousness, and Compassion are central, there is no end to God's qualities, the fullness of which is always increasing. The essence of God's divinity is Love, in which the divine attributes converge. God's creativity and the dynamism of transcendence are directed to integral perfection, the manifestation of the positive and fulfilling divine qualities at all levels of existence. Perfection is not a fixed goal, but goes beyond itself so that this transformation, too, is endless and ever-transcending.

In apparent paradox, it is God's Infinity that makes God intimately knowable to finite living beings, including ourselves. It is just because God is boundlessly free and powerful that God can limit God's Being and become finite in, and as, God's creation. At the same time that God is infinite and unknowable, God is also everywhere present and accessible. Those who seek God, each according to his or her own disposition, find that God approaches them and is known by them in the way or ways for which each person has an affinity. The many-sided divine availability is a demonstration of God's Love and Compassion for God's creation, and is also one of the ways in which God's limitless and ever-expanding nature expresses itself in the continuing cosmic process of God-manifestation. Sri Chinmoy stresses the personal aspect of God, or God with form, not only because this aspect is more accessible to human persons, but also because it is to the world, to the realm of form, that God-manifestation belongs. This open-ended transformation towards perfection is an ethical commitment essential to his philosophy as a whole. It is also at the heart of his vision of the nature of God.

NOTES

1. Sri Chinmoy uses the term "soul" as generally equivalent to the Sanskrit *ātman, jīvātman* or *jīva* of Indian traditions.

2. *Twenty-Seven Thousand Aspiration-Plants,* Part 8 (New York: Agni Press, 1983), No. 778.

3. Ibid., No. 751.

4. *Yoga,* 7.

5. *God-Life: Is It a Far Cry?* (New York: Agni Press, 1974), 45.

6. *Eternity's Breath: Aphorisms and Essays* (New York: Agni Press, 1975), 77. The aphorisms in this book were written in 1963, shortly before Sri Chinmoy came to the United States from India in 1964.

7. Sri Chinmoy makes this statement frequently throughout his writings.

8. *God's Hour* (New York: Agni Press, 1973), 7.

9. *The Garden of Love-Light,* Part 1 (New York: Agni Press, 1973), 13.

10. The word "Being" will be used here to refer to God in a general manner and to the totality of God's aspects or attributes, rather than to indicate *Sat* in particular in the context of *Sat-Cit-Ānanda,* since Sri Chinmoy usually renders *Sat* as "Existence" (as well as "Reality" or "Truth").

11. *The Vision of God's Dawn* (New York: Agni Press, 1974), 31.

12. Ibid., 1.

13. *Everest-Aspiration* (New York: Agni Press, 1978), 57.

14. This ineffability is declared in the Upaniṣads, see, for example Katha Up. 2.3.12 and Taittīriya Up. 2.4.1.

15. *Canada Aspires, Canada Receives, Canada Achieves,* Part 2 (New York: Agni Press, 1974), 59.

16. Sri Chinmoy acknowledges the force of the well-known saying *"Neti, neti"* or "Not this, not that" (see Bṛhadāraṇyaka Upaniṣad 2.3.6) in discriminating truth from falsehood, the unreal from the Real, and also as conveying a spirit of renunciation. At the same time, while giving immense importance to "Silence" in his own discourse, he is not an adherent of the apophatic approach or *via negativa,* though recognizing its validity as an element of the yoga of knowledge or *jñāna.* He rather advocates positive language in referring to God, as this chapter explains. See *Commentaries,* 57.

17. *Eternity's Breath,* 39.

18. Ibid., 38.

19. "The Fount," in *Europe-Blossoms* (Santurce, Puerto Rico: Aum Press, 1974), No. 512.

20. *United Nations Works,* Vol. 1, 12.

21. *Everest-Aspiration,* 97.

22. Opening invocation of Īśa Up., also Bṛhadāraṇyaka Up. 5.1.1.

23. *The Summits of God-life: Samadhi and Siddhi* (New York: Agni Press, 1974), 1–2, 4.

24. *Oneness of the Eastern Heart and the Western Mind,* Part 2 (2004), 49. The three volumes of this series collect Sri Chinmoy's lectures given at universities around the world 1968–2001.

25. *My Lord's Secret's Revealed* (New York: Herder and Herder, 1971), 78.

26. "Ecstasy," in *Europe-Blossoms,* No. 61.

27. *God's Hour,* 3.

28. *Service-Boat and Love-Boatman,* Part 1 (New York: Agni Press, 1974), 3.

29. *Service-Trees,* Part 44 (2005), No. 43,362.

30. See Kusumita Pedersen, "This *Prema* Dwells in the Heart of Them All: Swami Vivekananda on Love and Compassion," in *Vivekananda: His Life, Legacy and Liberative Ethics,* ed. Rita D. Sherma (New York: Lexington Books, 2020) 103–124. *Prema Sāgara* is the title of a book in Hindi by Lallū Lāla published in 1810, while he was engaged in translation and research at Fort Williams College, Kolkata; it is a translation of a work by Chaturbhuja Miśra in Braj Bhāsa based on the 10th Book of the Bhāgavata Purāṇa. See Lallū Lāl Kavi, *Premu-Sāguru or Ocean of Love, Being a Literal Translation of the Hindi Text of Lallū Lāl Kavi* as Edited by the Late Professor Eastwick, Fully annotated and explained Grammatically, Idiomatically and Exegetically by Frederic Pincott (Westminster, UK: Archibald Constable, 1897).

31. *Songs of the Soul* (New York: Herder and Herder, 1971), 69.

32. "One truth speaks," in *Europe-Blossoms,* No. 294.

33. *God's Hour,* 73.

34. *United Nations Works,* Vol. 1, 37.

35. *Eternity's Breath,* 9.

36. *Service-Boat and Love-Boatman,* Part 1, loc. cit.

37. This phrase occurs throughout his writings in all periods.

38. *The Oneness of the Eastern Heart and the Western Mind,* Part 2, 129. Text restored to original, *My Ivy League Leaves* (New York: Sri Chinmoy Lighthouse, 1972), 12.

39. Ibid., 4.

40. *God and the Cosmic Game* (New York: Agni Press, 1977), 6.

41. *The Oneness of the Eastern Heart and the Western Mind,* Part 1 (New York: Agni Press, 2003), 304.

42. *God and the Cosmic Game,* loc. cit.

43. John Berthrong.

44. *Professor-Children: God's Reality-Fruits* (New York: Agni Press, 1997), 11–12.

45. God's measureless attributes such as Light or Delight can be thought of as having "formless form;" they are particular but still "formless" in the sense that they

do not have limited shape such as an anthropomorphic shape, and do not appear as "personal."

46. *Fifty Freedom-Boats to One Golden Shore,* Part 3 (New York: Agni Press, 1974), 74.

47. *The Oneness of the Eastern Heart and the Western Mind,* Part 2, 437.

48. *Canada Aspires,* Part 2, 23.

49. Ibid., 66.

50. *Fifty Freedom-Boats to One Golden Shore,* Part 2 (New York: Agni Press, 1974), 98.

51. *Service-Trees,* Part 12 (1999), No. 13,478 and No. 13,479.

52. *Aspiration-Plants,* Part 3 (1983), No. 225.

53. *Service-Trees,* Part 10 (1998), No. 9,410.

54. *God-Life,* 39–44.

55. *Summits,* 127–128.

56. Ibid., 15–16.

57. *Upaniṣads,* tr. Patrick Olivelle (New York: Oxford University Press, 1996), 167.

58. Patrick Olivelle. "Heart in the Upaniṣads," *Rivista di Studi Sudasiatici,* 1 (2006): 51–67.

59. *Yoga,* 101.

60. *God's Dawn,* 9–11.

61. Ibid., 9.

62. Ibid., 10.

63. *Yoga,* 101.

64. *Service-Trees,* Part 5 (1998), No. 4,564.

65. *Commentaries,* 60.

66. *Seek My Face, Speak My Name* (Northvale, NJ: Jacob Aronson Inc., 1992), 65.

67. *Major Trends in Jewish Mysticism* (New York: Schocken Books, 1961, reprinted from the 3rd revised edition, 1954), 261.

68. Peter Heehs in his article "The Kabbalah, the Philosophie Cosmique and the Integral Yoga: A Study in Cross-Cultural Influence" (*Aries* 2, no. 2 (2011): 219–247) describes how Mirra Alfassa, who was to become the Mother of the Sri Aurobindo Ashram, in 1904-1908 when she was in her twenties studied the "Philosophie Cosmique" of Max Theon (c.1848-1927) and his wife, known as Sybil Altima Una. This teaching has many elements of Lurianic Kabbalah; Theon came from Eastern Europe and his father had been a rabbi. Heehs examines the similarities between the Philosophie Cosmique and the Integral Yoga of Sri Aurobindo and the Mother, while stressing that Sri Aurobindo's main influences are Vedāntic, as he himself stated.

   Heehs concludes that there is no direct influence of Kabbalah on Sri Aurobindo, but indirect influence of the Philosophie Cosmique on the Integral Yoga on certain points may be possible. He comments that "Aurobindo's idea of 'exclusive concentration of consciousness-force' [in *The Life Divine*] is remarkably similar to the Lurianic idea of *tsimtsum.* This cannot be explained by direct or indirect influence, since Aurobindo never read any kabbalistic texts, and the Philosophie Cosmique, of which he had indirect knowledge, does not contain anything like *tsimtsum.* This would seem to be a case of independent inspiration, due perhaps to Luria and

Aurobindo having caught the same idea during spiritual reflection or experience. The idea of an originating contraction or separation occurs also in the writings of other mystics, for example Jakob Böhme and William Blake. This suggests that a certain line of mystical thought or experience can lead to a similar concept in different cultural contexts" (243–244).

69. *God's Dawn*, 40.

70. *Yoga*, 14–15.

71. *Pole-Star Promise-Light,* Part 2 (New York: Agni Press, 1975), 23.

72. Ibid., p. 40.

73. *Service-Trees, Part 8,* 1998, No. 7,060.

74. *The Garden of Love-Light,* Part 1, 2.

75. *Fifty Freedom-Boats to One Golden Shore*, Part 6 (New York: Agni Press, 1975), 22–23.

76. *The Doubt-World* (New York: Agni Press, 1977), 31.

77. *Fifty Freedom-Boats,* Part 6, 24. See also *Earth-Bound Journey and Heaven-Bound Journey* (New York: Agni Press, 1975), 54–55.

78. *Yoga*, 18.

79. See *Commentaries,* 218–222; *Eternity's Breath,* 21, 38, and *God's Dawn,* 21–23.

80. *Eternity's Breath,* 22; see also *Yoga,* 71: "...these gods and goddesses are simply different manifestations of the Sole Absolute. Each deity embodies a particular aspect or quality of the Supreme."

81. In Hinduism, this concept is first mentioned in the Bhagavad Gita 4.6-8 and is especially associated with Vaiṣṇavism. In English it is often rendered as "divine Incarnation."

82. Especially the series *Seventy-Seven Thousand Service-Trees*, Parts 1–50, 1998 through 2009. I am grateful to Kakali Atkin for help with references in this section.

83. Op cit., Part 31 (2003), Nos. 30,270 and 30,271.

84. *Service-Trees*, Part 4 (1998), No. 3,238.

85. *Service-Trees*, Part 20 (2001), Nos. 19,197 and 19,198.

86. *The Oneness of the Eastern Heart and the Western Mind,* Part 2 (2004), 437.

87. *Service Trees*, Part 7 (1998), No. 6,017.

88. *Service-Trees*, Part 6 (1998), No. 6,306.

89. *Service-Trees*, Part 4 (1998), No. 3,204.

90. *Service-Trees*, Part 2 (1998), No. 1,076.

91. *Service-Trees*, Part 44 (2005), Nos. 43, 363–365.

Chapter 3

Creation and Evolution

THE CREATOR AND THE CREATION

The universe comes from the Supreme, who is the ground of its existence and has sovereignty over all. The One becomes the Many in a conscious and willed process of creation. Throughout his writings Sri Chinmoy speaks of "God the Creator" and "God the creation," making clear that the world is not separate from the Supreme but is itself God in other forms —forms which are multiple but also one through their indwelling divinity and because of the single Source of their reality. This chapter explores the nature and purpose of the divine action that brings the world into being, the ontological continuity of the One and the Many, evolution or the unfolding progress of the cosmos, and the ethical significance of evolution as God's increasing manifestation in creation, moving towards integral perfection.

THE PURPOSE OF CREATION: THE JOY OF THE LĪLĀ

Why did God create the world? Sri Chinmoy consistently gives the answer that the One wanted to become many in order to fulfill Itself through the cosmic Līlā, the Play or Game of the universe. The sense of the Sanskrit word embraces spontaneous play which is done for its own sake, a game with rules and assigned roles, and the performance of a drama. The purpose of the Līlā is the joy or delight (ānanda) of the play itself.[1]

Rather than simply saying that the one God "became many," Sri Chinmoy declares in many similarly worded accounts that God "wanted to become many." The divine impulse towards fulfillment in multiplicity is central to his concept of creation and reaffirms two statements in the Upaniṣads: "In the

45

beginning this was Being alone, one only without a second . . . . It thought, May I be many, may I grow forth."[2] In the same passage in the Chāndogya Upaniṣad the sage Uddālaka Aruni then says, "All these creatures have their root (*mūla*) in Being. They have Being as their abode, Being as their support." He continues with the great utterance or *mahāvākya* "*Tat tvam asi,*" "You are That," declaring the oneness of the soul or *ātman* of every creature with the Supreme Brahman.[3] As well, the Taittirīya Upaniṣad says, "He desired: Let me become many, let me be born. He performed austerity [*tapas*]. Having performed austerity he created all this, whatever is here. Having created it, into it, indeed, he entered. Having entered it, he became the actual and the beyond."[4]

Sri Chinmoy says: "God originated Himself out of His own Silence. He was One but He wanted to become many in order to divinely enjoy the Cosmic Game,"[5] and "God was originally One. With His Aspiration, God wanted to become many. He wanted to divinely enjoy and supremely fulfill Himself in and through an infinite number of forms."[6] As the Game cannot be enjoyed with only one player,[7] "He created Himself in millions of forms and shapes."[8] In a Bengali song he says:

One has become many	Ek sājiyache bahu
For aspiration's enjoyment supreme;	Nijere karite āswādan
Many have become one	Bahu sājiyache ek
For manifestation's enjoyment supreme.	Nijere dānite pramodan
Many and one	Bahu ār ek jāni
Are inseparably one	Abhinna hiyā nibedan.[9]
In Reality's Perfection-Fulfulment-Light.	

In the play of manyness, there is an increase of joy, a joy that is different from the joy of divine aloneness. "By becoming Many, the Supreme tastes His own Truth . . . . in infinite forms. And finally, when He has manifested and fulfilled Himself fully in infinite forms here on earth, the Supreme goes back to His original Source. The Game is complete."[10] It is "complete" in the sense that it is whole—and yet the Game is not "over." With the passage of time, manifestation of the Divine in the world achieves perfection and perfection brings forth satisfaction, or fulfillment. But perfection, as Sri Chinmoy often says, is not a fixed goal but is ever-transcending. "Today's goal is tomorrow's starting point," and the perfection of the present will be surpassed by the perfection of the future as the universe continues to evolve.

THE ONE AND THE MANY

For Sri Chinmoy divine creation is a process of becoming. He states that God "becomes" the world rather than that God commands it to come into existence. While an early aphorism says, "The Self-division of the Supreme proclaims the birth of creation,"[11] this division is not fragmentation but an expansion into plurality, sometimes called "projection." He images this becoming as growth from a seed: "The whole universe came into existence from Brahman the Seed."[12] Speaking of a seed and its growth emphasizes the continuity of substance between origin and outcome. The primal unity of the One is not affected when the One becomes many: "God was one, but He wanted to become many. When He became many, He did not lose His oneness. The dance of God's unity in multiplicity and multiplicity in unity we call God's eternal Game."[13] Moreover, the divine Plenitude is not diminished: "When the Supreme started the creation, it was from an iota of His entire Being. Everything in the creation . . . is a very infinitesimal portion of the Supreme"[14]—as Krishna says in the Bhagavad Gītā, "I support this entire universe constantly / With a single fraction of myself."[15] Both the One and the Many are "forms" of God. "The One is many in Its universal form. The Many are One in their transcendental form,"[16] Sri Chinmoy says, and "God is One. At the same time, He is Many. He is One in His highest Transcendental Consciousness. He is many here in the field of manifestation. At the highest, He is Unity. Here on earth, He is Multiplicity. . . . He is manifesting Himself in infinite ways and in infinite forms."[17]

The oneness of God with God's Creation is at the heart of Sri Chinmoy's vision. He declares, "God can never be separated from His creation. Creator and Creation are one, inseparable."[18] Throughout his writings he uses the metaphor of a tree for this oneness-and-multiplicity; here we should remember the intimate connection with trees that he established in his childhood, climbing them and wandering in the groves and forests of Chittagong. We might also note that the archetype of the World Tree is found not only in Indian sources but also in many traditions globally.[19] Sri Chinmoy says that when God wishes to experience God's Self as the Many in countless forms, the emergence of the Many is "like the seed that eventually grows into a banyan tree. When the seed grows into a huge tree, we see millions of leaves and thousands of fruits and flowers. But it started its journey as one single seed."[20] The tree comes from only one seed and when fully grown has a single trunk and root system, but also many branches bearing the myriad leaves, flowers, and fruits, here compared to the numberless beings of the universe. The branches, leaves, flowers, and fruits are essential to the tree's fully developed life; each is an integral part of the whole organism though they are of different appearances, made of different tissues and perform different functions. Overall the image of the tree vividly displays the existence of the One and the Many as a natural, coherent and living unity.

THE TRANSCENDENTAL AND THE UNIVERSAL

In the following passage Sri Chinmoy links the image of the seed and tree to his even more frequent description of creation as Silence giving rise to Sound: "The Creator is at once the Silence-seed and the Sound-tree. As the Silence-seed, as the Silence of the Transcendental Height, He embodies His own highest height and deepest depth. And as the Sound-tree, he offers to His creation His own achievement. Silence prepares; Sound reveals. Sound offers what Silence is."[21] (Note that in this passage "height" and "depth" are both aspects of "Silence.") Answering the question of a child, "How did God get His first beginning?" Sri Chinmoy replies:

> God got His first beginning from His Silence. . . . When he was in Silence, He was One alone. He felt no loneliness as we do when we stay alone. Even when He was alone, He was complete because He Himself was Silence and He Himself was both the Observer and Enjoyer of that Silence. God started His first beginning with Silence. Then He became many with His Sound-Light. With His Silence-Light He was one. With His Sound-Light He became many.[22]

In the very beginning, "Before the Supreme created the Universe, He created Himself,"[23] "God originated Himself out of His own Silence"[24] and then, "When He wanted to become the sound-life, He projected Himself into many forms."[25] In this process, "universal Sound" comes forth from "transcendental Silence;"[26] the "projection" and self-multiplication of God's Being—the One becoming the Many—is the birth of Sound from Silence:[27] Especially in his poetry, Sri Chinmoy consistently uses "Sound" to refer to the manifest creation and "Silence" to refer to the unmanifest Source. In this poem he uses the phrase "silence-seed" to bring together the cosmological figures of speech.

Unity is good.
Unity with multiplicity is better.
Unity in multiplicity is by far the best.

Who owns unity?
The climbing heart.

What is unity with multiplicity?
The vision of the soul
In the manifestation of life.

Where is unity in multiplicity?

In the Silence-seeds,
Time-flowers
And
Sound-fruits of God.[28]

This poem illustrates Sri Chinmoy's distinctive way of articulating a philosophical reflection that has a number of moving parts in a concise, structured, and meaning-packed lyrical statement, in this case drawing on the tree metaphor. "The climbing heart" refers to aspiration, the upward-mounting inner flame, cry, or hunger for a greater and more perfect reality; in human life Sri Chinmoy locates aspiration primarily in the spiritual heart, which he very often calls the "aspiration-heart." Aspiration impels evolution, as will be more fully related below.

In reflections on Sound and Silence and the creation of the universe, the mantra Aum (or Om) is prominent in a few early passages: "Aum is the soundless sound. It is the vibration of the Supreme. It is called the Seed-Sound of the Universe, for with this sound, the Supreme set into motion the first vibration of His creation. The teeming universe is sustained perpetually by the creative vibration of the Divine Aum."[29] Aum is the form in sound of the ultimate Reality: "Brahman is the imperishable Infinite. Another name for Brahman is Aum. Aum is the Creator. Aum is the creation. Aum is beyond the creation."[30] Note that Sri Chinmoy says that Aum not only brings creation into manifestation, but also is "beyond" or prior to manifestation and creation. "Aum is the real name of God. In the cosmic manifestation is Aum. Beyond the manifestation, farthest beyond is Aum."[31] Aum bridges the Infinite and the finite, the formless and form, and thus is paradoxically known as the "soundless sound."[32]

In the process of cosmogonic becoming, it is the interior dimension of universal existence that emerges first from the transcendent Source. We have already learned that, "The universal Heart originated in God's Silence. When God was absolute Silence, inside this Silence something was growing. . . . The universal Heart came into existence before God's sound-life came into existence. And where is the universal heart? It is deep inside us, where reality constantly grows."[33] And we have also seen that, "When I look at God's Eye, / I clearly see/ That His Eye is transcendental," and "When I feel God's Heart, / I unmistakably feel/ That His Heart is universal."[34] And so the poet can say: "God's Eye / Multiplies God's Heart / Into Infinity," distilling into seven words a description of the beginning of cosmic creation.[35]

Sri Chinmoy adds that it is within the universal Heart that the soundless Sound first arises along with Delight or *Ānanda*; they come into being as God is creating Himself.[36] Since "God expresses Himself through silence. God expands Himself through Light," and "Light is the birth of God,"[37] the emergence of form through soundless Sound and Delight is simultaneous with the appearance of form as Light, which in Sri Chinmoy's writings can often be understood as a synonym for Consciousness. To summarize, within the primordial Silence there grows the Universal Heart, and within the Universal Heart emerges the Soundless Sound, Delight and the primordial Light. They arise together as *Sat-Cit-Ānanda*, which is "between" Silence and Sound and partakes of both as it expresses Itself. Sri Chinmoy alternatively puts it this way: "There are three realities: God, Soul and Life. God is the Transcendental Reality. Soul is the Inmost Reality. Life is the Universal Reality. God reveals the soul; the soul reveals life. God the Reality lives in His creative Will. Soul the Reality lives in its sustaining Will. Life the Reality lives in its fulfilling Will."[38] This passage is striking because of its emphasis on "Will" or conscious agency. From God the Transcendent there is "revealed" the universal and *inner* existence—the reality growing "deep inside us;" here "Soul" stands for the universal Heart as the interiority of all being. Then "Soul" by its Will brings forth or reveals the *outer* universal existence here called "Life," which in Sri Chinmoy's philosophy has the sense of integral, multi-dimensional and manifested existence.

In the following lines, the whole sequence is set forth in the "reverse" order, moving upwards, in Sri Chinmoy's most condensed style: "What is existence? Existence is God's Body. What is God's Body? God's Body is Infinity's Life. Infinity's Life is God's Dream. What is God's Dream? God's Dream is His Transcendental Reality's embodied Inspiration and revealed Aspiration."[39] Here "Dream" occupies the same position as "Soul" in the previous passage. The ascent from the outer world of manifestation and the return to the Source are delineated in a few words. If one is acquainted with the terms used here, which are poetic yet philosophically precise, these lines convey in a mantric or *sūtra*-like manner a brief but dense and highly structured ontological statement.[40]

To a child who asks, "Who made God?" Sri Chinmoy speaks of "Dream" and "Reality" as equivalent to unmanifest Silence and manifested Sound, adding that our own enjoyment of God's Presence is a culminating purpose of the divine Play. Significantly, this is also said to be God's enjoyment of God's Self through us.

> God Himself made God. God the Silence made God the Sound. Who is God the Silence? God the Silence is God the Dream. God the Sound is God the Manifested Reality.
>
> Who made God? God's Silence. God made Himself because he wished to enjoy. What was He going to enjoy? He was going to enjoy His universal Presence. That is to say, He wanted to enjoy His presence everywhere—inside

everyone, inside everything. Why did He want that? He wanted that because if He enjoyed His Presence everywhere, then one day the human beings he would create would also be able to enjoy His Presence.

When He was One, He was happy. But He wanted to become many because He wanted to be happy in a different way. . . . When God was alone, He created Himself alone, and He was happy. He thought that He should have some other way to become happy so He created Himself in many forms, in infinite, countless forms.[41]

Sri Chinmoy also refers to the creation as a form of divine art and God as the Supreme Artist.[42] This metaphor is evocative since even in human life art is an open-ended, self-transcending activity. An important aspect of the divine artistry is God as the Supreme Musician, which refers back to Silence and Sound. It might be supposed that since creation begins with Sound, creation would be described as initiated by the making of music, but this is not so. Rather, God's music is not merely Sound but Being in its totality, both the universal manifest and the transcendent unmanifest because—again paradoxically—Silence itself is a form of music. "Silence is the source of everything. It is the source of music and it is music itself. Silence is the deepest, most satisfying music of the Supreme,"[43] Sri Chinmoy says; "God the Musician knows that His Music is His transcendental Self-communion . . . . God's Music tells us that music is the realisation of the universal Soul."[44] God is the divine Player of the cosmic music in all of its modes, and the play of the universe is spoken of as a dance as well as a song: "God's Unity-Song wanted to be transformed into God's Multiplicity-Dance,"[45] also called "the dance of life."[46]

Sri Chinmoy is clear that even when the universal Life exists fully externalized in all its multiplicity and concreteness, its totality is contained *within* God's infinite Being: "Where is the universe? It is within God's Life. Where is God's Life? It is within His all-illumining Love."[47] God "holds the universe within Himself" while also living within the heart of the human person, an inner space that is boundlessly vast, as we already have seen.[48] "To know that the Lord is within the cosmos, without the cosmos and beyond the cosmos is to know everything,"[49] Sri Chinmoy says. As stated in chapter 1, this ontological structure is "panentheism."[50] It cannot be characterized as "pantheism," the view that God is equated with all that exists and is not more, since Sri Chinmoy continually affirms the transcendent and declares that "The universe in its entirety is but a tiny spark of His Infinite Magnitude."[51] Further, God's Love, which *contains* God's Life, is not an "attribute" of God but as stated above is God's whole Being, uncreated and created, as God is "made of" Love.[52] Indeed, God is Love, and "Truth is in all, but Love is all."[53]

ILLUSION AND "NOTHING"

Sri Chinmoy explicitly denies that the world, or universe, which is God's Body,[54] is an "illusion." Commenting on Śaṅkara, he says, "Shankara never did say that the world is a cosmic illusion. What he wanted to say and what he did say is this: the world is not and cannot be the Ultimate Reality."[55] Unillumined human beings indeed do not see the world as it really is, but our awakening will enable us to see that the world is not an "illusion," if this is taken to mean that it is unreal. Rather, when we transform our own limited and distorted vision, which causes the so-called illusion, we will see that the world is real since it is an integral part of God's Reality, with which it is continuous, as has been stressed. The world of appearance and of physical existence as such is not unreal or ontologically deficient; it is indeed real even though it may seem imperfect. Sri Chinmoy declares:

> The world is not an illusion. True illusion can never be comprehensible, whereas the world is easily comprehensible when we go deep within and look at it with our inner eye. It is the illusion that is unreal and not the world of ours.
>
> As my body is real, even so is my God's Body, the world.
>
> Nothing comes out of an empty void. God has projected the universe out of His Existence-Consciousness-Bliss. He has created the world. He has become the world. He wills and He becomes. He smilingly unveils without what he is silently within.[56]

It is helpful to recall that the understanding of the world as "God's Body" is a central theme in the philosophy of Rāmānuja.[57] In prioritizing this view as well as upholding the idea that creation is God's Līlā or Play, Rāmānuja denies that the world is unreal or mere appearance. Sri Chinmoy has said,

> God the Creator and God the creation have to be accepted at the same time. When we pray we feel that God is in heaven, but we do not feel that the same God is inside our heart and all around us, so we neglect God the creation. When we look at the beauty of Nature we must feel that it is the living Presence of God. When we look at a tree, when we look at a plant or when we enter into a garden, we must feel that it is God Who has taken incarnation as a beautiful flower, a most beautiful flower . . . we must accept everything as a manifestation of God.[58]

The term "incarnation" is not only congruent with Rāmānuja and Hindu tradition more generally, but needless to say has a profound resonance with Christianity and theologies of creation.

The question of illusion brings us to the question of creation "from nothing." Sri Chinmoy contests the very concept of creation "from nothing" because creation by God is a process of becoming rather than of *fiat*—and also because in the beginning, there was no "nothing" (which may be another way of saying the same thing). In the Chāndogya Upaniṣad immediately before he describes how the One has become many, Uddālaka objects, "Some people say 'in the beginning there was non-being [*asat*] alone, one only; without a second. From that non-being, being was produced.' But how, indeed, my dear, could it be thus? Said he, how could being be produced from non-being?"[59] Sri Chinmoy does allow for the use of the word "non-being" but only with searching reflection. In the following passage he stands the idea of "nothing" on its head and then dismantles and reinterprets it.

> We see the world within us; we see the world without us. In the world within there is a being, and in the world without there is also a being. These two beings are called "non-being" and "being" [*asat* and *sat*]. From non-being, being came into existence. The very idea baffles our minds. How can non-being create being? Non-being is nothing. From nothing, how can something come into existence? But we have to know that it is the mind that tells us that from non-being being cannot come into existence. We have to know that this "nothing" is actually something beyond the conception of the mind. "Nothing" is the life of the everlasting Beyond. "Nothing" is something that always remains beyond our mental conception. It transcends our limited consciousness. When we think of the world or of being coming out of non-being, we have to feel that this Truth can be known and realised only on the strength of our inner aspiration, where the mind does not operate at all. It is intuition which grants us this boon of knowing that 'nothing' is the song of the ever-transcending Beyond, and 'nothing' is the experience of the ever-fulfilling, ever-transcending and ever-manifesting existence.[60]

The true nature of "nothing" or "non-being" has to be grasped by intuition beyond ordinary thought, a kind of knowing which is attainable through yoga (as discussed below in our chapter on knowledge). And as already mentioned, the Void or great Emptiness (*mahāśūnya*) is none other than the divine Fullness or Infinity (*pūrṇam*), which is the ultimate Reality. He at times quotes the Upaniṣadic invocation "Infinity is that. Infinity is this. From Infinity, Infinity has come into existence. From Infinity, when Infinity is taken away, Infinity remains."[61] "Nothing" or *asat* is to be construed as the Infinite or the *Pūrṇam,* to *Sat-Cit-Ānanda* and "the song of the ever-transcending

Beyond."[62] With an allusion to the utterance on Delight from the Taittirīya
Upaniṣad (3.6, see below), he says "From Nothingness-Fulness / We came. /
To Fulness-Nothingness / We shall retire."[63]

ASPIRATION AND EVOLUTION

The process of creation as becoming is portrayed, as we have seen, by
complementary key phrases and images. God creates as a divine Play or as the
Supreme Artist, especially the Supreme Musician. The tree of creation grows
from "Brahman the Seed." Sound emerges from Silence. God also creates by
meditating: "The universe is God's Creation . . . is God's Compassion . . . is
God's concentration . . . is God's meditation . . . is God's contemplation."[64]
Again, creation is God's "Dream" or "Vision" which becomes reality. As
God Dreams, God creates by His Will: "He wills and He becomes."

God's Dream and God's Will are also God's Aspiration. "God had a
glowing Dream. The name of that Dream was Aspiration. Man has a climbing
cry. The name of this cry is also aspiration. God was originally one. With
His Aspiration, God wanted to become many."[65] Aspiration, the longing for
a higher, vaster and more perfect reality, is the driving impulse of cosmic
progress and is a central principle of Sri Chinmoy's worldview. God's
Aspiration is God's own inherent and continuous self-transcendence; in Its
own highest, the divine Reality eternally expands Its own Infinity and goes
beyond Itself to a new Reality. God also aspires through creation, which is
another mode of divine expansion. The self-transcendence of God's Reality
in the divine Silence and its expansion in Sound are both intrinsic to the
dynamism of the divine nature.

> Aspiration is a world. In the world of aspiration, God, who was at the very
> beginning one, wanted to become many. When He wanted to become many,
> He sang the song of self-transcendence. By fulfilling Himself in the world of
> multiplicity, He offers us the dance of perfection. It is in the aspiration-world
> that we see God the One and God the Many, God the eternal Silence and God
> the infinite Sound.[66]

God's wish to experience God's own Reality as the Many is God's own
Aspiration for an ever-growing increase of Delight through the cosmic
Play. Sri Chinmoy at times quotes this passage on Delight or Bliss from the
Taittirīya Upaniṣad: in his own translation, "From Delight we came into
existence. In Delight we grow. At the end of our journey's close, into Delight

we retire."[67] The world is born from God's Delight, evolves in and manifests Delight, and returns to its Source of divine Delight.

The following poem tells us that the evolutionary process of cosmic God-manifestation is impelled by Love and eventuates in Delight as the fullness of perfection and satisfaction. This process of transformation attains to the "deathless" state of being that has transcended ignorance or inconscience, lack of the light of consciousness.

Sound is the universality
Of the created universe.

Silence is the universality
Of the unborn universe.

Love is the universality
Of the progressive universe.

Delight is the universality
Of the deathless universe.[68]

The poem focuses our attention on the universe, the macrocosm at its most vast, also on the interior dimension of the universe, and as well on its dynamism through time in the greatest narrative of creation and transformation.

In an early dialogue the poet asks God, "Who asked You, who compelled You, who inspired You to be the Creator of the world?" God answers, "My Concern asked me to be the Creator of the world. My Realisation compelled me to be the Creator. My Compassion inspired Me to be the Creator."[69] The passage expresses an anticipation of God's relation with God's creatures: a relation of loving concern and compassion, formed by God's "realisation," which may be construed as God's identification with God's Self. The passage seems to hint that the creation, even before it exists, somehow asks to be brought into existence. We have already seen that "The universe is God's Compassion" and that God is Love. Sri Chinmoy says, "God is constant and eternal Concern. The moment He created Himself, Concern was there; and the moment He created your soul, Concern was there . . . the source of Concern is oneness. God is the all-pervading One and His Concern comes from His all-pervading oneness. . . . When He has oneness, He has to offer something, and that something is His Concern."[70] This fulfillment through self-offering takes place only in relationship and so requires the presence of another, to be found in the personal and interpersonal dimensions of the Many. When God experiences God's own Reality through countless forms, one paramount way is through loving relationship. God's Concern, Compassion, and Love are therefore an essential aspect of the Joy or Delight of divine fulfillment which is the very reason for creation.

The cosmic process of God-manifestation takes place through the involution of the Divine "into" Matter and the evolution of the Divine "out" and "up" from Matter. The following passage identifies God with the divine attribute of Bliss or Delight.

> Bliss is the creation of life and bliss is the life of creation. The creation of life is the Silence-God. The life of silence is the Sound-God. Creation enters into inconscience and then gradually comes back to its Source, and regains its Source. When it enters into inconscience, into the lowest chasm of reality, we call this involution. And when from that lowest chasm creation again climbs up high, higher, highest, we call this evolution. The Silence-God has another name, Spirit; and the Sound-God has another name, Matter. Progress requires involution of Spirit and evolution of Matter.[71]

Spirit is "implicit," literally "folded up," and Matter is unfolded or "explicit;"[72] so that Sri Chinmoy says, "Life is evolution. Evolution is the unfoldment from within"[73] (the word "evolve" literally means to unfold and roll out). The Formless "involves" into form, the Infinite into the finite, and then through unfoldment of its inner divine nature, the finite existence of form "evolves" back into the Formless.[74] This process is not perceived in the biological study of evolution, but proceeds parallel to it and is observable through yoga. "Everything is evolving," Sri Chinmoy says, "The essence of evolution is an inner and outer movement."[75]

Evolution is "the veiled determination of an apparent unconsciousness seeking conscious formation and growth. . . . Nature is the evolving phenomenon, while consciousness is its guide in evolution."[76] This guiding consciousness within Nature is ultimately none other than the Divine, as God has entered into creation to participate in the Play and acts in and through the soul or inmost self of each individual existence.

> It is a true truth that life was fast asleep in matter, and mind was fast asleep in life; now without the least hesitation we can say that something lies fast asleep in mind. The wheel of evolution ever moves—it stops not.
>
>   Fast asleep in mind lies the Consciousness Divine, fully illumined and patiently awaiting the moment of its unveiling.[77]

While Sri Chinmoy does use the word "evolution" for this process of cosmic awakening, his more usual term is "manifestation." The purpose of the cosmic Play is this very "God-manifestation," as greater and greater joy comes not only from the multiplicity and variety of creation, in which God is immanent, but also from the ever-increasing concrete presence in finite existence of the qualities of the infinite Divine such as Light, Delight, Peace, Power, and Beauty. This is an open-ended process taking place through great expanses of time, and is seen as a cosmic progress intended by God. God-manifestation is the ongoing transformation of all life in the gradual achievement of perfection, leading to growing "satisfaction." Perfection, as already mentioned, is not a fixed state with a final definition, but is "ever-transcending" as is the divine Reality Itself.

The implications of this vision for the human condition are immense, for within the context of ongoing cosmic progress, human beings as we exist at present are "a transitional being" as Sri Aurobindo says,[78] a stage on the way to a more perfect being which will appear in the future as the outcome of evolution. The human will eventually be "divinized," transformed into a far more illumined and perfect being than ourselves, of boundlessly greater goodness, beauty, capacity and fulfillment—or to use a phrase that occurs many times in Sri Chinmoy's poetry, the human being will become "another God."

THE PLANES OF EXISTENCE

As creation begins in the transcendent plane, God's inseparable triune attributes are *Sat-Cit-Ānanda,* Existence, Consciousness, and Bliss or Delight, sometimes called "the triple Consciousness." These three primordial "attributes" are nondifferent[79] and their "division" is concomitant with "descent." When Sri Chinmoy mentions the "self-division" of the Supreme, he adds that "Creation is the descent of Consciousness."[80] It is at this point we begin to speak of the "levels" of existence.

The use of spatial metaphors for ontology (and for other subjects) is seemingly inherent in human thought and language. This is a large and profound subject of cross-cultural significance which here we cannot inquire into at any length. Ontological levels—and higher and lower "worlds"—are characteristic of traditional cosmologies in many cultures (though not of a modernist or secular worldview). Briefly put, towards the transcendent Reality is said to be an upward direction in a "vertical" dimension, and away from that Reality is downward, while the universal is an ontological breadth or "horizontal" dimension. To perceive or to go "within" is to access the interior depth of one's self or of another being, which adds a third dimension of ontological "space." Knowledge of the different planes as objective "worlds" is attainable through yoga, as Sri Chinmoy avers with many others,[81] while he also comments that "height" and inner "depth" are part of the mental consciousness and that "ultimately height and depth become one."[82] Spatiality and also time are conditions of the manifested world or creation, while "beyond" the creation (another spatial metaphor) these conditions do not apply or are experienced so differently that ordinary language cannot indicate them directly. Only metaphor, words bearing mantric efficacy or words having a special mystical sense can gesture towards the experience of higher realities and the transcendent realm.[83]

When fully manifested, the universal existence of the phenomenal world is said to be organized as a series of higher and lower levels or "planes," and on each plane, there is also an inner and outer dimension. Each of the planes has sublevels, and the cosmological structure corresponds to the parts of the human being as macrocosm does to microcosm; in general outline from higher to lower, these are the psychic, the mental, the vital, and the physical modes of existence. All of the planes of existence are "universal" and macrocosmic as well as individual; for example, the existence of "mind" is not limited to the individual thinker or the personal "subjective;" there is also "the universal Mind."[84] The different modes of ontological substance are described in the *Taittirīya Upaniṣad*[85] as a series of "selves" (*ātman*) made of "food" or physical matter, of life-energy, of mind, of consciousness and of bliss. These correspond to the view developed in later Indian tradition of the *kośa*-s or "sheaths" covering the *ātman* or soul, namely the *annamaya kośa, prāṇamaya kośa, manomaya kośa, vijñānamaya kośa* and *ānandamaya kośa*.[86] These modes of substance ultimately have a single common nature or substratum of being, as they have a common origin, God or Brahman. The "stuff" comprising the many worlds of the universe is *both* conscious and material and is not bifurcated into thought and insentient matter (as in some Western thought); rather the kinds of substance are ranged in their levels along a continuum from the more "gross" and less conscious in one direction, to the more "subtle" and "refined" and more conscious in the other.

The highest of the planes of existence is the Absolute Supreme or Existence-Consciousness-Delight, the infinite Source. Below this is "the soul's world," spoken of as "a sea of immense peace"[87] and then the "psychic" plane which corresponds to the heart, that is, the spiritual heart or heart chakra. "Emotion" is found on all levels and is of respective kinds with different qualities. Below the psychic plane are the levels of "mind," including intuitive mind and then what is more familiarly called "mind," including the intellectual mind and the "physical mind," which is directly bound to and "governed" by experiences of the physical senses. Below the levels of "mind" are those of "the vital" or life-energy and of the physical. The vital comprehends both broader or "nobler" emotions above and aggressive and compulsive energetic drives at the lower levels. The physical plane includes the "subtle physical" and then the "gross physical" of our everyday sense life. This cosmology with roots in

Vedic tradition is extensively developed by Sri Aurobindo in his major works and is affirmed overall by Sri Chinmoy.[88]

As all existence has its Source in the Absolute, for Sri Chinmoy there is not an ultimate dichotomy between Spirit and Matter or *Puruṣa* and *Prakṛti*. In an early series of aphorisms he stresses this point.

> The eternal Truth can never be the monopoly of the Spirit. Dauntless Matter, too, has every right to claim her equal share.
>
> Our present faith in Matter is not enough. It must needs be stronger. We must see eye to eye with the Upanishads and declare that Matter also is Brahman.
>
> Our absolute Freedom will come into existence from the Spirit. But Matter's giant breast will be the field of our full manifestation.
>
> "All this is Brahman."[89] The oneness of Matter and Spirit is the only affirma-tion of the Brahman. Therefore neither Matter nor Spirit can dwell beyond Its fond and boundless clasp.[90]

Sri Chinmoy describes Puruṣa or Spirit as "pure, witnessing consciousness," while Prakṛti, Matter, or Nature, "is the evolving and transforming consciousness" (note that Matter is said here to be a mode of consciousness). "Matter is the primordial substance. Matter is ever changing. Spirit is always static. Matter is the possessor of infinite qualities. Spirit sees and sanctions. Matter does, grows, and becomes. Spirit is Consciousness. Spirit is the Witness. Matter is the Creativity infinite."[91] These two are inseparable[92] and "neither Spirit nor Matter is superior to the other"[93] because both are aspects of the creation and ongoing God-manifestation: "In and through Prakriti is the fulfilment of the cosmic Play."[94]

Indeed, Sri Chinmoy declares that "Realisation says that there are no such things as the bondage and freedom which we so often refer to in our day-to-day lives. What actually exists is consciousness—consciousness on various levels, consciousness enjoying itself in its varied manifestations."[95] The integral transformation of God-manifestation through evolution calls for acceptance of all levels of existence from the highest to the lowest, as all are aspects of God's full Being. Sri Chinmoy says, "The absolute Grace of the Supreme has given birth to the transcendental Reality and the universal Reality. Man's constant inner cry reaches the transcendental Reality, which is the acme of perfection, in the Beyond, and at the same time manifests the universal Reality in the core of each aspiring individual on earth."[96] With our aspiration-cry we journey forward and our transformation culminates in love: "Progress is our inner assurance of a deeper manifestation. Progress is founded upon evolving experience and manifesting experience. When we cry for God the Absolute Reality, we grow into the evolving experience. When we, as divine lovers, become inseparably one with our supreme Beloved, we become the manifesting experience."[97] In the divine Play of evolution and manifestation, each person has a unique role: "Here on earth the message of the permanent Truth, the transcendental Truth has to be fulfilled, for God has chosen earth as His field for Manifestation. The eternal Light has to be manifested here on earth, and we, all of us, have to become conscious instruments of God."[98]

NOTES

1. The concept of the divine Līlā does not seem to derive from the Upaniṣads and tracing its origins is beyond the scope of this study. But let us note that the Brahma Sūtras (or Vedānta Sūtras) take up the question of creation's purpose: since Brahman cannot lack anything outside Itself and therefore does not create in order to obtain anything, it is said that Brahman's creative activity is sport or *Līlā* (2.1.33). Both Śaṅkara and Rāmānuja mention the games that kings or princes play as sport. Rāmānuja says that "even as children play out of fun, so Brahman, without any purpose to gain, engages Itself in creating this world of diversity as a mere pastime." The Līlā does not have any purpose external to itself. It is its own reward—the delight of the play is the very reason for its existence. See *The Vedānta Sutras of Bādarāyana with the commentary by Śaṅkara*, tr. George Thibaut, Part 1 [*Sacred Books of the East*, ed. F. Max Muller, Vol. XXXIV] (New York: Dover Publications, 1962), 356; Rāmānuja, *Brahma Sūtras Śrī-Bhāṣya*, trans. Swami Vireśwarānanda and Swami Ādidevānanda, (Kolkata: Advaita Aśrama, 2012), 237. The concept of the divine Līlā is prominent in Vaiṣṇavism.

2. Chāndogya Upaniṣad 6.2.1-3.

3. Chāndogya Upaniṣad 6.8.4-6 and following through 6.16.3.

4. *Taittirīya Upaniṣad* 2.6.1. For these passages I refer to Sarvepalli Radhakrishnan, *The Principal Upaniṣads*, trans. and with an Introduction (New York: Humanities Press, 1953).

5. *The Oneness of the Eastern Heart and the Western Mind*, Part 2, 128. On the use of the masculine pronoun for God, see above, 37.

6. *Flame Waves: Questions Answered at the United Nations*, Part 12 (New York: Agni Press, 1978), 15.

7. Idem; also *The Vision of God's Dawn*, 1.

8. *The Vision of God's Dawn*, loc. cit.

9. *Illumination-Song and Liberation-Dance*, Part 1 (New York: Agni Press, 1976), 21; the poet's own translation.

10. *God-Life: Is It a Far Cry?* (New York: Agni Press, 1974), 7.

11. *Eternity's Breath*, 3.

12. *Commentaries*, 84. Chinmoy's use of the word "seed" and also his phrase "seed-form," bring to mind the cosmogonic *hiraṇyagarbha*, the "Golden Embryo" or "Golden Womb" first mentioned in the Rig Veda (10.121), and in other Vedic and later sources; see F. D. K. Bosch, *The Golden Germ: An Introduction to Indian Symbolism* (New Delhi: Munshiram Manoharlal Publishers, 1994), Ch. 2. In some accounts

hiraṇyagarbha becomes the "world egg;" the cosmic egg, like the World Tree, is an image occurring across traditions; see Venetia Newall, "Egg," in *Encyclopedia of Religion,* Editor in Chief Mircea Eliade, 5 (1987): 36–37. Sri Chinmoy mentions *hiraṇyagarbha* only once, saying "It is there that the seed of creation originally germinated" (*The Body: Humanity's Fortress* [New York: Agni Press, 1974], 3.) The metaphor of a tree, discussed below, makes the connotations of the word "seed" more self-evident. Radhakrishnan comments, "The names and forms of the manifested world are latent in the egg as the future tree is in the seed" (*Upaniṣads,* 61).

13. *The Oneness of the Eastern Heart and the Western Mind,* Part 1, 48.

14. *God and the Cosmic Game,* 9.

15. 10.42. *The Bhagavad Gītā,* tr. Winthrop Sargeant, Revised edition edited by Christopher Chapple, Foreword by Christopher Chapple (Albany, NY: State University of New York Press, 1994), 452. Krishna uses the word "seed" (*bījam*) for the Creator: "I am that which is the seed of all creatures" (10. 39), Ibid.; Sri Chinmoy quotes this verse in *Commentaries,* 207.

16. *The Oneness of the Eastern Heart and the Western Mind,* Part 2, 40.

17. Ibid., 67.

18. *The Oneness of the Eastern Heart and the Western Mind,* Part 1, 304.

19. *Katha Upaniṣad* 2.3.1, *Bhagavad Gītā* Ch. 15; see also Pamela R. Frese and S. J. M. Gray, "Trees," in *The Encyclopedia of Religion,* Editor in Chief Mircea Eliade, Vol. 15 (New York: MacMillan Publishing Company, 1987), 26–33.

20. *United Nations Works,* Vol. 1, 138.

21. Ibid., 120.

22. *I am Telling You a Great Secret: You Are a Fantastic Dream of God: Children's Questions on God* (1974), 29–30. Note that in this passage both Silence and Sound are forms of "Light."

23. *Vision of God's Dawn,* 31.

24. Ibid., 1.

25. *A Life of Blossoming Love* (1992), 8.

26. "Eternal Surrender," in *The Golden Boat,* Part 5 (New York: Agni Press, 1974), 45.

27. In one English poem he refers to "rest" and "motion." "Motion and Rest," in *The Golden Boat,* Part 5, 2.

28. "Unity and Multiplicity," in *The Wings of Light,* Part 1 (New York, Agni Press, 1974), 32.

29. *Eternity's Breath,* 1–2.

30. *Commentaries,* 194.

31. Ibid., 236.

32. For detailed historical study of Aum, see Finnian McKean Moore Gerety, *This Whole World Is Om: Song, Soteriology, and the Emergence of the Sacred Syllable,* Ph. D. dissertation, Harvard University, 2015.

33. See above, 24.

34. *Service-Trees,* Part 31 (2003), Nos. 30,270 and 30,271.

35. *Service-Trees,* Part 33 (2003), No. 32,193.

36. *The Vision of God's Dawn,* 31.

37. *Commentaries*, 32.

38. *The Oneness of the Eastern Heart and the Western Mind,* Part 2, 130.

39. Ibid., 5.

40. Since Vedic times mantra has been used in Indic traditions in ritual and as a focal point in meditation; it is a form of sacred speech and sound that is believed to have the capacity to concretely connect the one who utters or thinks of it to a deity or spiritual being. Jeffery D. Long explains *sūtra* as "the root text of a system of Indian philosophy (*darśana*). Traditionally, a *sūtra* is written in a style so terse as to require a commentary (or *bhāṣya*) in order to be comprehensible. It is likely that *sūtras* originated as mnemonic devices developed to preserve the oral teachings of the founding figure that established the system of thought to which a *sūtra* belonged." *Historical Dictionary of Hinduism,* 2nd ed. (Lanham, MD: Rowman & Littlefield, 2020), 367–368.

41. *I am Telling You a Great Secret*, 7–8.

42. *Eternity's Breath,* 70–71.

43. *God the Supreme Musician*, 16.

44. *Eternity's Breath*, 112.

45. *I Am Telling You a Great Secret*, 10.

46. The title of a 1,000-poem series of twenty parts of fifty poems each, written in 1973.

47. *God's Hour* (New York: Agni Press, 1973), 6.

48. Ibid.,18.

49. *Commentaries,* 219.

50. For reflections on panentheism, see Philip Clayton and Arthur Peacocke, eds., *In Whom We Live and Move and Have Our Being: Panentheistic Reflections on God's Presence in a Scientific World* (Grand Rapids, MI: William B. Eerdman's Publishing Company, 2004) as well as Biernacki and Clayton. On pantheism, see Michael P. Levine, *Pantheism: A Non-theistic Concept of Deity* (New York: Routledge, 1994).

51. *Commentaries*, 205, referring to Bhagavad Gītā 10.42.

52. See above, Ch. 2.

53. loc. cit.

54. *The Oneness of the Eastern Heart and the Western Mind,* Part 2, 17.

55. Ibid., 22. This statement is from a 1969 university lecture, "The Vedanta Philosophy." On another occasion, in informal conversation he was asked "Shankara never really disavowed the existence of the phenomenal world. Am I right in saying this?" Sri Chinmoy agreed, saying, "The general conception of Maya has been misinterpreted in the East…[but] some of the modern Indian thinkers came to the conclusion, after throwing considerable light on Shankara's philosophy, that he did not actually mean . . . that the world is a colossal illusion." He does not name these modern Indian thinkers, but seems to be referring to Sri Aurobindo and those aligned with him. This is one of the very few times that Sri Chinmoy refers to Śaṅkara. *Earth's Cry Meets Heaven's Smile,* Part 1 (Santurce, Puerto Rico: Aum Press, 1974), 64.

Anantanand Rambachan in his book *The Advaita World View* (Albany, NY: State University of New York Press, 2006) states that "Śaṅkara does not describe the world as an illusion . . . He challenges the claim that what appears to be outside the mind is an illusion and argues for the objective nature of the world" (76), in the section "Is the World an Illusion?" and see all of Chapter 7, "Brahman and the World."

56. *Songs of the Soul* (New York: Aum Publications, 1998 [1971]), 44.

57. See Julius Lipner, *The Face of Truth: A Study of Meaning and Metaphysics in the Vedāntic Theology of Rāmānuja* (Albany, NY: State University of New York Press, 1986), especially Ch. 7.

58. *A Tribute to Monsignor Thomas Hartman* (New York: Agni Press, 2017), 42–43.

59. *Chāndogya Upaniṣad* 6.2.1-2, trans. Radhakrishnan, 499.

60. *Commentaries*, 57–58.

61. Iśa Upaniṣad opening invocation and Bṛhadāraṇyaka Upaniṣad 5.1.1.

62. He also says, "People often wonder how God creates life from nothing. However, the word 'nothing' is incorrect here. God does make life out of something and that something is His Light, His Consciousness-Light. The Source of Life is His Consciousness-Light. Stone life, plant life, animal life, human life, divine life, universal life: everything comes from God's Consciousness-Light." *The Vision of God's Dawn*, 5.

63. "From Nothingness-Fulness," in *Flower-Flames*, Part 70 (1983), No. 6,995.

64. *The Oneness of the Eastern Heart and the Western Mind*, Part 1, 138.

65. *The Oneness of the Eastern Heart and the Western Mind*, Part 2, 128.

66. *The Oneness of the Eastern Heart and the Western Mind*, Part 3, 9.

67. *Taittīriya Upaniṣad* 3.6.

68. "Universality," in *The Wings of Light*, Part 11 (New York: Agni Press, 1974), 44.

69. *My Lord's Secrets Revealed* (New York: Aum Publications, 1998 [1971]), 79.

70. *The Vision of God's Dawn*, 33–34.

71. *The Oneness of the Eastern Heart and the Western Mind*, Part 1, 76.

72. "Like You I Wish to Be," in *The Wings of Light*, Part 19 (New York: Agni Press, 1974), 23.

73. *Yoga*, 47.

74. Ibid, 25.

75. *Commentaries*, 195.

76. *Eternity's Breath*, 3, 5.

77. *Eternity's Breath*, 19.

78. "Man: A Transitional Being," in *The Collected Works of Sri Aurobindo*, Vol. 17. http://www.collectedworksofsriaurobindo.com/index.php/readbook/02-Post-content-Vol-17-the-hour-of-god-volume-17.

79. See *Life-Tree Leaves* (New York: Agni Press, 1974), 59–60, and *God, Avatars and Yogis* (New York: Agni Press, 1974), 11–12.

80. *Eternity's Breath*, 3.

81. The chakras or centers of the "subtle body" described in various yoga traditions are portals to the macrocosmic dimension of these different planes or levels when "opened" or actively functioning.

82. *Meditation: Man-Perfection in God-Satisfaction* (New York: Agni Press, 1978), 74–75.

83. See Kusumita P. Pedersen, "The Poetry of Sri Chinmoy: A Philosopher in the Heart," in *Antonio T. de Nicolás: Poet of Eternal Return,* edited by Christopher Key Chapple (Ahmedabad: Sriyogi Publications & Nalanda International, 2014), 299–309.

84. *United Nations Works,* Vol. 1, 257.

85. *Taittirīya Upaniṣad,* 2–3.

86. For a detailed overview and interpretation of concepts of the "subtle body" and related questions in a number of traditions, see Geoffrey Samuel and Jay Johnston, eds., *Religion and the Subtle Body in Asia and the West* (New York: Routledge, 2013); also Shamini Jain, Jennifer Daubenmier, David Muehsem, Lopsang Rapgay and Deepak Chopra, "Indo-Tibetan Philosophical and Medical Systems: Perspectives on the Biofield," *Global Advances in Health and Medicine* 4, suppl (2015):16–24; doi: 10.7453/gahmj.2015.026.suppl.

87. *Eternity's Soul-Bird,* Part 2 (New York: Agni Press, 1974), 30.

88. The foregoing account is based on references throughout Sri Chinmoy's writings, but see especially *Eternity's Soul-Bird,* Parts 1 and 2, and *Death and Reincarnation: Eternity's Voyage.* For a detailed account of Delight's descent through the planes, employing the terminology of "Supermind" and "Overmind" forged by Sri Aurobindo, see *Commentaries,* 50–51; the phrase "governed by the physical" is used for the physical mind. Concerning the roots in Vedic tradition of this cosmology, this is especially in reference to the modalities of substance often equated with the *kośa*s and corresponding stratified worlds or "planes" – while bearing in mind that a hierarchy of "higher" and "lower" realms, while indeed found in Indic traditions, also occurs in others.

89. *Chāndogya Upaniṣad* 3.14.1.

90. *Eternity's Breath,* 38–39.

91. *Commentaries,* 219.

92. Ibid., 220.

93. *Eternity's Breath,* 38.

94. *Commentaries,* 169.

95. *Yoga,* 36.

96. *United Nations Works,* Vol. 1, 103.

97. *The Oneness of the Eastern Heart and the Western Mind,* Part 1, 64.

98. Ibid., 148.

Chapter 4

The Soul's Journey

THE SOUL

What is the soul? Sri Chinmoy describes the soul as the "representative" of God. He also says, "The soul is a conscious portion of God. It came directly from God, it remains directly in God and it will go back to God. The soul is the light which is called consciousness."[1] This divine representative is the individual soul residing in all beings, the *atman* or "self" of Vedantic tradition, also called the *jīva* or *jīvātman*. In the Upanisads the *ātman* is spoken of as the inmost subject of awareness which as the true knower of all our experiences employs the outer senses and other faculties.[2] It is this soul that reincarnates from one life to another, while the one Absolute does not and is called the *Paramātman* or the Supreme Self. In his poetry Sri Chinmoy consistently speaks of two divine qualities of the soul: light or illumination, synonymous with consciousness, *cit*, and delight or bliss, *ānanda*. He invites us, "Discover your soul's / Ever-illumining light / And ever-deepening delight"[3] and says that, 'Delight / Is the soul's / Natural state,"[4] "Delight is an unlimited capacity / Which our heart has / And our soul eternally is."[5] The soul is a drop of the Ocean of *Sat-Cit-Ānanda*, Existence-Consciousness-Bliss—and "the tiniest drop has a right to feel the boundless ocean as its very own, or to cry to have the ocean as its very own."[6]

When God the One becomes the Many, God enters into the countless forms of creation as a part, so to speak, of God's own Being. Sri Chinmoy says, "The soul is present in the heart of all creatures. The soul is in each object, in each individual creation: in the mineral kingdom, in the plant kingdom, in the animal kingdom, in the human kingdom."[7] An "individual creation" can be flexibly identified, since there is a soul in material objects, parts of the body, places such as a city or country, works of art, oceans, the planet Earth and in spiritual beings such as deities or angels.[8] Sri Chinmoy was once asked, "A chair has a soul. If you chopped up the chair into little pieces of wood, would those pieces of matter each have their own soul?" He answered, "Yes, but you have to know that those souls would have practically no development. In those pieces of wood there would be only the tiniest spark of consciousness. True, everything and everyone has a soul, but the consciousness of the soul is a matter of development."[9] He also says, "The difference between the souls of things and the souls of humans is a matter of their degree of evolution, the degree to which they manifest their divine potentialities. It is through the process of reincarnation that the soul gradually manifests its hidden powers within, and eventually reaches its absolute Fulfilment."[10]

THE SOUL'S JOURNEY OF EVOLUTION

When the universe of space and time first comes into existence, consciousness is deeply "involved" in matter and is little manifested externally. At the same time, at even the most elemental material level, the Divine is fully present as immanent: Sri Chinmoy says that "No atom is empty of God's Will,"[11] and "Every atom / Embodies the smiles and tears / Of the whole world."[12] The soul enters into the interior of matter, or involves, as an entity of light or consciousness and through reincarnation it evolves; evolution is a spiritual as well as a biological process. Sri Chinmoy explains, "The soul enters into the chasm of inconscience in order to participate in the cosmic Lila."[13] A Bengali song says:

From a distant world	*Sudur hate bhese āsi*
Floating I came into the heart	*Ei dharanir buke*
Of this world.	*Swarupe mor bhule gechi*
I have forgotten my Self-form totally	*Andhakāre dhuke*
In the eyeless darkness-life.[14]	

In a more extended narrative, the whole drama of the soul's journey is vividly related:

> Each soul needs involution and evolution. When the soul descends, it is the soul's involution. When the soul ascends, it is the soul's evolution. The soul enters into the lowest abyss of inconscience. The soul evolves again into *Sat-Cit-Ānanda*—Existence, Consciousness, Bliss—the triple consciousness.
>
> The soul enters into inconscience. For millions of years it remains there, fast asleep. All of a sudden, one day a spark of consciousness from the ever-transcending Beyond opens its eye, and then the hour strikes for self-inquiry.

"Who am I?" it asks. The answer is *Tat twam asi*, "That thou art."[15] The soul is thrilled. Then again it falls asleep. Again it enters self-oblivion. More questions arise after some time:

Whose am I? I am of That.
Where have I come from? From That.
To Whom am I returning? To That.
For Whom am I here on earth? For That.

Then the soul is satisfied. The soul is now fully prepared for its journey upward—high, higher, highest. At this moment the soul sees the Self, an exact prototype of the Supreme Being here on earth, and the evolution of the soul starts properly. From the mineral life, the soul enters into the plant life, from the plant life to the animal life, from the animal life to the human life, and from the human into the divine life.[16]

When the soul enters into the physical world, it accepts ignorance or "self-oblivion" and forgets its true nature. It "falls asleep." It then passes through different forms, going from one body to another in a series of repeated births, deaths, and rebirths. Each time the physical body dies; the soul passes upward through the vital world, the mental world, and the psychic world or heart's world, casting off the respective "sheaths" of matter, life-energy, mind, and psychic substance before coming to the soul's world. There, during a short or longer period of rest, it assimilates the experiences of the previous life and considers in what environment it will next take birth. Before it returns to this world it comes before the Supreme and tells what it achieved in its preceding life and its wishes for the next incarnation. It either receives permission from God or must make another choice, and sometimes God makes a request to the soul to accomplish certain things.[17] As it comes back to the earth plane, the soul takes a new heart, mind, vital and body. Moreover, the conditions and events of its life will be determined to a great extent by the law of karma, or action and result.[18] Sri Chinmoy explains that "Each time the soul comes into the manifestation it gains considerable experience, and when it goes back to the soul's region after each incarnation it takes with it the essence of all its experiences."[19] In this way, "the soul grows, enriching itself, making its divinity more integral, more harmonious and more perfect."[20] In the first part of this journey of many centuries, the soul's progress is impelled by an urge to self-transcendence that is not yet fully aware of itself; it is "aspiring unconsciously."

In the vast plan of the divine Play, each soul has its own part. Sri Chinmoy explains, "All souls possess the same possibilities, whether they are housed in the lowest or the highest forms of life. We have to remember, however, that the Supreme manifests Himself in infinite ways through the different souls. They express His varying aspects of Divinity. For example, one soul may manifest Light, another Power, a third Beauty, and so on."[21] All are necessary to collectively make the cosmic Game complete in a plenitude of complementary qualities. "Each soul / Is absolutely necessary / In God's Cosmic Game,"[22] Sri Chinmoy affirms, because "Each human soul is destined / To play a unique role / In God's manifestation."[23] To the question, "Has your soul a special mission?" the answer is that it does, and that "there are as many missions as there are souls."[24]

HUMAN LIFE AND CONSCIOUS ASPIRATION

It is in human life that conscious aspiration for oneness with the Source awakens at the destined moment of readiness, and indeed, it is God Who awakens us.

> The flame of our aspiration is kindled by God Himself. The fruit of our realisation, too, we get from God directly. God is the Inspirer in us. God is the Eternal Giver. God is the eternal Receiver in us. God uses aspiration to take us to Himself. God uses realisation to bring Himself to us.[25]

Throughout his writings Sri Chinmoy locates aspiration in the heart, constantly referring to the "aspiration-heart," "heart's aspiration," the "heart's cry" and the "mounting flame" of aspiration within the heart. He says:

> Aspiration does not come from the mind. No! It comes directly from your heart. The heart can give you everything. Aspiration is the harbinger of realisation or illumination. In aspiration is the seed of realisation. Aspiration comes from the heart because the illumination of the soul is always there. And when you meditate on the heart, not only do you get aspiration, but you also get the fulfilment of that aspiration: the soul's infinite Peace, Light and Bliss.[26]

He reflects on the fact that aspiration and realization are actually different aspects of a single process of spiritual evolution: "What we call aspiration is realisation on another plane of consciousness. Here on earth we call it aspiration, but that very thing is realisation on another plane. Similarly, what we call realisation on another plane, on this earth-plane we call aspiration. Realisation is nothing but a continuous act of ever-transcending aspiration."[27] Here we recall his statement that, "Realisation says that there are no such things as the bondage and freedom which we so often refer to in our day-to-day lives. What actually exists is consciousness—consciousness on various levels, consciousness enjoying itself in its varied manifestations."[28]

He powerfully affirms the all-embracing, integral nature of aspiration: "Aspiration houses the outer world and the inner world, the world of realisation and the world of manifestation, the world of ego and the universe of universal oneness."[29]

When the soul takes human incarnation and begins to aspire consciously, it strives to illumine the different parts of the person and meets the challenge of the relative lack of light in the outer being, which may be unreceptive. "While in the human life, the soul brings down peace, light, and bliss from Above. First it offers these divine qualities to the heart, then to the mind, then to the vital, then to the gross physical. When illumination takes place, we see it in the heart, in the physical mind, in the vital and in the gross physical body."[30] The human person in this world is composed of the "parts of the being," which in addition to the soul are the body, vital, mind, and heart. As mentioned above, these correspond to the macrocosmic planes of matter or the physical, the vital plane of life-energy, the mental plane, and the psychic plane. On earth all of these co-exist. In its untransformed state, the body is characterized by lethargy and inertia, the vital by aggression and craving, the mind by doubt and suspicion, and the heart at times by insecurity and timidity. When transformed by the light of the soul, the heart will assume its true nature of boundless love and oneness. The mind will become clear and vast, and will search for truth. The vital will become dynamic and spacious instead of aggressive and "strangling," and the body will be awakened and active.

THE EGO

In the human condition of ignorance one of the main reasons that the outer being is unaware of the soul, resists the soul's light and even denies the soul's existence is the ego. Sri Chinmoy explains:

> The ordinary human ego gives us a sense of separate identity, separate consciousness. No doubt, a sense of individuality and self-importance is necessary at a certain stage of development. But the ego separates our individual consciousness from the Universal Consciousness. The very function of the ego is separation. It cannot feel satisfaction in viewing two things at a time on the same level. It always feels that one must be superior to the other. So the ego makes us feel that we are all separate weaklings, that it will never be possible for us to have the Infinite Consciousness. The ego, finally, is limitation.[31]

As in everyday speech, the ego is described as full of pride, seeking name and fame, craving attention and admiration, practicing "self-advertisement," and trying to dominate. It enjoys the misfortunes of others and is without sympathy, which belongs to the heart.[32] Tellingly, Sri Chinmoy observes that "Despair / Is a form of / Ego-exhibit,"[33] and that "My mind enjoys / My ego tantrums."[34] While ego exists on different levels, it is firmly established as a structure of the mind, and while we are in the mind it blocks us from a larger perspective. Sri Chinmoy refers to its frequent "hurtful hallucinations."[35] The ordinary mind functions in terms of separation, division, and limitation: "The mind lives / Inside a tiny ego-cage"[36] and indeed, "The mind loves to live / In its tiny ego-bubble."[37] Limitation caused by the ego is itself the reason for less light or consciousness and more darkness or ignorance: "A darkness-mind / Is a product / Of ego-supremacy."[38]

When asked, "How do we weaken the ego and ultimately subdue it?" Sri Chinmoy answers, "By thinking of God's all-pervading Consciousness."[39] A poem says, "Ego dies only when / Our mind is eager to fly / In Infinity's Sky."[40] Ego is transformed by such aspiration, and most especially by love, oneness and self-giving—by what expands our consciousness and our sense of "I-ness." Sri Chinmoy speaks quite often of the "death" of the ego, and its apparent demise is surely necessary at a certain point on the spiritual path. Yet the small ego "dies" to be reborn as "the divine ego," which feels itself to be God's child, offers itself in the service of others and can identify with the whole universe.[41] A song says, "*Khudra āmire hārāite habe brihāt āmire labhite*: I must lose the little 'i' to get the big I."[42] Echoing the teaching of Sri Ramakrishna on the "unripe ego" and the "ripe ego,"[43] Sri Chinmoy says in a poem, "The unripe individual ego tells me / That I am the possessor. / The ripe universal ego tells me / That God is the only Possessor / And the only Possession."[44]

To become fully effective, this transformation must take place through conscious aspiration for a spiritual goal and the practices of yoga. Entering the spiritual life is a step that a seeker takes at the moment determined by the Supreme and the soul: "Our acceptance of the spiritual life / Is not personal—/ God-aspiration beckons us / To enter the spiritual life."[45] Once in the spiritual life, the aspirant becomes aware that there is an inner self from which guidance comes, can work to strengthen faith in this guidance, and through the practice of prayer and meditation can cultivate the inner silence in which this guidance can be discerned. For its own part, the soul is making every effort to offer this guidance. Sri Chinmoy says, "There is not a single moment / When my soul does not encourage / My body, vital, mind and heart / To do the right thing / And become the right thing."[46] He adds, "When the soul guides us, / We are safe, / For the soul receives guidance / Directly from God,"[47] but "The soul does not / Command us. / It only whispers."[48] We must listen attentively and focus on our heart to hear the soul: "Silently, softly, sweetly / My soul speaks / To my heart, mind, vital and body;"[49] however,

"When the soul whispers, / Only the heart can hear—/ Not the mind, not the vital / And not the body."[50]

THE HEART

It is not possible to overstate the importance of the heart in Sri Chinmoy's philosophy. He always described the path that he taught—the path of love, devotion, and surrender—as "the path of the heart." In an early talk he explains,

> The heart is strikingly significant because inside it is the living presence of the soul. True, the consciousness of the soul permeates the entire body, but the actual location of the soul is inside the heart. The soul has everything: Peace, Light and Bliss in infinite measure. We get these divine qualities inside the heart directly from the soul. And from the heart, we can bring them to the mind, to the vital and to the physical proper.[51]

The heart can thus be the main vehicle of transformation for human beings, not just in meditation proper but at all times: "The possibilities of the heart / Must be utilised at every moment / In our day-to-day life."[52] We have already learned that the heart is the site of aspiration and that it owns the profound silence of meditation. And the heart, above all, has the power of identification or oneness and self-giving love.

When Sri Chinmoy refers to the heart, this is not the physical heart but "the spiritual heart" or heart chakra, located in the center of the chest in the subtle body described in different yoga traditions. In these traditions the chakras function as portals from the microcosmic individual person to the macrocosmic planes of existence, to which they correspond. The spiritual heart when fully developed is boundlessly vast; it "embodies" and "houses" the Universal Consciousness.[53] In *nirvikalpa samādhi*, one of the very highest states of *samādhi* or absorption in meditation, "we feel that our heart is larger than the universe itself . . . we see the universe like a tiny dot inside our vast heart."[54] In the Upaniṣads the *ātman* is repeatedly said to reside in the heart—*hṛd* or *hṛdaya*—or in the *guhā*, the "cave" or secret place understood to be the heart center; the soul is also said to be "within" or *antar*.[55] Therefore Sri Chinmoy urges, "Each seeker must discover / The secret and sacred passageway / From the aspiring heart / To the illumining soul."[56]

At the same time, as a portion of the Supreme and partaking of its infinitude, the soul can be experienced as larger than the body, and in various forms:

The soul is a flood of light and this flood of light will eventually illumine the teeming ignorance in the physical body. When we aspire, when we go deep within, we actually see the physical body inside the soul. The soul is in touch with the Highest, the Absolute, the All-Pervading, but the physical right now is not; the physical is limited, very limited. When we remain in the limited consciousness, we feel that the soul is inside the body and the soul is very tiny. Some will say it is as big as a thumb.[57] Our scriptures say it is smaller than the smallest, and, at the same time, vaster than the vastest.[58] There are many different conceptions of the soul. On the strength of our oneness with the highest Truth, we can see the soul with form and at the same time in the formless state.[59]

When one acquires full knowledge of the soul and enduring identification with it as one's true self, one attains God-realization, or conscious oneness with God, because one's own soul is a portion of God; God-realization and self-realization are one and the same.

Concerning the unique relation of the soul and the heart, Sri Chinmoy states that it is the heart that makes it possible for the soul to be immanent in the world. When asked, "You have said that everything has a soul. What things have a heart? For example, I am sure animals have a heart, but do plants have a heart? Do rocks have a heart?" he explained,

Everything has to have a heart because the soul remains inside the heart. Here is a wooden table. Inside it there is a soul, but the soul does not live directly inside the wood. Inside the wood there is a heart, and inside the heart the soul resides. *Without the heart, the soul cannot breathe.* The soul-consciousness can be everywhere, but the soul has to have a proper place to live, and that place is the heart [emphasis added].[60]

The soul is a drop of the infinite Divine and the heart provides a space for its presence in the manifested world. The heart enables the soul to "breathe"— "breath" is the necessary, living connection between the heart and the soul.[61] This is an important point in Sri Chinmoy's cosmology. He uses the word "breath" to indicate the very essence of something and also to express the most intimate kind of relation. At times he speaks of God's Breath and concerning the soul, says that "The soul / Breathes in / God's own Breath."[62] As the heart breathes, the heart's breath too is of God: "My Lord's Eye / Is / The breath of my heart."[63] The following lines image the flame of aspiration as *within* the breath of the heart: "I shall feed my sacred flame, / Inside the breath of my heart, / Soulfully and devotedly."[64] For a spiritual seeker it is important to remain in the consciousness of the heart as much as possible; one reason is that this can be practiced on a daily basis, while to experience the soul directly is far more difficult.

SPIRITUAL PRACTICE

For Sri Chinmoy, "the spiritual life" or yoga is a life of regular prayer and meditation and also of active work and service to society, without withdrawing from the world. Both meditation and service are ways of transcending the ego and receiving the soul's light, eventually expanding one's consciousness into the Infinite. While honoring the monastic vocation, Sri Chinmoy did not initiate his disciples into *sannyāsa* or renunciation, as was also true of Sri Aurobindo and the Mother. He comments, "True, at a certain stage of the spiritual journey, the renunciation of the gross material life is necessary, but at a higher stage it is no longer necessary. At the highest stage, we neither seek nor renounce anything."[65] Acceptance of the world is a central principle of his philosophy and is the subject of our final chapter. Overall he commends a life of simplicity and restraint, with vegetarian diet and avoidance of drugs and alcohol. He also places strong emphasis on physical fitness for health and gives great importance to the arts and the experience of beauty. During his lifetime he became known for recommending participation in sports, in ways appropriate for each individual, as an aspect of spirituality and a venue for self-transcendence.[66] As mentioned in chapter 1, he held that meditation is a capacity inherent in every person, and that no special qualification is needed. The practice of meditation is not limited to any religious tradition or culture, and to meditate one may be affiliated to any religion or to none. With this egalitarian and interfaith approach, he also advocated that for the betterment and transformation of the world, as many people as possible should take up contemplative practices.

Sri Chinmoy gave detailed instruction for many years on the methods of meditation and prayer, including personal replies to numerous questions. In his writings he is clear that there is not one specific method or technique that can be adopted by everyone and offers a rich array of procedures from which the practitioner can choose while learning what works best. There are certain basic methods that do need to be implemented and these are daily regularity, sitting with the spine straight, quieting the mind, and for his own path, concentrating on the heart and offering gratitude. Concentration, or focusing on a single object, is a necessary foundation for meditation, as genuine meditation depends on establishing inner silence which enables an expansion of consciousness. While the approach is flexible according to individual dispositions and different occasions, a strong commitment to contemplative practice is synonymous with the spiritual life. He says, "I like the old kind / Of spirituality—/ That means long hours / Of meditation / Every day,"[67] and also states encouragingly, "There is no such thing as / An unproductive meditation."[68] He also makes what may seem to be a radical suggestion: "You pray early in the morning

/ And meditate early in the evening. / Indeed, this is your conventional approach / To the spiritual life. / But if you feel that this approach / Is not offering you / Satisfactory results, / Then try an unconventional approach: / Pray and meditate / At any time of day or night / Until God-hunger tortures / Your entire being."[69] This advice may at first seem striking and exceptional, yet it draws on the foundation principle of flexibility while stressing the paramount importance of aspiration. If aspiration is intense, then everything else can be achieved.

THE DIVINE PLAY AND IGNORANCE

In the course of the soul's journey, both before entering the spiritual life and while on the spiritual path, we encounter adversity and suffering as well as limitations and moral failure, even malevolence. When asked why suffering and evil exist, Sri Chinmoy consistently gives the same answer to this question. First, "evil" is a word that he sees as problematic and he often says that the word "evil" is misleading. For example:

> What you call evil, that very thing I call ignorance. There is a great difference between ignorance and evil. Ignorance is an experience and this experience ultimately will lead me to a higher truth. We go from the lesser light, to the greater light, to the greatest light. What you call evil and sin are actually experiences of bondage and imperfection.[70]
>
> What is evil? Evil is darkness. What is darkness? Darkness is nothing but very limited light. If you really enter into the inner world, you will see that in darkness also there is a very small, subtle light…there is some light, infinitesimal light, because God is everywhere. If He is omnipresent, how can He not be inside even the most abysmal darkness? He is there, but He is manifested there to a very limited extent. So evil, which is very insignificant light, will gradually, in the bosom of Infinity and Eternity, be illumined and grow into light.[71]

What is called "evil" is a part of the totality of existence since it is within the world, which is "God the creation." If the whole creation is the projection of God the Creator, then nothing can be said to exist outside of God or apart from God. And precisely because even in the deepest darkness there is still some presence of light, all darkness can be illumined. Even the tiniest particle of light can expand and grow. There is nothing that cannot eventually be transformed—and faith in this ultimate transformation must never be abandoned.

It was God's intention that the creation would evolve from relative darkness through lesser light to more and more light: "What God wanted to do was go through ignorance to Knowledge, through limitation to Plenitude, through death to Immortality."[72] But in the very beginning there was only Light. How then did darkness and ignorance arise? In his account of the origin of ignorance and so-called "evil," Sri Chinmoy invariably uses the phrase "limited freedom."

In the beginning there was only Silence, and Light, infinite Light. Then each individual was given a limited amount of freedom, but we misused that limited freedom.

The evil force is in our mind, not inside our aspiring heart. The mind wants to taste the whole world infinitesimally, piece by piece. The heart wants to embrace the whole world as a unit. The heart feels that the whole world belongs to it. But the mind says, "This is mine, that is yours." The more the mind can separate, the greater joy the mind gets. Evil is a sense of separativity. When there is union, there is no evil; but when there is separation, at that time evil starts. If we have good will, love, a feeling of oneness, then instead of destroying the world, we shall try to embrace the whole world.

It was not God's intention that there should be undivine forces, hostile forces. No! But many things happen in the creation that are tolerated. It is one thing for something to be fully sanctioned and another thing to be just accepted or tolerated .[73]

When the One becomes the many, the Infinite multiplies itself and countless finite beings come into existence; this is the very nature of the divine Play. As soon as they exist, individual souls possess "limited freedom" and this, too, is part of the Play.[74] "There was no ignorance in the beginning"[75] but once God had given freedom to finite individual beings, creatures did diverge from their original state as first created by God. This has brought about a world which does have more ignorance, suffering and destruction than God originally intended. This departure from God's plan is not something God "sanctions" or approves but rather "tolerates," a crucial distinction for understanding the meaning of God's Will for the world.

Some individual beings or forces refused the life of expanding light and oneness, seeking instead to strengthen the life of separation, domination and violence. These are the "hostile forces" or "undivine forces." There are "spirits" and "vital beings," of which Sri Chinmoy says, "Some were once part of a human being, but some are only part of the universal existence. These entities do not want the soul's light. These beings get pleasure in creating mischief and destruction."[76] Hostile forces of any kind may attack human beings, both physically and also in thoughts and emotions. They may seek to use human beings as their channels or instruments; the most powerful are demonic powers capable of immense harm. Such entities are a familiar part of traditional religious cosmologies both East and West, which also recognize good, beneficent spiritual entities.

"Evil is a sense of separativity" and when the unillumined ego or sense of individuality generates desire to build up one's own separate existence, the result is the wish to dominate and even destroy others. But "the part of us that is keeping a sense of separativity, the small portion that wants to enjoy its sense of individuality or personality, is not actually evil," Sri Chinmoy says. "It is creating problems for us because it is unwilling to become unlimited."[77] Sri Chinmoy emphasizes that "the mind," and especially the human mind, is a significant factor in the emergence of so-called evil. "The root of evil is ignorance. What is ignorance? Ignorance is the dark mind."[78] We have already described the role of the ego: once the mind has come into existence, it clings to its own limitation and creates division, and may also receive influences from without that make these patterns more pronounced.

The point that evil does exist but is nonabsolute is of central importance. Equally important is the recognition that even the worst evil is contained inside the ongoing process of world-transformation, which is still incomplete. In the totality of the process, evil is not a cosmic principle opposed to the Divine but an imperfection which God, in and through God's creation, undergoes as part of the Play. Sri Chinmoy explains, "God is in everything. The universe is God's manifestation. But it is not yet God's Perfection. By His Self-revelation God is proceeding towards His Self-Perfection. Perfection has not yet taken place. . . . The harmony is not yet perfect; nothing is perfect yet."[79] It would be wrong to say that God wills any evil. Rather God has created relative light and darkness, ignorance and knowledge, and now allows or "tolerates" the refusal of light and expansion and clinging to their separateness by partially free finite creatures. This partial freedom of finite creatures, in which God seems to limit God's own omnipotence, is a condition of the Play, and as self-aware human beings, we can choose how to use our freedom although this freedom is limited.

Sri Chinmoy therefore minimizes use of the word "evil," although he does at times use it in his poetry. There are two reasons for this. The first is ontological accuracy, since evil has only a relative existence and nothing is absolutely evil. The second reason follows directly from the first. Words matter—and because the word "evil" has considerable potency, the force of the word and the idea that it expresses can mislead us and influence us to essentialize. And once we reify evil we give it a stronger hold over our minds, which is exactly how it acquires and increases its power. This can lead us to look down on others as inferior[80] and also make us doubt the possibility of our own transformation, which is a very grave danger to our life of aspiration.

SUFFERING AND ITS TRANSFORMATION

Creation and God-manifestation, Sri Chinmoy says, are still "unfinished."[81] In this evolving and imperfect world, there is suffering of many kinds for finite beings in a physical body (note that "suffering" is an inclusive concept and that physical pain is only one aspect of suffering). Suffering may be experienced as less acute if it is freely chosen and more distressful if it is involuntary. Sri Chinmoy's counsel is to see suffering in the largest possible context, indeed in the context of the soul's whole journey in all its vastness.

> Something may be painful to us, but in God's Eye it is not like that; it is an experience. And that experience is like a stepping-stone . . . . We have to know that we are making progress; we are proceeding towards the Light. Right now there is a tunnel of suffering before us, but at the end of the tunnel there is light.
>
> Suffering is not the beginning and suffering is not the end. Light and Delight were the beginning and they will be the end. In the process of evolution, the forces of suffering are making us stronger. . . . But if you ask, "Why should suffering exist at all?" then I wish to say that you call it suffering, but God does not call it suffering. He takes it as an experience, and when we become one with His Will, we also will take it as an experience. Right now we are not one with His Will, so suffering is suffering and joy is joy. We are separated from God by our limited mind. But if we remain in the wave of the cosmic Will, then we shall see that everything is an experience helping us to realise the Absolute.[82]

He explains further, "God does not need ignorance for Himself, / But he acts in and through our ignorance / For our liberation and perfection."[83] And this being so, "Is there any earthly problem / That does not have / A purifying and illumining purpose?"[84] which can be seen when the problem is understood in the largest context.

It is also helpful to understand the specific causes of suffering. Suffering does not have just one cause but can have many, and in any given instance the reasons for an experience of suffering are particular. It is sometimes supposed that all suffering can be explained by one's karma, but Sri Chinmoy states that this is not the case, although to be sure much suffering is the result of our own actions of body, speech, and mind, as generally believed in Indic traditions. He first cautions that, "The law of karma is not simple; it is very, very complicated."[85] He then explains that while it is true that the universe is governed by the law of karma[86] and "in the case of an ordinary, unaspiring person, karmic dispensation is unavoidable and inevitable,"[87] it is also true that

If we shed bitter tears and cry for forgiveness . . . . God's infinite Grace can nullify the results of one's bad karma and expedite the results of one's good karma. Also, not all suffering is the result of past karma. When undivine, hostile forces that are hovering around behave like mad elephants or enter into a person, the person suffers. A mad elephant, no matter how nice and sincere you are, will simply destroy you. Sometimes what happens also is that even when one has not done anything wrong, the soul wants to have the experience of suffering. Our soul wants to enter into the depth of pain just to know what pain is.[88]

Since disruptive or malevolent forces outside ourselves can cause undeserved suffering, we need to be vigilant and pray for protection. There may also be the illumined wish of an individual soul to experience suffering, as this can enable one to understand what suffering is, empathize with the suffering of others, and develop compassion.[89] As well, a person may sacrificially take on suffering karmically destined for others and willingly bear this experience for them. Sarada Devi says that "Even Avataras, saints and sages have to undergo the ordeal of suffering, for they take upon themselves the burden of the sins of omission and commission of ordinary human beings and thereby sacrifice themselves for the good of humanity."[90] In another domain, Sri Chinmoy has even mentioned incidents from his own experience where animals have sacrificed themselves to prevent or delay the suffering of others such as the human beings they are close to, praising the self-sacrifice of the animals and adding that such deeds are not uncommon.[91]

Suffering may have its own value. "Every experience in life can be meaningful and beneficial if we accept it properly."[92] Suffering is not necessarily purifying, but if there is suffering for whatever reasons, for as long as it lasts it can be utilized as a means of spiritual progress: "Although suffering is not our goal, through suffering we try to become pure."[93] Sri Chinmoy advises that if suffering does occur, we should not prolong it, let alone glorify it, but strive to overcome it. It must be faced with courage and resolution: "The more we can endure suffering, the sooner the strength of our suffering dies out. Therefore, let us sow the seed of endurance inside our aspiring heart."[94] And indeed, suffering can contribute to our inner strength: "Sorrows not only deepen / But also strengthen / Our heart-power."[95]

Sri Chinmoy repeatedly counsels that when there is suffering, we should deal with it by "taking it as an experience." He further says that we should take it not as our own experience but as an experience that God is having in and through us. The effort to know that it is God Who is the real Experiencer and Doer in us should not be held in reserve for times of drastic suffering and applied sparingly as a kind of exceptional remedy or advanced practice. It is a spiritual discipline that should be applied even in the midst of ordinary daily activities that do not afford us "excruciating pangs" but just humdrum aggravation, boredom and stress. That Sri Chinmoy says this spiritual discipline should be constant—no matter how great or small, serious or minor our suffering is—shows that the point is important in his philosophy as a whole, as does the frequency with which he repeats it. We have seen that the concept that God, as the *ātman* or Self, is the true Experiencer in us is found in the Upaniṣads, while the teaching that one should be God's "instrument" is found in the Bhagavad Gītā (11.33), to which Sri Chinmoy often refers in this connection. Sri Chinmoy explains, "When we say, 'God is the Doer; I am just His instrument,' then ego disappears. But if we feel we are the doers, ego comes into existence." From an egotistical sense of agency, he says, desire grows.[96]

Since suffering stems from desire and clinging, and these in turn arise from the ego's sense of agency, changing our consciousness of "who is acting" is a path to liberation. Indeed, it is not only the path to liberation from suffering but also from ignorance itself. Sri Chinmoy consistently affirms that the path of egoless action in surrender to God's Will leads to the supreme goal of God-realization. Surrender, however, does not depend on knowing exactly what God's Will is in every given instance, but on identification with God's Will and on knowing that one is God's instrument. This does not mean that one was not God's instrument before; one was all along but now one has become conscious of it.

With the awareness that one is playing a part in the Līlā, painful experiences can be accepted if they are necessary and inevitable according to God's "cosmic Will." It is here that the key to the transformation of suffering is to be found. With this wisdom, a poem expresses acceptance in a spirit of austere detachment:

I condemn no one
  Because
I know no person is the real doer.
  God is the real Doer.

I console no one
  Because
I know no person is the real sufferer.
  God is the real Sufferer.[97]

Beginning to understand that God is the real Doer and Experiencer brings us to a wider vision of the cosmic Play or Game. This in turn leads to a deeper level of experience in which the suffering is itself can be transformed into a kind of satisfaction or delight.

God is experiencing in us either suffering or joy. God has formed a circle and He is moving around the circle. This moment we call it joy; the next moment we call it sadness or sorrow, and the next moment we see that this is only His Game. Perfection is in accepting the suffering as such and the joy as such. We have to become conscious instruments of God to give Him the satisfaction of experiencing suffering or joy. If we have a higher realisation, we do not see imperfection in God's creation. We see that what we call imperfection or suffering is something that has to be transformed into permanent ecstasy or delight.[98]

From a similar perspective, Sri Aurobindo says that the creation is "a masked form" of *Sat-Cit-Ānanda* and because "Life is an energy of His conscious-force, the secret of all its movements must be a hidden delight inherent in all things"—yet because of "egoistic division" this delight may actually be "represented as its own opposite."[99] Thus the seeker after truth must eventually understand the deeper nature of both suffering and joy. Experiences of pain and sorrow do not cease to be distressful, yet are no longer experienced as "suffering" as they were before. In the same way, joy can be apprehended as an aspect of the divine Delight. All experiences are necessary for the ultimate satisfaction in the Play of the universe. As Sri Chinmoy says, "Joy and sorrow / Badly need each other / For their perfection."[100]

THE JOURNEY'S GOAL

In its long evolutionary journey the soul usually determines the different experiences that a person will have in a given lifetime and Sri Chinmoy observes that if we consciously put ourselves "into the spontaneous flow" of the experiences the soul wants to give us, we will eventually grow into "abiding peace, joy and fulfillment."[101] He adds,

> The soul is uncovering what it has always known. But at the same time, it is growing and enriching itself by taking into itself the divine essence of its earthly experiences. Meanwhile, the physical consciousness is becoming more and more conscious of the soul's unlimited divine capacity. In essence, the soul, being one with God, is uncovering what it has always known. But in the process of evolution, its *becoming* and *knowing*, *knowing* and *becoming*, move together and are complementary processes in the lap of the Supreme Truth.[102]

It takes time for the outer being to become receptive to the guidance and light offered by the soul, especially because the ego and "division-mind" can delay the soul's manifestation. But this resistance will not last indefinitely. The practices of prayer, meditation and selfless service eventually bring the seeker to advanced stages of yoga, including union with the object of contemplation and *samādhi*, deep and total absorption. In these states of spiritual attainment the limitations of the outer being are transcended and one can see with inner vision the reality of the soul and its true nature as a portion of God's Being.

The goal of God-realization is achieved when the heart, mind, vital and body are all illumined by the soul in an integral transformation. Sri Chinmoy says,

> A day will come when the soul is in a position to exercise its divine qualities and make the body, mind and heart feel that they need their self-discovery. The physical and the vital will consciously want to listen to the soul and be instructed and guided by the soul. Then, here in the physical world, we will have an immortalized nature, an immortal life, for our soul will have become totally and inseparably one with the Divine on earth. At that time we will have to offer our inner wealth to the world at large and manifest our soul's potentialities.[103]

The soul always knows that it is one with God, and because of their aspiration eventually the heart, mind, vital, and body surrender to the soul and also become conscious of this unity. At the same time they realize their oneness with the countless other souls who exist, entering into a universal communion of all beings. This conscious oneness with both God the transcendent Creator and God the universal creation is the culmination of both knowledge and love, which converge in this realization.

NOTES

1. *Eternity's Soul-Bird*, Part 1 (New York: Agni Press, 1974), 10.

2. See for example, *Bṛhadāraṇyaka Up.* 2.4.14, 3.4.2; *Chāndogya Up.* 8.12.4; *Praśna Up.* 4.9.

3. *Service-Trees*, Part 40 (2004), No. 39,994.

4. *Service-Trees*, Part 33 (2003), No. 32,060.

5. "Delight is an unlimited capacity," in *Flower-Flames*, Part 37 (1982), No. 3,621.

6. *Yoga*, 17.

7. Ibid., 11.

8. *Yoga*, 119–120; *Sri Chinmoy Answers*, Vol. 1, 2nd ed. (Oxford and Lyon: Ganapati Press, 2015), 670–671; *Sri Chinmoy Answers*, Vol. 2, 2nd ed. (Oxford and Lyon: Ganapati Press, 2015), 985.

9. *Eternity's Soul-Bird*, Part 1, 8.

10. *Yoga*, 119–120.

11. *Service-Trees,* Part 23 (2001), No. 22,814.

12. *Service-Trees,* Part 3 (1998), No. 2,523.

13. *United Nations Works*, Vol. 1, 44.

14. "Sudur Hate Bhese Āsi," in *Belā Chale Jāi* (New York: Agni Press, 2010 [1979]), No. 46.

15. Chāndogya Upaniṣad 6.8.7 through 6.16.3. *Tat* or "That" refers to the one Absolute or Brahman.

16. *Commentaries*, 93–94.

17. *Death and Reincarnation: Eternity's Voyage* (New York: Aum Publications, 1973), 127–128; 76–77.

18. Ibid., 109–113.

19. *Eternity's Soul-Bird*, Part 1 (1974), 5.

20. *Yoga*, 45.

21. *Yoga,* 125–126.

22. *Service-Trees,* Part 49 (2008), No. 48,497.

23. *Aspiration-Plants,* Part 188 (1993), No. 18,761.

24. *Yoga*, 32.

25. *The Oneness of the Eastern Heart and the Western Mind,* Part 2, 38.

26. *Mind-confusion and Heart-illumination*, Part 2 (New York: Agni Press, 1974), 5–6.

27. *The Oneness of the Eastern Heart and the Western Mind*, Part 3, 14.

28. See above, 59.

29. *The Oneness of the Eastern Heart and the Western Mind*, Part 1, 60.

30. *Commentaries*, 94.

31. *Yoga*, 104.

32. *Chandelier* (Pondicherry: Sri Aurobindo Ashram, 1959), No. 247.

33. *Service-Trees,* Part 10 (1998), No. 9,067.

34. *My Silver Jubilee Rainbow-Heart-Whispers* (New York: Agni Press, 1989), No. 24.

35. *Aspiration-Plants,* Part 144 (1991), No. 14,343.

36. *Service-Trees*, Part 3 (1998), No. 2,880.

37. *Service-Trees*, Part 24 (2002), No. 23,031.

38. *Service-Trees*, Part 33 (2003), No. 32,192.

39. *Yoga*, 105.

40. *Service-Trees*, Part 32 (2003), No. 31,308.

41. *The Doubt-World* (New York: Agni Press, 1977), 43–44; *Ego and Self-Complacency* (New York: Agni Press, 1977), 31.

42. *Four Hundred Song-Birds: Blue, Green, White, Red,* Part 3, No. 21 (1996).

43. *Gospel*, 269.

44. *Aspiration-Plants*, Part 191 (1993), No. 19, 061.

45. *Service-Trees*, Part 49 (2008), No. 48,639.

46. *Service-Trees*, Part 36 (2004), No. 35,237.

47. *Service-Trees*, Part 47 (2007), No. 46,059.

48. *Aspiration-Plants,* Part 253 (1993), No. 25,299.

49. Ibid., No. 25, 203.

50. *Service-Trees,* Part 33 (2003), No. 32,980.

51. *Our Path* (New York: Sri Chinmoy Lighthouse, 1970), 1.

52. *Service-Trees*, Part 49 (2008), No. 48,567.

53. *Kundalini: The Mother-Power* (Santurce, Puerto Rico: AUM Press, 1973), 18–19.

54. *Summits*, 82–83.

55. Mentions of these terms are very numerous and in a number of different Upaniṣads. For an initial inquiry, see Olivelle, "Heart in the Upaniṣads."

56. *My Christmas-New Year Vacation Aspiration-Prayers*, Part 7 (New York: Agni Press, 2002), 71.

57. Katha Up. 2.12.12-13, Śvetāśvatara Up. 3.13.

58. Śvetāśvatara Up. 3.20, Katha U. 1.2.20.

59. *Eternity's Soul-Bird*, Part 1, 7–8.

60. *Sri Chinmoy Answers*, Volume 2 (Oxford and Lyon: Ganapati Press, 2015), 1067–1068.

61. *Prāṇa*, often translated as "breath," is a cosmological principle in the Upaniṣads and understood as life-energy in yoga traditions more generally. "Breath" in the world's cultures and religious traditions is a vast subject, which we can barely touch on here. It is often understood on multiple levels, not only as air physically inhaled and exhaled, but also as life in different modalities, construed as various kinds of life-energy in the body, and life as a spiritual reality akin to "soul." "Breath" is the principle or ultimate Source of life itself, associated with the creation of the universe, the Breath or Spirit of God or the One. For example, see Ṛg Veda 10.129, and Genesis 1–2.

62. *Service-Trees*, Part 20 (2001), No. 19,179.

63. *Service-Trees*, Part 39 (2004), No. 38,527.

64. "I Shall Feed," in *A Soulful Cry versus a Fruitful Smile* (New York: Agni Press, 1977), 546.

65. *Yoga*, 83.

66. See Kusumita P. Pedersen,"Uniting Sports and Spirituality," *Hinduism Today*, April/May/June 2018, 56–63.

67. Both basic and more advanced teachings are collected in *Meditation: Man-Perfection in God-Satisfaction* (New York: Agni Press, 1989 [1978]); see also Kusumita P. Pedersen, "Sri Chinmoy on the Nature and Goals of Contemplative Practice," in *Contemplative Studies and Hinduism: Meditation, Devotion, Prayer, and Worship*, ed. Rita D. Sherma and Purushottama Bilimoria (New York: Routledge, 2021), 67–84.

68. *Service-Trees*, Part 47 (2007), No. 46,494.

69. *Service-Trees*, Part 33 (2003), No. 32,979.

70. *Aspiration-Plants*, Part 5 (1983), No. 448.

71. *The Hunger of Darkness and the Feast of Light*, Part 1 (New York: Agni Press, 1974), 9.

72. *Earth's Cry Meets Heaven's Smile*, Book 1 (Santurce, Puerto Rico: Aum Press, 1974), 72–73.

73. *Sri Chinmoy Speaks* (Oxford and Lyon: Ganapati Press, 2015), 83.

74. *Realisation-Soul and Manifestation-Goal* (New York: Agni Press, 1974), 8.

75. *Earth Cry Meets Heaven's Smile*, Book 2, 104–105.

76. *Astrology, The Supernatural and the Beyond* (New York: Aum Publications, 1973), 53.

77. *Sound and Silence*, Part 1 (New York: Agni Press, 1982), 44.

78. *Miracles, Emanations and Dreams* (New York: Agni Press, 1977), 45.

79. *God-Life: Is It a Far Cry?* (New York: Agni Press, 1974), 22–23.

80. *Sri Chinmoy Speaks* (Oxford and Lyon: Ganapati Press, 2015), 69.

81. *Aspiration-Plants*, Part 64 (1984), No. 6,384; *Service-Trees*, Part 33 (2003), No. 32,017.

82. *Aspiration-Glow and Dedication-Flow*, Part 1 (New York: Agni Press, 1977), 5.

83. *Aspiration-Plants*, Part 149 (1991), No. 14,853.

84. *Aspiration-Plants,* Part 144 (1991), No. 14,382.

85. *Death and Reincarnation*, 9.

86. *Yoga,* 126.

87. *Death and Reincarnation,* 112.

88. Ibid., loc. cit.

89. Ibid., 109; *The Meditation-World* (New York: Agni Press, 1977), 51–52.

90. Swami Vireśwarānanda, *Teachings of Sri Sarada Devi, The Holy Mother* (Chennai: Sri Ramakrishna Math, 1983), 5–6.

91. *Sri Chinmoy Answers*, Volume 2 (Oxford and Lyon: Ganapati Press, 2015), 1065–1066.

92. *Problems! Problems! Are They Really Problems?* Part 1 (New York: Agni Press, 1974), 32.

93. *A God-Lover's Earth-Heaven Life,* Part 1 (New York: Agni Press, 1974), 46.

94. *Tomorrow's Dawn* (New York: Agni Press, 1982), 44.

95. *Service-Trees,* Part 7 (1998), No. 6,098.

96. *Sri Chinmoy Speaks* (Oxford and Lyon: Ganapati Press, 2015), 80.

97. "The real doer," in *Europe-Blossoms*, 585.

98. *Sri Chinmoy Answers,* Volume 1 (Oxford and Lyon: Ganapati Press, 2015), 732.

99. *The Life Divine*, 10th edition (Pondicherry: Sri Aurobindo Ashram Trust, 1977), 219.

100. *Service-Trees,* Part 47 (2007), No. 46,620.

101. *Yoga*, 121.

102. Ibid., 116–117.

103. *Death and Reincarnation*, 100.

Chapter 5

Knowledge and Realization

WAYS OF KNOWING

In the evolution of the cosmos, the soul is on a journey from forgetting back
to knowledge of its true nature, awakening to its own divine reality and also
to that of the entire world. Swami Vivekananda says, "In the innermost core
of the human soul is the centre of the whole universe," and that God, the
cosmic Intelligence, "gets involved in the minute cell, and evolves at the
other end and becomes God again. He it is that comes down and becomes the
lowest atom, and slowly unfolding His nature, rejoins Himself."[1] As countless souls progress through myriad states of existence over vast spans of
time, the universe as a whole is awakening as new forms of life emerge, and
through long ages it has grown more and more conscious in diverse ways.[2]
Hidden consciousness is revealed and "becomes God again," so that the process of evolution is also one of divinization and God-manifestation. Even in
darkness or inconscience, however deep, there is infinitesimal light that will
expand—as Sri Chinmoy often says, "Light, more Light, abundant Light,
infinite Light." In human beings, the universe has now become self-aware
in yet another new kind of knowing and understanding. Human cognition is
one element in the ongoing cosmic process of transformation. This cognition
is a many-faceted system of varieties and grades of awareness, ranging from
relative ignorance to the highest knowledge of God-realization.

"Wisdom gives ignorance its due value," declares Sri Chinmoy. Each
of the different ways of knowing is valid in its own sphere. No mode of
knowledge is entirely false and none is entirely true, short of God-realization.
"Ignorance, however abysmal, always has within it some seeds of truth,
however twisted and incomplete," he says, and "knowledge, however exalted,
until it founds itself in the Gnostic Consciousness, always contains some

element of ignorance." Ignorance is a kind of knowledge, "but infinitely
far from all-fulfilling," and knowledge is a kind of ignorance, but "holding
within itself the seeds of True Wisdom." The minute particles of light that are
present even in dense darkness have the inherent impulse of all existence to
grow and expand, and within the totality of Being, "the state of ignorance is
a conscious, groping aspect of Knowledge in the Divine."[3]

Each kind of knowledge has its own criteria of validity: "A theory must
be tested. A fact must be honoured. A truth must be lived."[4] Whatever is true
in any sense makes its claim on us: "a fact must be honoured" and "a truth
must be lived." At the same time we can and should make our own claims
on what is presented to us as true: "a theory must be tested." Such is Sri
Chinmoy's regard for an honest agnosticism that he once set to music "the
agnostic's prayer"—"Oh, God! if there be a God, save my soul! if I have a
soul."[5] A questing agnosticism can be generative: "Agnosticism is of various
types. Fruitful agnosticism has every right to its own teeming knowledge.
It is from agnosticism that we come to suspect that an Unknowable Reality
engenders all our values: physical, intellectual and spiritual."[6] And because
intelligibility in itself is a kind of value, even an atheist has a kind of "God."

> Each human being has a God of his own. There is no human being without a
> God. The total atheist does not believe in God. But fortunately he believes, or
> rather unfortunately he has to believe, in a certain idea, some concept of order
> or disorder. And that very idea, that concept, is nothing but God.
>
> Freedom, absolute freedom, must be given each individual soul to discover its
> own path. Mistakes along the path of spirituality are not at all deplorable, for
> mistakes are simply lesser truths. We are not proceeding from falsehood to truth.
> We are proceeding from the least revealed truth to the most revealed truth.[7]

Ignorance and knowledge are thus a continuum. What is all-important is
movement on a path toward truth, and there may be many paths. The choice
of a path is conceived pluralistically: any of an array of approaches may be
adopted, all of which can lead to apprehensions of truth, apprehensions which
may be different from one another but each still valid.

Even in the case of two persons who have the same degree of yogic
illumination, the spiritual knowledge attained may differ perspectivally; Sri
Chinmoy uses the analogy of two people who come into the same room but
from different doors. For one an object may be located "in the front right
corner," while for the other the same object may be in "the left back corner."
Both knowers may justifiably claim to be correct although their perspectives
are partial and complementary.[8] This account is similar to the Jain teaching
of *anekāntavāda,* defined by Jeffery D. Long as "the doctrine of the multi-
faceted, complex nature of reality" and the "metaphysical basis for the Jain

philosophy of relativity."[9] According to L. M. Singhvi, the Jain view is that "Absolute truth cannot be grasped from any particular viewpoint alone because absolute truth is the sum total of all the different viewpoints that make up the universe."[10]

The difference between relative ignorance and relative knowledge depends not only on external conditions, but also on the capacity of the faculties possessed by the subject. It is helpful to bring to mind the distinction made, again in Jainism, between life forms with only one sense faculty (touch), those with two (touch and taste), and those with three, four or five.[11] Microscopic organisms are thought to have less capacity of awareness than worms, worms less than bees, and bees less than elephants or humans. The scope and power of outer awareness are limited by the less complex physical structure of a being located earlier in the trajectory of evolution, where consciousness is more involved into matter and less externalized, although the intrinsic consciousness of the soul or *jivātman* is itself undiminished. There is also the slant or distortion caused by the knower's attitude, motivation or desire; this is not a matter of the awareness-capacity as such but its focus or skewing by an "instinctive" disposition that directs awareness to certain things in the world and omits others. In the same way in the lives of human beings, cognition is molded by both innate capacity and by focus or intentionality; ignorance, we might say, is more "twisted" while knowledge is more "straight."

Should it be feasible to experience fully all possible perspectives in an undistorted manner, even then the comprehension of reality would still be incomplete because of the self-transcendence of truth. As Mother Mirra Alfassa has said, "Humility is that state of consciousness in which whatever the realization, you know that the infinite is still in front of you."[12] Self-knowledge calls us to a sincere awareness of our own finitude as we contemplate a limitless Reality. "Truth is never complete because we are living in an ever-transcending universe," Sri Chinmoy explains. He adds, "What the teachers of the past have said is eternally true; what we are saying is also eternally true. But each truth has its own grade, and all the time we are evolving and progressing."[13] Because understanding is an ongoing progress, each generation may define God in its own way which differs from the past: "There is nothing wrong / With each and every generation / Defining God."[14]

KNOWLEDGE IN THE PHYSICAL AND VITAL BEINGS

A human person usually apprehends the world through the combined functioning of the physical senses, the vital energies and ordinary emotions, the mind and at times also the heart. Emotion is found at all levels with different qualities, as stated earlier. In the previous chapter it was mentioned that parts of the outer being may have limited receptivity to the soul's light. What is the nature of their limitations? With regard to knowledge on the physical plane, we know that Sri Chinmoy does not suggest that the material world as such is an illusion. He also acknowledges that both sense perception and natural science are veridical. While he does observe that the knowledge conveyed by the physical senses is intrinsically limited even when greatly extended by the methods of science, he does not belabor this point.[15] He dwells rather on the fact that sense-knowledge is formed by the ways that the senses respond to their objects in terms of pleasure and pain. And the response of sense-faculties to what gratifies or repels them is intensified by the vital's life-energy.[16] It is the vital that makes the senses "wild" and turns them into a "storm."[17] This is also at times the behavior of an animal which in order to survive and flourish must obtain certain things, and may strive for them vehemently. Sri Chinmoy often uses the phrase "the animal life" to refer to such appetitive and aggressive responses. Human beings, who have self-reflection, may behave in similar ways to preserve or enhance the sense of self, or ego, as well as to satisfy basic needs and desires. Impulses of grasping and avoidance distort a person's apprehension of any entity, since it is perceived in terms of possession and rejection rather than in terms of that entity's nature as it truly is. Here we find the familiar link of attachments and passions to defects of knowledge that has been an age-old concern of philosophical and contemplative traditions.

The senses, nevertheless, are instruments that can be used well and need not keep us in bondage. The phrase "the senses" in the passages that follow indicates the whole of external human experience: the physical senses as energized by the vital and guided by the mind. Senses are "tyrants," but they can also be "servants," Sri Chinmoy says.[18]

"In the abyss of the five senses, / The animal life does not / Know the right thing. /

The human life knows / But does not do / The right thing. / The divine life knows /

And always does / The right thing."[19] When knowing begins to depend more on deliberate intention and reflection, it draws closer to conscious aspiration. Spiritual disciplines that develop skill in awareness and enlarge it can be undertaken to achieve the transformation of our faculties. When asked, "How can we use the senses properly?" Sri Chinmoy answers:

> The proper fulfilment of the senses will come only from God. The body has the senses, but the body is not the owner, the real owner is God. . . . The senses are instruments, God's instruments. God originally entrusted us with these instruments, but we consciously chose not to ask God how to utilise these senses. . . . We could use our eyes, for example, to see the divine beauty in

humanity and in all of God's creation. We could see the divine Light everywhere. But instead, what do we do with our eyes? We use our eyes either to possess the world or reject it. When we see something that pleases us, immediately we try to possess it. When we see something that displeases us, immediately we try to reject it. The universe is all Light, but we do not see it.[20]

The senses are transformed not by withering or destroying them but through practices that train them away from the behavior of grasping and rejection. Sri Chinmoy is clear that suppression is a wrong and ineffective approach, and that our physical and emotional faculties must not be forced, starved, or impaired but kept intact. He explains:

> If we suppress something today, tomorrow we will be subjected to its revolt. Suppression is not the answer. We must not suppress our emotion. What we have to do is illumine it. While we are illumining it, we shall feel real joy. By suppressing it, what do we actually accomplish? Nothing. We are only forcing ourselves beyond our capacity and sincere willingness. As we have a desire to enjoy a life of pleasure, so also we have a desire to suppress it. A life of gross pleasure and a life of suppression are equally bad. They are followed by frustration. Frustration ends in destruction.[21]

"Suppression" in this context is understood as coercion which is in fact itself a kind of desire or aggression. It can effect no real or lasting change. Sri Chinmoy adds: "Do not kill your senses; / Illumine them./ Make them ready for God / To utilise them."[22] As Sri Chinmoy's philosophy is founded on the principle of integrality, the senses have to be accepted and then transformed: "Do not go to extremes. / Accept the body / And the five senses / Only use them spiritually, / Divinely and soulfully."[23] Sustained practice of appropriate methods of discipline achieves restraint, purification and control eventually leading to mastery. In this process, the intention of awareness should be directed to experiences of joy rather than pleasure. Pleasure is grasping, limited and transitory, and followed by frustration—and "frustration is destruction."[24] Joy in contrast is spontaneous, leading to peace, and expanding to more joy, abundant joy, infinite joy.[25]

This approach displays the association of practices of restraint that are often called "ascetic" with the attainment of expanded and more lucid knowing and also the experience of joy.[26] Spiritual practice deals with consciousness, and its goals are both cognitive and affective. When transformed, the senses can and will experience a kind of consciousness that is radically different from what they had previously. This cry will be fulfilled: "Alas, / When will all my senses awaken / To feel God's Presence / All around me?"[27] As will this prayer: "My Lord Supreme, / My soul prays to you: / May my five senses / Be totally illumined / So that I can be / A constant, dedicated, / Surrendered servitor to you."[28] The yogic practices of restraint and cultivation of the virtues, along with prayer, concentration and meditation eventually accomplish the passage from a limited sense of self, identified with the outer being, to the widened sense of self-identified with the whole world and its divine Source—an epistemology of transformation.

THE MIND

The mind has a central role in the constitution of knowledge and in its transformation. Sri Chinmoy says, "For an ordinary human being, the mind is the highest stage in the process of evolution;"[29] it is "the highest part of our ordinary human consciousness."[30] If we regard the mind as superior to the physical and ordinary emotional parts of our being, we tend to give it authority (at least in theory) to direct our lives and allow it to be the judge of what is true and false. But for human consciousness to be transformed by spiritual practice and higher modes of knowledge to be attained, the mind's dominance must give way to the rule of the soul, exercised through the heart as described above. The relation of the mind and the heart is a constant theme in Sri Chinmoy's philosophy, and the need for the mind, because of its limitations and defects, to surrender to the heart. Though often extremely resistant, when it becomes receptive to an authority higher than itself, the mind can aspire and become illumined.

When Sri Chinmoy speaks of the mind as an obstacle in the spiritual life he usually means the "physical mind" in its ordinary unenlightened state. The physical mind, as the phrase indicates, is engrossed in the external material world: "This mind constantly thinks of what you are going to eat, what you are going to say, what clothes you are going to wear and so on. The most limited, gross daily activities are the realm of the physical mind,"[31] he explains. The normal functioning of the physical mind is necessary for everyone. "We remember not to touch the hot stove with our hand. If it is chilly, we remember to wear a coat. We count our change when we buy something. Our physical mind is operating harmlessly in all these things,"[32] Sri Chinmoy says. As stated above, even limited modes of knowledge have validity in their own proper domains. The ordinary mind makes plans and anticipates tasks and problems, thinking of how to do them and solve them. It also deals on the vital plane with our cravings and emotions and can either be very helpful as a guide, or can be captured by our unhelpful responses of anger, fear, jealousy, and gratification: "My ego-mind sings / My vital's attachment-song."[33] The intellectual mind engages in reasoning and deals with abstractions, but even when it does this in a sophisticated manner, in its unillumined state it is "one step removed from the purely physical consciousness."[34] The human mind, whether sense-engrossed, emotional or intellectual, has inherent limitations in its functioning which render it incapable in any efforts to reach modes of knowing which are beyond itself. In sum, "The human mind / Is nothing short of / A thick ignorance-blanket."[35] Attempts to use it "as is" to deal with spiritual matters and to come to these higher levels of knowledge are bound to be counterproductive. As a song says, *"Maner atite jete habe jāni manere karate joy*—I know, beyond the mind I must go to conquer the mind."[36]

One crucial limitation of mental functioning is that it deals with its objects sequentially and in separate parts, and invariably compares these divided entities with each other, often to suspect and criticize. Sri Chinmoy, as we have seen, calls this the "division-mind." He comments, "The worst quality / Of the human mind / Is its enjoyment of negativity."[37] The ordinary, unenlightened mind

> does not allow us to expand ourselves. It always says, "One at a time, little by little, piece by piece." The mind seems to go very fast, but . . . thinks of only one thing at a time. It does not want to embrace existence as a whole. The mind sees things part by part. If Infinity appears before the mind, the mind will take a part out of the whole and say, "This is the truth." It will take a portion of the Vast rather than accept the Vast in its own way. It will try to scrutinise Infinity itself to see if there is any imperfection in it.[38]

And in this way, with stubborn recalcitrance, "The mind's eye / Sees Divinity in all / But does not want to accept it."[39]

Another shortcoming is that the mind, however swift, sharp, or agile it may be, does not have within itself principles that give it stability and reliability. As Sri Chinmoy often says, the mind doubts anything and everything, and then, thinking, "Maybe I was wrong," doubts its own doubt. "The mind constantly contradicts itself and we must dance on the waves of its ever-changing surface."[40] Indeed, "The mind even doubts its own existence and its own formulation of thought."[41] Although the mind is capable of doubting itself, it often quite inconsistently refuses to cede authority to the heart or soul, although they have superior knowledge. This refusal is due not only to the inertia of habit, but to the mind's pride in its entrenched authority even when permitted to function appropriately in its own domain: "The partition-loving mind / Is always / Rebellious."[42] A song puts it, *"Jānte chahi mānash āmar shikte chāhi nā*—My mind wants to know, but does not want to learn."[43] The mind may just be doing its job, but it does not know when to stop—or is simply unable to stop. The mentally formed sense of self, or ego, is the chief obstacle to higher modes of knowing and to spiritual progress, as explained in the previous chapter. The mind is "power-hungry," and even "desires world-domination."[44] Paradoxically self-doubt, still a form of ego, is even more harmful than self-assertion, and is the one defect that Sri Chinmoy is most likely to speak of as a spiritual death that brings the life of aspiration to an end: "Doubt is dangerous, / And self-doubt / Is infinitely more dangerous"[45]—"Self-doubt / Is the beginning / Of self-destruction."[46]

When the intellect and physical mind receive light from higher planes we may begin to speak of "the illumined mind," remembering that this illumination admits of degree. This enlightened mind is often used in the practice of philosophy. Throughout his life Sri Chinmoy esteemed philosophy highly and also affirmed that poetry can be a vehicle for philosophy, as is true in many traditions, saying, "The philosopher is a poet in the mind. The poet is a philosopher in the heart."[47] He even stated on one occasion that philosophy is "on the same level as music in its capacity to reveal and manifest the Divine here on earth."[48] The mind, when it aspires for truth, becomes "the searching mind." Sri Chinmoy comments, "Our mind can get astounding answers / To its questions / If it is ready to surrender / To a new light."[49] The aspiring mind develops spiritual qualities of clarity and vastness and Sri Chinmoy avers, "The clearness of the mind / Is, indeed / The nearness of God."[50] Further, "When the mind becomes sincere, the mind opens itself consciously, devotedly and soulfully to the Vastness. When sincerity dawns in the mind, multifarious encouraging and inspiring experiences of the world descend from Above through the mind and prepare the mind for its universal opening to the transcendental Heights."[51] Addressing the mind in an early prose poem, he says, "O my mind, no earthly chain can fetter you. You are always on the wing. No human thought can control you. You are forever on the move. … Yours is the arrow of concentration. Yours is the soil of lightning intuition. Yours is the unhorizoned peace."[52]

IMAGINATION AND INTUITION

Sri Chinmoy views imagination in an extremely positive way. For him, dismissive expressions such as "It was only my imagination" would be trivializing and mistaken. "Imagination is no self-deception," he says.[53] "Imagination is not / A whim of the mind. / It is a reality in its own right,"[54] so "Do not discard imagination. / Imagination is a solid power. / Imagination is a reality / In the higher worlds."[55] Imagination is a creative capacity that by making an "image" (as the word implies) of a given reality begins the process of invoking that reality, calling it into more concrete existence. Imagination is not a mental process in an ordinary narrow sense; "The dancing eye / Of a soaring imagination / Carries the mind / To the farthest destination."[56] Mental fabrications can certainly be false, but Sri Chinmoy employs the term "hallucination" for such phenomena and reserves "imagination" for use only with a positive connotation.

> Imagination is not mental hallucination. Hallucinations come from the subconscious plane. This subconscious plane can be in [i.e., function in] the mind, it can be in the vital, or it can be in the gross physical. But when you imagine, there already reality exists. There would have been no scientific discoveries if there had been no imagination. Imagination itself is a reality, but you have to be in the flow of imagination. There is a world of imagination. Either you have to enter into that world, or you let that world enter into you.[57]

Imagination is also connected to memory in a significant manner. When we wish to bring back a positive spiritual experience in order to rise above inertia or dejection and get joy and inspiration, we should use the power of imagination to recall the experience we previously had and then actually recover it.[58] As for dreaming, dreams experienced during sleep do not necessarily have any special epistemological status, since there are many kinds of dreams; they may be on any "level" of knowing, from trivial and quite meaningless to bearers of valuable insight and even visionary dreams.[59]

Sri Chinmoy thus consistently advocates the constructive use of imagination. "Imagination is not wishful thinking. / Bring down the fruits of imagination / From its reality-tree."[60] Imagination is essential to spiritual progress and lack of imagination may be an impediment.

> Divine imagination is not a false way of looking at truth; it is the proper way to look at the truth. People who do not have the capacity to imagine cannot go very far. We see a poet and we may think that he is living in the world of imagination, but it is the poet who enters into the world of reality with his inner vision. Today's imagination is tomorrow's aspiration. Tomorrow's aspiration is the realisation of the day after tomorrow.[61]

Imagination correctly used not only can enable us to transcend the limitations of the ordinary mind, but also can strengthen our aspiration and contribute directly and significantly to contemplative practice.

Above all, levels of mind proper is the plane of intuition, which in Sri Chinmoy's use of the word is not actually part of "mind" at all and not to be equated with it. "When one has intuition, one lives in the light of divine existence," he says. "But the mental brilliance or natural intelligence that we notice in our daily lives does not have its source in the world of intuition. Intuition is something far deeper and higher."[62] Intuition is:

> the direct perception of Truth, which needs no mental help. It is knowledge without thought or mental form. It is direct and spontaneous. It makes you feel

what it is. Normally, you see something and then you give it a mental form, saying, "This is what it is." But intuition makes you feel its true existence at once. Intuition houses the depth of Vision and the wealth of Realisation all together.[63]

In English there are very few words for spiritual knowledge and "intuition" must fill part of this lack. It is also important to note that the word "feel" plays a key role in Sri Chinmoy's epistemology and is often used to refer not only to imagination and also, as in the passage above, to the direct vision of intuition but as well to the centrally important cognitive experience of the heart, to be discussed shortly.

He elaborates, "The intuitive capacity does not and cannot function when the physical mind is too active. . . . When the seeker begins to aspire and consciously prays and meditates, the physical mind is transformed into the illumined mind. At that time, the dormant intuitive faculty bears fruit."[64] Intuitive perception often occurs, as is at times observed, as a sudden flash in which we see something—or many things at once in their interrelation— in a way that is not possible for the physical mind. The visionary poetry of the Vedic seers was born from their intuition, "their full and conscious awareness of direct and immediate Truth."[65] Sri Chinmoy also comments that "A scientific achievement need not be from the mind, not even from the intellect; the greatest scientific achievements come directly from the intuitive plane."[66] Intuition working within science is a great augmentation of human knowledge and facilitates its self-transcendence. Using the term "materialism" to indicate an epistemological materialism or physicalism, Sri Chinmoy says, "Materialism has begun to far exceed the limits of sense-knowledge. With this obstruction fading away, the march of materialism is now quite safe and satisfactory towards its unimagined Goal."[67]

Intuition is a far higher form of knowing than imagination. Sri Chinmoy says that while intuition is not the same thing as the full functioning of the *ājña* chakra or "third eye," there is a relation: "Intuition / Is the fondest child / Of the third eye."[68] Even beyond intuition is "vision," compared to divine Vision or God's Seeing, and described as follows:

Vision comes directly from the third eye. The source of vision is infinitely higher than the source of imagination. With His cosmic Vision, God created this world. Imagination can be high, higher, highest. But if we are touched by God's infinite Grace, we can know what His Vision is or even be endowed with God's Vision.

There is a great difference between inner vision and imagination. Imagination has a reality of its own; it can be very high, very lofty and very deep. Imagination can come from a very, very high realm of consciousness. But the source of vision is infinitely higher than even the highest plane of imagination. . . . When we imagine, usually our mind operates. I am not saying it is the earth-bound mind; it can be the higher mind. . . . But when we use our vision or third eye, at that time the Source of creation is operating in and through us.[69]

It is important to emphasize once more that Sri Chinmoy holds that our powers of knowing are by no means confined to the outer faculties of the physical senses, the ordinary emotions and the mind; it is not through them that "the Source of creation is operating" in a direct, comparatively unmediated way. "There are worlds beyond the senses,"[70] he says, and there are other faculties, "inner senses," that we may not normally employ but which we can learn to use. He elaborates:

> In the field of consciousness, truth proves its own existence. In the outer life, truth does not prove its own existence. That is because we relate to the outer world with our outer senses. . . . But *we also have inner senses*. The mind has one foot in the inner world and one foot in the outer world. As an inner sense it is inadequate, and as an outer sense it is incompetent [emphasis added].

> If you want to see something in the outer world, you have to go to the place where it is being shown. In the inner world it is also like that. . . . Everything has to be seen or judged in its own world. . . . Physical truth has to be seen in the physical world and spiritual truth has to be seen in the spiritual world.[71]

He says, "The outer world is very limited in comparison to the inner world,"[72] and "The inner world / Is truly much vaster / Than the outer world."[73] A "world" may be described as a trans-individual domain of existence and consciousness, and in each world the appropriate abilities or "senses" of that type of consciousness must be employed to experience the realities of that world.

The external "body-consciousness" of a human being is very limited, as are ways of knowing that depend on it. To have knowledge of inner worlds and what is in them, awareness must turn inward, "go deep within," as Sri Chinmoy often says. The need to turn consciousness inward in order to see deeper reality has been established in Indic traditions at least since the time of the Upaniṣads.[74] As training is necessary to understand their principles and to do work in the fields of music, science, sports or literature, so likewise training in yoga is necessary to enter into the inner "worlds" of spiritual experience. Their principles and concrete aspects are learned through lengthy instruction and practice of the methods of introspection known in contemplative traditions. The practitioner needs to acquire mature skill in order to attain spiritual perception. This training is by no means just a matter of technique, though techniques must be mastered, but is a reorientation and change of the whole person and sense of self. As already explained, one lays aside a provisional and less real "self" to identify with the true self, the soul, called in Vedāntic tradition the *antarātman,* the "inner self" or "self within."

Those who have not experienced or "seen" God, the soul or other inner realities cannot validly dismiss the testimony of those who have had such experiences simply because they themselves have not had them. The analogy is given of a person who has visited another country and gives a description of it; the mere fact that some other individual has never been there and may not presently have the opportunity to go does not mean that this country does not exist —even if the skeptical person has difficulty imagining this place or for some reason wants to deny its reality.[75]

Indeed, "For a genuine seeker, / The inner world / Is infinitely more real / Than the outer world"[76] and thus this yogic or spiritual epistemology cannot be accurately presented without an adequate framing cosmology and ontology (such as has been offered in the previous chapters). As Swami Vivekananda says,"One party says thought is caused by matter, and the other says matter is caused by thought. Both statements are wrong; matter and thought are coexistent. There is a third something of which both matter and thought are products."[77] This "something" is Brahman or *Sat-Cit-Ānanda*, in which Consciousness and the Real are nondifferent. Because Brahman or God has become the whole universe, all of its "worlds"—both inner or outer—are forms of consciousness-existence and constitute the totality of "God the creation."

THE HEART

The heart is for Sri Chinmoy preeminent among the "inner senses" and is a faculty of knowledge as well as of emotion and the center of love, affection, and compassion. Sri Chinmoy often refers to the heart's knowing as "feeling," a word which takes on special significance for him because, as just mentioned, English lacks more precise terms for spiritual knowledge. The heart's subtle, pure emotions are a kind of cognition, while the heart's ability to "feel" may at times even be similar to intuition. The heart often is said to feel the presence of something or someone, and especially God's Presence; Sri Chinmoy states on a number of occasions that is it is easier to feel God's Presence than to "see" God.[78] The heart above all has the power of identification and the feeling of oneness: "The heart can identify with anything, small or large," he says.[79] The mind does not have the heart's capacity of identification, and since the very goal of spiritual practice is the realization of oneness, this is a crucial limitation. "The mind makes you feel that we are all separate, but the heart makes you feel that everybody belongs to you. If you use the heart immediately you will see the entire universe—Infinity itself—*within you*. But if you use the mind, you see anything vast as outside yourself. If you think of the Infinite with your mind, it is no longer infinite; it is all limited. Beyond a certain point, the mind's conceptions do not extend" (emphasis added).[80]

With regard to actual practice, Sri Chinmoy recommends locating one's awareness "in the heart" during prayer and meditation as well as at other times, as we have seen. This means both to focus awareness on the heart center, and also to cultivate the modes of consciousness of the heart—the feelings of love, sympathy, compassion and oneness, as well as the heart's peace and silence. The heart of a person is like a door or gateway of entry into the cosmic Heart or universal interiority (Sri Chinmoy often refers in his poetry to the "heart's door"). The individual's capacity to attain wisdom through the connection to the universal Heart must be increased over time:

> The spiritual heart is larger than the universe itself. The whole universe is inside the spiritual heart . . . the heart is like a globe which encompasses the whole universe. Inside the heart is the plane for love, the plane for light, the plane for peace.
>
> One has to develop the spiritual heart. Everybody does not have the same capacity. Everybody has potentiality, but it must be developed. It is not like our oneness with God, which is something we all possess equally but have misplaced. No, the capacity of the spiritual heart is something we have to achieve in the process of evolution. Gradually it grows from a seed to a plant to a huge banyan tree, as our oneness with God increases. With unconscious oneness we come into the world. Through the process of prayer, meditation, love, devotion and surrender, we develop conscious oneness. . . . When we have developed the spiritual heart, at that time we come to realise our identity with the Mother and Father of the universe.[81]

Sri Chinmoy speaks of "the eye of the heart," an expression also found in Sufism and Christian tradition,[82] and says "To see the ultimate Truth / We must open / Our heart-eye," and declares that "The vision / Of the heart-eye / Is unlimited."[83] The heart's wisdom has been acknowledged since Vedic times: the famous Creation Hymn of the Ṛg Veda says that "Searching in their hearts through inspired thought, poets found the connection of the existent in the nonexistent" (*Sató bándhum ásati nír avindan hṛdí pratīṣyā kaváyo manīṣā́*, 10.129.4);[84] while the Bṛhadāraṇyaka Upaniṣad affirms, "Through the heart one knows truth—*hṛdayena hi satyam janati*" (3.9.23).[85]

SAMĀDHI AND GOD-REALIZATION

The term "*samādhi*" (literally, "completely held together") is used in Indic traditions with the general meaning of a state of profound, one-pointed absorption in the object of meditation.[86] In different contexts there are more specific meanings and definitions of different kinds of *samādhi*. Sri Chinmoy describes *savikalpa samādhi*[87] as a state in which some thoughts may remain but ordinary human consciousness is transcended and the experience of time and space completely altered; although some thoughts may occur, they do not affect the dynamism of the *samādhi*.[88] In *nirvikalpa samādhi* there are no thoughts of any kind. Following is Sri Chinmoy's description based on his own experience; he cautions that it is necessarily an inadequate account since no words can be adequate to the experience itself.

> In *nirvikalpa* samadhi we have no mind. We see the Creator, the Creation and the Observer as one Person. There the object of adoration and the person who is adoring become totally one. We go beyond everything and at the same time we see that everything is real. . . . When we enter into *nirvikalpa* samadhi, the first thing we feel is that our heart is larger than the universe itself. Now we see the world around us, and the universe seems infinitely larger than we are. But this is because the world and the universe are now perceived by the limited mind. When we are in *nirvikalpa* samadhi, we see the universe like a dot within our vast heart.

He adds that in this *samādhi* there is indescribable Bliss or Delight and inconceivable power.[89] His poem "The Absolute," quoted in chapter 1, lucidly expresses this state of consciousness: "No mind, no form, I only exist; / Now ceased all will and thought . . . A realm of Bliss, bare, ultimate; / Beyond both knower and known." This experience of the formless Ultimate is one of many different aspects of God-union and cosmic communion which he has expressed in his poetry. Here are just two examples:

Bachan maner atite
Nitya jyotir nadite
Dubiche chitta more
Khule geche āj sahasra āñkhi
Ruddha jatek dor

Beyond speech and mind,
Into the river of ever-effulgent Light
My heart dives.

Today thousands of doors, closed for millennia,
Are opened wide.[90]

Chetanā āmār ākāshe bātāse
Miliyā nritya kare
Sāgare jale kheliyā berāi
Āmi thāki giri pāre
Nāi konā thāi jethā āmi nāi
Bishwā bhubana mājhe
Ātma jiban āhuti ditechi
Paramer sebā kāje

My consciousness dances
With boundless sky and air.
It also sports with the waves of the sea.
And I am on the top of the mountain peak.
No place there is on earth
Where my consciousness is not.
I am offering my self-form
To the service of the Absolute Supreme.[91]

Exalted as such states are and difficult to attain, Sri Chinmoy is explicit that *samādhi* is not equivalent to God-realization. "There is no comparison between *samādhi* and realisation," he says. "Samādhi is a state of consciousness in which one can stay for a few hours or a few days. . . . But once one has achieved realisation, it lasts forever. And in realisation, one's whole consciousness has become inseparably and eternally one with God."[92] When realization is attained, it is an irreversible awakening to the truth that the soul is one with God, a "conscious portion" of God, and realization also means that the entire being, not only the soul, is conscious of this oneness.

It is possible to experience temporarily what this is, yet "seeing God" is not the same as "realising God." Sri Chinmoy explains, "Conscious union with the Highest is called realisation. But if we just get a glimpse of the highest Truth, this experience is infinitely inferior to realisation. Experience tells us what we will eventually become. Realisation makes us conscious of what we truly are: absolutely one with God, forever, throughout Eternity."[93] How does one know that God-realization has indeed taken place? Sri Chinmoy answers this question by using the example of eating a mango.

When you eat a mango, you know that you have eaten it. If others say, "No, you have not eaten a mango," it does not bother you, for you know what you have done. . . . In the spiritual world also, when one has drunk the Nectar of realisation, one knows that one has really realised God. One feels infinite Peace, infinite Light, infinite Bliss, infinite Power in his inner consciousness.[94]

He adds, "This reality is more authentic than my seeing you right here in front of me. When one speaks to a human being, there is always a veil of ignorance: darkness, imperfection, misunderstanding. But between God and the inner being of one who has realised Him, there can be no ignorance, no veil."[95] He also says, "When you have discovered yourself, you have discovered the highest Truth, and that Truth is God . . . . In realisation, there is no feeling of loss or gain. You do not feel that you have lost something or gained something, but rather that you have become something, that you are one with something."[96]

When he was once asked, "Who is the Unmanifest?" Sri Chinmoy replied, "You yourself are the Unmanifest. That is to say, your highest Self is still unmanifest. You, who represent God on earth, and you, who in your highest consciousness are absolutely one with God, are still unmanifest."[97] Therefore, "God-realisation, or *siddhi*, means Self-discovery in the highest sense of the term. One consciously realises his oneness with God . . . he comes to know that he and God are absolutely one in both the inner and the outer life. God-realisation means one's identification with one's absolute highest Self"[98] and moreover, "To realise the highest Absolute as one's very own and to constantly feel that this realisation is not something you have actually achieved, but something you eternally are, that is called realisation."[99]

One can be God-realized to a greater or lesser extent. Sri Chinmoy uses the image of a tree, which one can just touch, climb up part of the way, or climb all the way to the top. Even a person who has only touched the tree is indeed realized, but this may be a "partial realisation," not as full as that of one who has gone to a higher height, has become more familiar with the body of the tree and may even have come back down to bring fruits of the tree to share with others.[100] And as discussed in chapter 2, one may realize God as "personal," "impersonal" or both and realization of more aspects is a fuller realization. Once one has touched the realization-tree, the increase of realization to greater completeness is possible if not inevitable. The state of liberation, or freedom from the bondage of ignorance, is short of realization as such, and liberation must be achieved before realization can be attained.[101] But when some degree of realization or conscious oneness is fully attained, one does not fall back into ignorance. Sri Chinmoy declares: "This victory is permanent and eternal. Nothing and no one can take away from you, nor can you lose it."[102]

Aspiration and the process of yoga achieve realization by bringing the "light" or consciousness of the soul into the other parts of the person through the heart, gradually bringing about an integral illumination. As mentioned in the previous chapter, the soul is already one with God, but seeks to manifest its self-knowledge by entering into the heart and enlightening the heart with its divine consciousness. Then, from the heart the light of realization expands into the mind, from the mind to the vital and from the vital to the physical body. When it permeates the physical, the vital, the mental and the psychic, all of them awaken to what they truly are and identify with their own highest reality.[103]

Throughout his writings Sri Chinmoy uses the term "another God." He says, "What is it like to be another God? / It is like attaining / Not only your unattained self / But also your unattainable Self."[104] As well, one could construe the phrase "another God" to mean conscious realization of "God" as the One alone and of "another" as a God among the Many—to become "another God" may mean an inclusive simultaneous knowledge of both the one Divine and also the manifold particulars within the world. It is the greater fulfillment of the One knowing Itself as "another" through the universal Play of the Many. This awakening is an illumination of the whole person that joins or weaves together all the different modes of human knowing. A poem narrates this integral transformation: "My mind-light / Has made me another sky. / My heart-light / Has made me another moon. / My soul-light / Has made me another sun. / My earth-light / Has made me another God."[105]

NOTES

1. *Collected Works*, Vol. 2, 157, 211.

2. "The awakening universe" is a phrase of theologian John F. Haught; see *The New Cosmic Story: Inside Our Awakening Universe* (New Haven: Yale University Press, 2017).

3. *Eternity's Breath*, 56. The phrase "Gnostic Consciousness" refers to Sri Aurobindo's description of the Supermind as "the Truth-Consciousness of the Infinite;" see *The Life Divine*, Book Two, Part Two, 967.

4. *Eternity's Breath*, 55.

5. Author unknown; see the "Wish I'd Said That" website at: https://wist.info/topic/atheist/.

6. *Eternity's Breath*, 20.

7. *Yoga*, 1.

8. *Why the Masters Don't Mix* (New York: Agni Press, 1974), 48.

9. *Jainism: An Introduction* (New York: I. B. Tauris, 2009), 194; the doctrine of *anekāntavāda* is discussed in detail in Ch. VII.

10. "The Jain Declaration on Nature," in *Jainism and Ecology: Nonviolence in the Web of Life,* ed. Christopher Key Chapple (Cambridge, MA: Harvard University Press, 2002), 220.

11. See Padmanabh S. Jaini, *The Jaina Path of Purification* (Berkeley: University of California Press, 1979), 109–110.

12. *Collected Works of the Mother,* 2nd ed., Vol. 3. Pondicherry, Sri Aurobindo Ashram, 2003, 175. Available at: http://library.sriaurobindoashram.org/mother/cwm03/chapter/39/.

13. *Summits,* 130.

14. *Service-Trees,* Part 1 (1998), No. 305.

15. *Yoga,* 52.

16. *The Illumination of Life-Clouds,* Part 2 (New York: Agni Press, 1974), 38–49.

17. *Service-Trees,* Part 5 (1998), No. 4737; Part 6 (1998), No. 5,840.

18. *Arise! Awake! Thoughts of a Yogi* (New York: Frederick Fell, 1972), 2.

19. "In the abyss of the five senses," in *Flower-Flames,* Part 14 (1981), No. 1,381.

20. *The Body: Humanity's Fortress,* 80–81.

21. *Earth's Cry Meets Heaven's Smile,* Book 2 (San Juan: Aum Press, 1974), 191.

22. *Service-Trees,* Part 13 (1999), No. 12,676.

23. *Aspiration-Plants,* Part 3 (1983), No. 224.

24. This phrase occurs frequently, as does the observation that pleasure is followed by frustration.

25. See, for example, "Joy," in *The Inner Hunger* (New York: Agni Press, 1976), 51–53; also "The Secret of Joy," in *The Oneness of the Eastern Heart and the Western Mind,* Part 1, 353–356.

26. Sri Chinmoy usually reserves the term "asceticism" for severe austerities, including the kind sometimes called "mortification." Practices of restraint (with a wide range of rigor), often generally referred to as "ascetic" or "asceticism," are found in all or most of the world's religious traditions. See for example Vincent L. Wimbush and Richard Valantasis, eds. *Asceticism* (New York: Oxford University Press, 1995); Walter O. Kaelber. "Asceticism," in *The Encyclopedia of Religion,* ed. Mircea Eliade, Vol. 1 (New York: MacMillan, 1987), 441–445; and Gavin Flood, *The Ascetic Self: Subjectivity, Memory and Tradition* (Cambridge: Cambridge University Press, 2004).

27. *Service-Trees,* Part 19 (2000), No. 18,477.

28. *Aspiration-Plants,* Part 187 (1993), No. 18, 686.

29. *Mind-Confusion and Heart Illumination,* Part 1 (New York: Agni Press, 1974), 84.

30. Ibid., 78.

31. *Mind-Confusion,* Part 1, 8.

32. *Mind-Confusion,* Part 1, 21.

33. *Silence Speaks,* Part 3 (New York: Agni Press, 1994), No. 8.

34. *Mind-Confusion,* Part 1, 8.

35. *Service-Trees,* Part 21 (2001), No. 20,017.

36. *Four Hundred Song-Birds,* Part 3, No. 16.

37. *Service-Trees*, Part 36 (2004), No. 35,607.

38. *Mind-Confusion,* Part 1, 11.

39. *Service-Trees*, Part 37 (2004), No. 36,454.

40. *Mind-Confusion*, Part 1, 22.

41. Ibid., 19.

42. *Service-Trees*, Part 23 (2001), No. 22,654.

43. *Four Hundred Song-Birds*, Part 1, No. 24.

44. *Service-Trees*, Part 1 (1998), No. 859, No. 895.

45. *Christmas-New Year*, Part 22 (2004), No. 5.

46. *Service-Trees*, Part 5 (1998), No. 4,433.

47. *Commentaries,* 16.

48. *Blessingful Invitations from the University-World* (New York: Agni Press, 1998), 27; on philosophy in this sense, see Chapter One, Note 68.

49. *Service-Trees,* Part 3 (1998), No. 2,821.

50. *Service-Trees,* Part 3 (1998), No. 2,836.

51. *United Nations Works,* Vol. 1, 235.

52. *Songs of the Soul,* 24.

53. *Meditations: Food for the Soul* (New York: Harper & Row, 1970), 59.

54. *Christmas-New Year*, Part 50 (2007), No. 48.

55. *Service-Trees*, Part 16 (1999), No. 15,443.

56. *Silence Speaks*, Part 3, No. 70 (1994).

57. *Conversations with the Master* (New York: Agni Press, 1977), 20–21.

58. *Meditation: Man-Perfection,* 122.

59. *The Journey of Silver Dreams* (New York: Agni Press, 1974), passim.

60. *Service-Trees,* Part 14 (1999), No. 13,694.

61. *God-Journey's Perfection-Return* (New York: Agni Press, 1975), 21.

62. *Mind-Confusion*, Part 1, 5.

63. *Yoga*, 99.

64. *Soulful Questions and Fruitful Answers* (New York: Agni Press, 1976), 15.

65. *Commentaries*, 6. Also, recall that in the reflection above (53) on the idea of "nothing" in the Upaniṣads, he says, "It is intuition which grants us this boon of knowing that 'nothing' is the song of the ever-transcending Beyond, and 'nothing' is the experience of the ever-fulfilling, ever-transcending and ever-manifesting existence."

On the poetry of the Rig Veda, Stephanie Jamison and Joel Brereton say, "India has a magnificent tradition of religious literature stretching over three and a half millennia, with a vast range of styles and subjects – from almost impersonal reflections on the mysteries of the cosmos, the divine, and humankind's relation to them to deeply intimate expressions of worship. This literature is justly celebrated not only within the various traditions that gave rise to the various works but around the world among people with no ties to those religious traditions. The Ṛgveda is the first of these monuments, and it can stand with any of the subsequent ones...India also has a magnificent literary tradition, characterized in great part by sophisticated poetic techniques and devices and a poetic self-consciousness that glories in the transformative work that words can effect on their subjects. Again, the Ṛgveda is the first monument of this literary tradition and at least the equal of the later literature." *The Rigveda: The Earliest Religious Poetry of India,* tr. Stephanie W. Jamison and Joel P. Brereton (Oxford: Oxford University Press, 2014), 2–3.

66. *Art's Life,* 35–36.

67. *Eternity's Breath,* 39.

68. *Service-Trees,* Part 49 (2008), No. 48, 179.

69. *My Heart-Melody* (New York: Agni Press, 1994), 7–8.

70. *Yoga,* 52.

71. *Mind-Confusion,* Part 1, 34–35, 38.

72. *Summits,*122.

73. *Service-Trees,* Part 42 (2005), No. 41,677.

74. We have noted above that there are numerous references in the Upaniṣads to the interiority of the heart (*hṛdaya*) and the secret place, the "cave" or *guhā,* often equated with the heart, as well as to the location in this inner space of the soul, the "inner controller" or *antaryāmin,* or the Person, *puruṣa.* This is a space which is a portal to the cosmic and transcendent. As well, the Bhagavad Gītā refers to the divine Presence in the hearts of all creatures (10.20, 15.15, 18.61).

75. *Yoga,* 76–78; *I Wanted to Be a Seeker of the Infinite* (New York: Agni Press, 2012), 91–93.

76. *Service-Trees,* Part 2 (1998), No. 1,095.

77. *Collected Works,* Vol. 5, Sayings and Utterances, No. 8,409.

78. This is true whether it is to see God's Face, see God's Feet, or "see God all around us." *Service-Trees,* Part 38 (2004), No. 37,389 and Part 49 (2009), No. 48, 379; Part 45 (2006), No. 44,155, and Part 42 (2005), No. 41,485.

79. *Mind-Confusion,* Part 1, 18.

80. *Mind-Confusion,* Part 1, 7.

81. *Summits,* 95–96.

82. See Andrée Affeich and Maya Azzam, "Sufi Terms and Their Translation from Arabic to English: Diwân al-Hallâž as a Case Study," *Terminalia* 19 (2019): 28–38; doi: 10.2436/20.2503.01.131; also Paul Gavrilyuk and Sarah Coakley, eds., *The Spiritual Senses: Perceiving God in Western Christianity* (Cambridge, UK: Cambridge University Press, 2012.

83. *Service-Trees,* Part 31 (2003), No. 30,095; Part 26 (2002), No. 25,806.

84. *The Rigveda; The Earliest Religious Poetry of India,* vol. 3, trans. Stephanie W. Jamison and Joel P. Brereton (New York: Oxford University Press, 2014), 1609.

85. Cited in Olivelle, "Heart in the Upaniṣads," 54–55.

86. The term is used in all of the Indic traditions, varying in its meanings within each tradition according to the terminology established for states of meditation.

87. *Savikalpa* and *nirvikalpa* are respectively with and without "*vikalpa,*" which can be rendered as "conceptualization" or "imagining;" see Christopher Key Chapple, *Yoga and the Luminous* (Albany, State University of New York Press, 2008), 144–145, 158, referring to Pantañjali's *Yoga Sūtra* 1.6, 1.9 and 1.42.

88. *Summits,* 76–77.

89. *Summits,* 82–83.

90. *Supreme, Teach Me How to Surrender* (New York: Agni Press, 1975), 88.

91. *Supreme, I Sing Only for You* (New York: Agni Press, 1974), 9.

92. *Summits*, 85–86.

93. Ibid., 62.

94. Ibid., 56.

95. Ibid., 13–14.

96. *Soul-education for the Family-World* (New York: Agni Press, 1977), 66–67.

97. *Summits*, 66.

98. Ibid., 12–13.

99. Ibid., 32.

100. Ibid., 73–75. The image of tree-climbing, including obtaining fruits and bringing them down to share with others, derives from Sri Chinmoy's childhood experience.

101. Ibid., 29–32.

102. Ibid., 109.

103. Ibid., 16.

104. *Aspiration-Plants*, Part 1 (1983), No. 66.

105. "My light has made me," in *Europe-Blossoms*, 381.

Chapter 6

Love

DIVINE LOVE

God is Love. The Supreme Being Itself is Love. Sri Chinmoy says, "Love is God's very essence. It flows from Him eternally."[1] Divine Love is infinite, unconditional, and boundlessly self-giving: "Divine Love makes no demand. It is spontaneous and constant. It is unlimited in every way. It is like the sun."[2] In God, "Love itself and its power of expression can never be separated;" they are simultaneous.[3] Oneness and Love are aspects of one another. Unity in multiplicity is the nature of all existence—and Love is the consciousness of this ontological oneness. It is also the life that shines forth from this consciousness; thus divine Love is "the fulfilment of oneness,"[4] construing fulfillment as expression or manifestation. Sri Chinmoy often speaks not just of "oneness" but of "the feeling of inseparable oneness," which is this fulfillment consciously experienced.[5] "Love in the process of its manifestation is conscious Truth enjoying itself,"[6] adds Sri Chinmoy. Delight (*Ānanda*) is enjoyment in Consciousness (*Cit*) of and by the Truth or Reality (*Sat*) of oneness. These triune aspects of the Absolute are none other than Love. The cosmos in its wholeness is held in Love: "Where is the universe? It is within God's Life. Where is God's Life? It is within His all-illumining Love."[7] Divine Love is eternal and is all in all: "There is only one thing that was, is and forever shall be, and that is Love: the Love that created, the Love that nourishes, the Love that sustains God's universe."[8]

God is all Love, Sri Chinmoy says again and again. Everything in his philosophy revolves around this understanding. God's infinite Consciousness—as the blissful knowledge of the oneness of all that is—is the divine Wisdom, and as both Silence and as Sound, this delight-flooded Wisdom is Love.

"There is no difference between divine Love and divine Wisdom," Sri Chinmoy says.

> Love itself is wisdom and wisdom is light. The moment the wisdom-sun dawns within us, we feel that the whole universe belongs to us. Our oneness with the universe becomes inseparable. If this is not wisdom, then what else is? This wisdom is founded on divine Love, which is the conscious expansion of our existence. . . . If we cultivate Love, wisdom will come, and if we aspire for wisdom, then Love will come and inundate us.[9]

When we love, we discover truth. "Knowledge comes only from God, who is Love,"[10] and "in the intensity of love, we can extend our knowledge."[11] In wisdom it is revealed to us what love truly is: "Love is oneness. / If we establish oneness, / We give according / To our utmost capacity."[12] Love is not only wisdom and the affective experience of oneness, but also is self-giving for the good of those we love. God is a "Self-giving Infinity"[13] and in giving ourselves we become like God. We have been made for this—"Life is for / Self-giving. / Self-giving is for / God-becoming."[14]

Because God knows that we and God are inseparably one, God loves us infinitely more than He loves Himself. On account of our ignorance, it is very difficult, if not impossible, for us to believe in God's limitless Love for us. Nevertheless,

> God loves us. He loves us constantly and unconditionally. No matter what we have done, what we are doing or what we shall do, He will always love us. God loves us much more than He loves Himself. To our thinking and doubting minds, this may seem hard to believe. But if we use our loving and surrendering hearts, then we are bound to feel that God loves us infinitely more than He loves Himself. Why does He love us so much? He loves us because He feels that His Dream remains unfulfilled without us, His Reality remains unmanifested without us; without us He is incomplete.[15]
>
> Divine Love tells us that we are greater than the greatest, larger than the largest; it tells us that our life is infinitely more important than we imagine. Divine Love means constant transcendence, not only of our human boundaries, but of God's own Realisation in us and through us. [16]

God has become the world to experience God's Self in infinite ways in countless forms for the every-growing joy of the divine Play. Each of us is one of these forms and is a God-in-becoming in the evolution of divine perfection. But we are not aware of this. Instead we are acutely aware of our imperfection, but God knows our future transformation: "I see myself as another stupendous failure. God sees me as another God."[17] God knows who and what we really are—an inseparable part of God's own largest Self—and so God needs us more than we need God and God loves us more than we can ever imagine. Astonishingly, we are Gods to God: "Aspiration tells us that we will be able to see the Truth of the Beyond. . . . Yoga tells us that the Truth of the Beyond is within us. Finally, God comes and tells us, 'My child, you are the Truth of the Beyond. You are My Beyond.' "[18]

GRACE AND COMPASSION

God's Love for us and for all of God's creation has different aspects. We have seen that "The absolute Grace of the Supreme has given birth to the transcendental Reality and the universal Reality."[19] Sri Chinmoy also says, "God used His Delight-Power when He created the world, and now He uses His Love-Power to protect the world and bring perfection to earth."[20] The Love that creates and preserves the world and cares for its ongoing existence is God's Grace, which pours out upon all of creation unceasingly: "God is / God's torrential Grace."[21] Sri Chinmoy at times distinguishes God's Love as Grace from God's Compassion, using "Compassion" to mean a focused and active Love that embraces and helps a particular person or people in need, responding to a cry or when there is an opening. "Grace is universal, while Compassion is individual,"[22] he says. When Compassion descends, to be effective it must be received. "When Compassion flows, it flies like an arrow and pierces the very veil of ignorance. Love touches ignorance; Love can even stay with ignorance. But Compassion will not stay there. Compassion has to be successful, otherwise Compassion will be withdrawn."[23] When Compassion is invoked and successfully received, there is nothing that it cannot and will not do for us: "God's Compassion / Carries its own / Absolute Will-Power."[24] If not received, Compassion will in time return to try again; there is no such thing as the permanent withdrawal of God's Compassion: "God has forgotten / To close / His Compassion-Door;" moreover "God's Compassion-Net / No human being / Can destroy."[25] Sri Chinmoy compares divine Compassion to a boundless Ocean into which God wants us to dive, often refers to God's "Compassion-Rain" and says in a song "*Kripā nāme akārane kripā sadā nāme*—Compassion descends always unconditionally, Compassion descends."[26]

Without God's Grace and Compassion, no one can traverse the full length of the spiritual path: "We achieve God-realisation / By virtue of God's / Unconditional Grace."[27] And when our understanding is complete, we will see that even the self-effort that we have expended to attain our realization is but another aspect of God's Compassion and Grace. "Personal effort has no existence of its own. It is the divine higher Power, the higher Power of the infinite Beyond, that secretly feeds and inspires us to exercise our personal effort, will and determination in all that we do, say and become."[28] We have been made by God's Grace and Concern, and "The moment God created us, / He stamped His Love, Affection / And Compassion / On our hearts."[29] Within this Love and Concern, we live and have our being: "There is only God's constant, selfless, unreserved Concern. This Concern is His glowing, flowing and descending Grace."[30]

JUSTICE AND FORGIVENESS

Sri Chinmoy states clearly that God's Justice is a form of God's Compassion: "Justice-Light and Compassion-Height are one, inseparably one."[31] Unlike human justice, the purpose of divine Justice is not punishment or retribution when there is wrongdoing, but illumination and more rapid progress. If divine Justice is never used, progress may be indefinitely delayed.[32] "Divine justice is Love. Divine justice is self-giving. Divine justice is fulfilment. . . . A transformed and perfected human being is the duty of divine Justice. A fulfilled and manifested God in man is the duty of divine Justice."[33] Almost all of the time, God uses Compassion, but "My Lord uses / His Justice-Light / As His Last Resort."[34] God shows God's aspect of discipline when Compassion has not worked in spite of repeated attempts. "Finally, when God sees that even His infinite Compassion does not solve the human problem, He will use His loving divine Authority, His divine Power." This Power does not destroy, but awakens and arouses the "dormant lion" of "our inner cry to know the ultimate Truth, to grow into the absolute Reality."[35]

Similarly, when Sri Chinmoy speaks of divine forgiveness he does not refer primarily to remission of the consequences of wrongdoing. Forgiveness is rather a way that God lifts up our whole existence to a higher level. Like Grace and Compassion, it is always present and available: "It is very difficult to believe—/ But very true—/ That God's Forgiveness-Heart / Is for the asking."[36] A song says, *"Tumije anādi khamar bāridhi nirabadhi*—Always You are Your beginningless Forgiveness-Ocean."[37] Indeed, God forgives our failings even when we are unaware of it: "God's Forgiveness-Heart / Touched the very core / Of your remorseful tears / Long before you became conscious / Of your tears."[38] At the same time, Sri Chinmoy places great importance on our cry for forgiveness and as well, our awareness that God forgives us. This cry and this awareness are a form of our love for God and gratitude to God; they create the receptivity in us that enables God to purify and transform us. Thus the experience of asking for and receiving forgiveness is associated with awakening, hope and new life: *"Tomār khamā amār hiyār naba jāgaran*—Your Forgiveness, my heart's new awakening."[39] Not only this, God's Forgiveness and Compassion are equated with life itself.

You forgive me.	*Tumi āmāi khama karo*
Therefore I am still alive.	*Tāito beñche ācchi*
You love me.	*Tumi āmāi bhālobhāsho*
Therefore I am still alive.	*Tāito beñche ācchi*
You have caught me by the hand.	*Tumi āmai dhareccho hāt*
Therefore I am still alive.	*Tāito beñche ācchi*
I am Your Compassion-Flute.	*Āmi tomār kripā bānshi*
Therefore I am still alive.	*Tāito beñche ācchi*[40]

Sri Chinmoy has written hundreds of poems on God's "Compassion-Eye" and God's "Forgiveness-Heart." This poem, which is also a song, expresses the certainty that they give us life: "My dear Lord, / How can I live / Without Your Life's Compassion-Eye? / My sweet Lord, / How can I breathe /Without Your Heart's Forgiveness-Sky?"[41]

We must not only constantly cry for and receive God's Forgiveness but also, as God has forgiven us, we must forgive ourselves: "If we do not forgive ourselves, we are unable to go forward. We are only looking backward. We have to forgive our past; otherwise we cannot enter into the future."[42] This has priority: "We must forgive ourselves first, / Long before we forgive / Our enemies."[43] Then we must forgive those who have wronged either ourselves or others. Indeed, we must learn to "forgive the world." Sri Chinmoy advises, "Learn the art of forgiving / And apply it to yourself first. / Then it becomes easy / To forgive others."[44] If we do not forgive ourselves we carry a burden of guilt, and if we do not forgive others we carry a burden of resentment. In both cases this can cause a spiritual obstacle which impedes our progress. But when we accept God's Love in the forms of Grace, Compassion and Forgiveness, God gives us everything.

Because of Your Grace	*Tomār kripār urdhe nāchi*
High in Heaven I dance.	*Tomār khama nimne bāñchi*
Because of Your Forgiveness	*Prem sāgare dub diyechi*
Here below on earth	*Tomār mājhe sab peyechi*
My life-breath breathes.	
I have dived deep	
In the sea of Love divine.	
I have received everything	
Inside Your Heart-depth.[45]	

We are brought to the sea of Love which is God by God's own Grace and Compassion, and these will give us the capacity to receive all that it holds.

THE PATH OF LOVE

Sri Chinmoy affirms that love is an unsurpassed way to God-realization and is the swiftest and most effective way to approach God.[46] As mentioned in chapter 1, he describes the spiritual path which he taught during his lifetime and which is set forth in his writings as the path of "love, devotion and surrender." In one of his early works he says:

Love is action. Devotion is practice. Surrender is experience.
Love is realisation. Devotion is revelation. Surrender is manifestation.
Love is the meaning of life. Devotion is the secret of life. Surrender is the Goal of life.
In my love, I see God the Mother. In my devotion, I see God the Father. In my surrender, I see God the Mother and God the Father together in one body.
Love without devotion is absurdity. Devotion without surrender is futility.
Love with devotion was my journey's start. Devotion with surrender is my journey's close.
I love the Supreme because I came from Him. I devote myself to the Supreme because I wish to go back to Him. I surrender myself to the Supreme because He lives in me and I in Him.[47]

We love God and are drawn to God because God is all Love, not because God is omnipotent or omniscient. It is love that is fulfillment and God's Love attracts us to God like a magnet, as our love for God likewise pulls God to us. "I love God, / Not because He is great, / Not because He is good, / But because He is my All / And I am His All."[48] The path of love, devotion and surrender is the path of the heart. Love and oneness in the heart are natural and spontaneous: "The heart knows how to love everything / And become everything."[49] The heart's capacity to love is boundless—"The heart can love / Not only unreservedly / But also unconditionally"[50]—and it is also self-transcending: "When the heart loves / It knows no limit."[51] What the aspiring heart loves, it also knows: "Reality can easily / Be seen and caught / By the streaming tears / Of the heart."[52] Not only this, "The love of the heart / Directly comes from / The Eye of God,"[53] from the highest Transcendent. Addressing his own heart, the poet-seeker says: "Nothing can be simpler than your pure longings. Nothing can be more spontaneous than your glowing feelings. Nothing can be more fulfilling than your selfless love. Nothing has a more immediate access to the Supreme than your inmost cry."[54]

We should offer to God whatever love we have, no matter how imperfect, and at the same time we should aspire to love God divinely. There is a great difference between ordinary human love and divine Love: "Human love desperately needs. Divine Love abundantly feeds."[55] The reason for the defects of human love is that "the instrument that we are using right now is our very limited consciousness. That is why we are limited in our love. But if we use the other instrument, which is very vast, if we use the Universal Consciousness, our capacity for divine love becomes unlimited."[56] Although "True human love, even if it is not spiritual, will have some psychic element in it,"[57] nevertheless untransformed human love is mixed to a greater or lesser degree with self-centered thoughts and feelings such as insecurity and jealousy.[58] There may be as well the feeling that our love is not returned adequately.[59] Unillumined human love is possessive, so it binds instead of liberating. In addition,

> In human love there is demand or, at least, expectation. Very often we start with demand, and when a higher wisdom dawns we no longer demand, but still we expect something from others. We convince ourselves that this expectation is justified. Since we have done something for others—offered our love—we feel it is quite legitimate to expect something in return.

> But in divine Love there is no such thing as demand or expectation. In divine Love we just give what we have and what we are. What we have and what we are is dedicated service. In the human life, before we give our love, we try to discover love in others—that is, their love for us. In the divine life, before we give our love to others, we try to discover Love in its reality and integrality within ourselves. Only then are we in a position to offer love to others. At first our satisfaction dawns when we feel that those to whom we offer our love accept it wholeheartedly. But there is an even higher form of divine Love when we go beyond this feeling, and give love just for the sake of self-giving. We give, and if our love is not accepted, we do not mind. We shall go on giving, for we are all love, our Source is all Love.[60]

Our love for God should grow into this kind of self-giving love that is without any expectation:

"A lovely child attracts our attention. We love him because he conquers our heart. But do we ask anything from him in return? No! We love him because he is the object of love; he is loveable. In the same way, we can and should love God, for He is the most lovable Being."[61] We must come to realize that "God is very simple / And very easy to love—/ Like a flower or a child,"[62] and "not only day by day / And hour by hour, / But moment by moment / Our love of God must increase."[63] We will eventually feel that "I love God because He is the only Love"[64] and that "I live on / God's unconditional / Love-Breath."[65] At last, "My love of God / Has to be / An undying inner fire."[66]

DEVOTION

Love, devotion and surrender are a continuum of the aspects of love. "Love, devotion and surrender cannot be separated. . . . It is love that contains devotion and surrender."[67] On the path of love, devotion and surrender are the way love grows, phases in the development of love for God. Sri Chinmoy says, "Devotion is a soul-stirring emotion. It dynamically permeates the entire consciousness of the devotee. Devotion is action. This action is always inspired by the devotee's inner being."[68] Thus devotion (*bhakti*) has both an inner and an outer aspect, or one may say, an affective and an active dimension. Inwardly devotion is intensity, intensity of longing in separation from the Beloved and intensity of adoration in the Beloved's presence. "My God-devotion / Is intensifying / My love of God."[69] This intensity expedites our progress: "Devotion-intensity / Is the fastest speed / In the spiritual life."[70] Intrinsic to love as devotion is the quality of sweetness: "Devotion is our inner sweetness. Devotion is our divine intensity. Devotion is our supreme dynamism."[71] The intensity, sweetness and sense of deep personal intimacy found in devotion swiftly bring the devotee closer and closer to God.

On the path of love, devotion and surrender, devotion is necessary for God-realization: "No devotion-breath, / No God-oneness-life,"[72] but "God gives Himself / Unreservedly and unconditionally / To a devotion-heart."[73] In fact, devotion by itself may suffice for realization: "My Supreme, my Supreme, my Supreme! / You are telling me / That a seeker does not need / Strict spiritual disciplines. / He does not need austerities. He does not need the highest / And deepest meditation. / What he needs to realise You / Is only pure, pure, pure devotion."[74] Yet at the same time the experience of devotion is its own fulfillment. It is best not analyzed but evoked through music and the words of poetry and prayer: "A devotee sees a circle which is God. He enters into it with his soul's cry. He then silently comes and stands at the center of the circle and grows into a tree of ecstasy."[75] The devotee entreats the Beloved,

My Lord,
Your Love has entrapped my eyes,
    My heart, my life and my all.
May I be allowed to entrap
The hallowed dust of Your Feet?

I am prepared
To come into the world
    Again and again

Only to fathom Your Love
Unfathomable.[76]

Indispensable as the heart is to the development of devotion, Sri Chinmoy says that devotion must be integral, in all parts of the person: "Devotion must have its root in all spheres of the being. Devotion only in the heart is not enough. Devotion also has to be in the mind, in the vital and in the physical. Only then does devotion become perfect."[77]

The outer and active aspect of devotion is self-giving or self-offering. "When we really love someone, we give that person all that we have and all that we are."[78] In everyday speech in English, "to be devoted" to someone or something has this same connotation of giving our attention, time, resources, care and concern to the object of our devotion. Sri Chinmoy repeatedly says, "Self-giving is God-becoming," and self-offering brings spiritual knowledge: "Wisdom depends on / Personal self-offering" and "Self-giving means / awareness / Of the highest height." It is even true that "My self-giving life / Looks at the highest Height / Only to become the Height itself."[79] Why is devotion expressed outwardly as service such a powerful means of spiritual progress? "Service is self-expansion," Sri Chinmoy says.[80] When we serve, in the true sense of the word "service," our actions are not for ourselves, not for our own benefit or for our ego, but for others. All concrete action in the outer life changes us in some way, and thus "selfless" service dedicated to others is a way of transforming the sense of self.[81] "In this expansion we feel that we are no longer for ourselves, but for all . . . so it is through service, dedicated service, that we consciously grow into the Vast, into Infinity's Light and Delight."[82]

Service of others can be thought of as sacrifice, but where there is love and the feeling of oneness there is no "sacrifice" as it is usually referred to. Rather, "Fulfilment is nothing but voluntary sacrifice. Where your sacrifice is, there will as well be your delight,"[83] and "What is to be sacrificed? One's life-breath. How to sacrifice? With a feeling of universal oneness . . . . Man's choice is Joy. Joy's choice is sacrifice. Sacrifice's choice is Nothing. This Nothing is verily the unfoldment of everything and the fulfiment of man and God."[84] The devoted offering of service to God in the world, for the welfare of the world and without attachment to the results, is the central teaching of Krishna in the Bhagavad Gītā. Sri Chinmoy explicitly affirms this teaching, declaring, "The Gita is God's Vision immediate. The Gita is God's Reality direct;"[85] and in his commentary on the Gita he says, "It is in dedicated service that we see the universal harmony, we grow into the universal consciousness. Our will becomes God's Will."[86] He says, "Everything about love, devotion and surrender is written in the Bhagavad Gītā."[87] He also points out that surrender of everything to God is the final teaching in the Gītā; it is Krishna's "supreme word" after everything else has been said.[88] And we should remember that in giving this teaching, Krishna also says, "You are surely loved by Me ...You dear to Me" (18.64 -65).[89]

SURRENDER

The third and culminating stage of the path of love is surrender. Surrender itself is not God-realization, but it is a prerequisite for realization, and when surrender is full and permanent, it leads directly to realization: "The ocean-vast God-realisation / You can have / If your surrender / Is utterly complete."[90] What is surrender? "Love and surrender / Are essentially and eternally / Only one thing." Sri Chinmoy says. "Love is / The beauty / Of surrender," and "Surrender / Is the fragrance / Of love."[91]

Surrender is not, as Sri Chinmoy often says, the surrender of a slave to a master, nor "the surrender of one army to another."[92] It is also not an inert compliance, "idle surrender or helpless submission"[93] but a dynamic acceptance and self-dedication. The Bengali word for "surrender," *samarpan*, means a full or complete offering or giving (*arpan*). Surrender, then, is in meaning very close to "self-offering" or "self-giving." Surrender is above all the perfection of oneness with God through identification with God's Will. Sri Chinmoy often says that the prayer of Jesus, "Your Will be done," is the highest of all prayers. He says, "There is no separativity / In surrender. / The finite simply / Recognises its own Infinity / And becomes inseparably one with it."[94] Genuine surrender comes from knowing that God is not other than ourselves, hence its proximity to God-realization. "Surrender means oneness, inseparable oneness with our infinite, eternal, immortal life. Without surrendering, we will not know that we are infinite, eternal, and immortal."[95] The infinite Reality cannot be attained if we try to grasp it; to become it we must give ourselves to it knowing that we are already part of it, like the drop claiming the ocean as its very own. Sri Chinmoy explains:

> Divine surrender to God's Will is a dedicated surrender, devoted surrender, loving surrender and unconditional surrender. In spiritual surrender there is no compulsion. It is our inner urge that compels us to reach the highest height . . . when we consciously give our lower existence to our higher existence, it is the surrender of oneness. This surrender we make to our own highest height; we offer our dedicated life to the highest Supreme, who is our very own. We offer our various limitations to our own perfections. We do not feel sorry, embarrassed or ashamed. We surrender one place which is our possession, to another place which is also our possession.[96]

This identification or sense of oneness is the manifestation of love: "Surrender is not / A sacrifice"—"Surrender is / The wisdom / Of God-love,"[97] and surrender is love itself: "Sleepless and breathless / Love of God / Is what God means / By unconditional surrender."[98]

Surrender, like devotion, must be integral. It needs eventually to be not only an inner recognition of oneness but also manifested in all aspects of our outer life at all times. Sri Chinmoy has called this distinction "theoretical surrender" and "practical surrender."

> My theoretical surrendered oneness says, "Lord, let Thy Will be done." But as soon as I am buffeted by the blows of earthly life, I withdraw my so-called surrendered oneness with my Beloved Supreme. I curse myself for having been eager to become one with Him. This is theoretical surrendered oneness.
>
> My practical surrendered oneness is totally different. In my practical oneness I experience what He experiences in and through me: life's failure and life's success, life's sorrow and life's joy, life in the process of recoiling and withdrawing, life in the process of becoming and transcending. All I accept with cheerful, devoted, unconditional and surrendered oneness.[99]

From the oneness of practical surrender springs the acceptance of God's Will in profound conviction of its goodness: "When we are identified with the Will of the Supreme, we feel that His Will is All-Compassion and All-fulfilment."[100] This kind of identification is direct knowledge by intuition, through love: "Surrender is the purest devotion that sees through the eye of intuition…Surrender is the wisdom that sees and becomes the Truth."[101]

Obedience to God's Will is a precondition of surrender. To accept and act according to God's Will even reluctantly is a greater degree of surrender than to reject it, as is needless to say. Consistent sincere effort to maintain obedience in all things both small and great is thus indispensable if our goal is oneness with God. Because God's Will is for our good and our progress—as God's Love for us and knowledge of us are perfect—to depart from God's Will is to reject our own good. To discern what God's Will is in any given situation, the regular practice of prayer and meditation is essential, with the cultivation of inner silence: "My heart / Is a direct line / To God's Will."[102] As well, the guidance of a qualified spiritual teacher, if the seeker has one, should play an important role. Outer obedience and inner obedience are both necessary, but inner obedience is far more difficult, Sri Chinmoy observes, because it requires obedience of the mind and overcoming doubt. Like devotion and surrender, obedience is an aspect of love and is integral to the path of love. Sri Chinmoy says:

> Inner obedience is the conscious recognition of one's higher life, higher reality, higher existence. Inner obedience is a supreme virtue. Inner obedience is the achievement of one's true knowledge. When we obey the higher principles, higher laws, we love. When we love, we become.

We obey our Inner Pilot not because He is all-powerful, not out of fear that He will punish us. We obey Him because He is all Love. . . . Our existence wants to be one with the infinite Love. We are a streak of light that enters into the vast sun. We offer our individuality and personality to our highest Source and then we become the song of universality. Our limited life, our limited consciousness, becomes universal and the universal becomes the unlimited, the Infinite One. From the finite we go to the Infinite and from the Infinite we go to the Transcendental Absolute.[103]

It is very important that Sri Chinmoy at times refers to God's Will as "the Cosmic Will" of God, or God's "all-loving, all-pervading universal Will."[104] Our identification with God's Will therefore takes us beyond our accustomed small context and confined consciousness to make us increasingly aware that we are part of a something higher and vaster.

Surrender, on the foundation of obedience, should ideally be cheerful, willing and also unconditional. That is, it should not place conditions or limitations, expect something in return or ask for an explanation of why or how something is asked of us by God. While these themes of obedience and surrender are prominent in theistic spiritualities of love in which the Divine is understood as personal, nonetheless total, unconditional, and cheerful surrender would seem to be a difficult state to attain for almost any individual. How is surrender possible? Surrender calls for great inner strength and in the beginning of the spiritual path doubtless it will be a far cry. Yet Sri Chinmoy tells us that when time has matured, with the aid of God's Grace and Compassion, surrender can be established:

> There comes a time in our spiritual life when we realise that we are not satisfied with what we have, whether it is material wealth or inner wealth, or with what we are. At that time we are ready for surrender. How does one surrender? It is very easy. When we feel the need for surrender, automatically the means will come. If we are desperately in need of surrender, if we feel the soul's inner urge, if our entire being wants to surrender to God's Will, then we will be given more than the necessary capacity, assurance, Compassion and Light from above and within . . . . Surrender to God's Will entirely depends on our necessity. If we feel that our life is meaningless, that we won't be satisfied or fulfilled without surrendering our earthly existence to God's Will, then surrender will be possible for us.[105]

He adds that at first the conscious effort to surrender is interior and is made during meditation. It then permeates the outer being of the aspirant and finally becomes constant.[106] "Surrender is an unfoldment. It is the unfoldment of our body, mind and heart into the Sun of divine Plenitude within us."[107] To surrender is to experience blissful fulfillment: "Surrender is / Oneness-heart-ecstasy."[108] Sri Chinmoy often refers to "surrender-delight" and "surrender-joy." Moreover, "Surrender is freedom. The more we surrender, the vaster becomes our freedom,"[109] and "To surrender to God's Will / Is to enjoy / The freedom of Infinity."[110] In sum, "If we can surrender in absolute silence, we shall ourselves become the Reality of the Real, the Life of the Living, the Centre of true Love, Peace, and Bliss. We shall become an incomparable blessing to ourselves."[111] Surrender is the pinnacle of the spiritual life and abides in the core of ultimate Reality. Sri Chinmoy declares: "Love-life never dies. / Devotion-life ever lives. / Surrender-life transcends / Both death and life. / It lives in the heart / Of beginningless silence / And / Endless sound."[112]

GRATITUDE

Throughout his writings Sri Chinmoy stresses the paramount importance of gratitude, which is at the core of his philosophy. He says, "Gratitude is a miracle-action in us. This miracle-action strengthens our physical body, purifies our vital energy, widens our mental vision and intensifies our psychic delight."[113] He has even said that "A moment of gratitude offered to God is equal to an hour of most intense meditation on God."[114] He explains, "Gratitude is self-expansion. Gratitude is God-expansion within us. Once we offer an iota of gratitude to the Supreme in us, to the Inner Pilot within us, our heart is immediately expanded. There is no better way to expand our heart than to offer gratitude."[115] We recall that the spiritual heart can become large enough to hold the universe and in the expanded heart, "Gratitude / Is the vastest ocean / Of our inner life."[116]

Sri Chinmoy says continually, with many poetic variations on this theme, that our gratitude is incomparably precious to God and connects us to God immediately and intimately: "To God / Nothing is more significant / Than my gratitude-heart" and "God tells me that / My heart's gratitude-tears / Are His most precious treasures."[117] Two phrases that frequently occur together in his poetry are "gratitude-heart" and "surrender-life," indicating that gratitude is the inner dimension or source of surrender, while surrender is the outer manifestation of the interior attainment of gratitude. Gratitude is a way of experiencing our life-reality that liberates us from the small sense of self, or ego, by reversing its smallness and selfishness, enabling it to see that I am in the midst of vastness and that "my" self does not actually belong to me. Our gratitude awakens to and embraces the fact that we owe our very existence to God and so, "I shall offer gratitude / To my Lord Supreme / Just for being."[118] "Our gratitude-heart," Sri Chinmoy says, "feels that its very existence on earth is an unconditional act of God's Grace" and therefore it surrenders: "Our gratitude-heart knows that its acts are for God and God alone."[119]

Gratitude sees the worth of everything and so it loves all. It loves God who is the Source of all and accepts as good all that comes to it from the Source, Who is Love. Inherent in gratitude are aspiration, the inner urge of self-transcendence, and also the life of self-offering.

> In this world we are apt not to value anything or anyone, but our gratitude-heart always values everything in God's creation. It values God the Creator and God the creation. It values God's Compassion and it values God the Compassion. It also values God's Justice-Light and God the Justice-Light, for it knows that God, our beloved Supreme, is always the Author of all Good. Our gratitude-heart never fails God. It carries with it flaming aspiration, the burning inner cry and a constant self-giving reality. At every moment God pleases our gratitude-heart with His boundless Concern, Compassion and all-loving Oneness.[120]

Gratitude is not a stage on the path or a phase on the continuum of love. Instead it is itself the fundamental attitude of love, devotion and surrender. It is the key to them and empowers them. We must never underestimate the power of gratitude—"My Lord Beloved Supreme, / You have given / My finite gratitude-heart / The capacity / To bind Your universal Life / And Treanscendental Self / At the same time."[121] Sri Chinmoy declares, "Gratitude / Is the highest and deepest self-offering / To the Absolute."[122]

In the divine Play there is an exchange of Love in which God gives us God's Love in the forms of Grace, Compassion, and Forgiveness, while God has bestowed on us the capacity to offer our love to God in return in the form of gratitude. Both kinds of Love are equally necessary. In the mutual give and take of Love, gratitude is another name for the way that human beings can most perfectly love God: "Love is the essence of God's Divinity: Gratitude is the essence of man's Divinity."[123]

NOTES

1. *Sri Chinmoy Speaks* (Oxford and Lyon: Ganapati Press, 2015), 117.
2. *Service-Boat and Love-Boatman,* Part 2 (New York: Agni Press, 1974), 4.
3. *Sri Chinmoy Speaks,* 117.
4. *Service-Boat and Love-Boatman,* Part 1 (New York: Agni Press, 1974), 4.
5. *Our Path,* 3.
6. *Eternity's Breath,* 9.
7. *God's Hour,* 6.
8. *Fifty Freedom-Boats,* Part 2 (New York: Agni Press, 1974), 57.

9. *Service-Boat,* Part 2, 7–8.

10. Ibid., Part 1, 10.

11. *Eternity's Breath,* 57.

12. *Service-Trees,* Part 14 (1999), Nos. 13,784-85.

13. "Peace," in *Flower-Flames,* Part 4 (1979), No. 354.

14. *Aspiration-Plants,* Part 137 (1990), No. 13,681.

15. *Fifty Freedom-Boats,* Part 3 (1974), 1.

16. *Service-Boat,* Part 2, 6.

17. *Meditations: Food for the Soul* (New York: Harper & Row, 1971), 16.

18. *United Nations Works,* Vol. 1, 29.

19. Ibid., 103.

20. *Fifty Freedom-Boats,* Part 3 (1974), 3.

21. *Service-Trees,* Part 37 (2004), No. 36,808.

22. *Inspiration-Garden and Aspiration-Leaves* (New York: Agni Press, 1977), 22–23. See also *Service-Boat,* Part 2, 30–32.

23. *Service-Boat,* Part 2, 31.

24. *Service-Trees,* Part 34 (2003), No. 33,088.

25. *Service-Trees,* Part 34 (2003), No. 33,116 and Part 33 (2003), No. 32,219.

26. *Four Hundred Song-Birds,* Part 2, No. 14.

27. *Service-Trees,* Part 11 (1999), No. 10,359.

28. *Service-Boat,* Part 1, 8–9.

29. *Service-Trees,* Part 33 (2003), No. 32,461.

30. *United Nations Works,* Vol. 1, 14.

31. *Everest-Aspiration* (New York: Agni Press, 1978), 18.

32. Ibid., 17.

33. *United Nations Works,* Vol. 1, 39–40.

34. *Service-Trees,* Part 35 (2004), No. 34,254.

35. *United Nations Works,* Vol. 1, 42.

36. *Service-Trees,* Part 49 (2008), No. 48,355.

37. *Khama Karo,* (New York: Agni Press, 1987), No. 41.

38. *Aspiration-Plants,* Part 41 (1984), No. 4004.

39. *Four Hundred Blue Green White Red Song-Birds,* Part 1, No. 5.

40. *Supreme, Teach Me How to Cry* (New York: Agni Press, 1974), 4.

41. *Sail, My Heartbeat, Sail,* Part 1 (New York: Agni Press, 1998), No. 26.

42. *Sri Chinmoy Answers,* Vol. 1, 659.

43. *Service-Trees,* Part 40 (2004), No. 39,812.

44. *Aspiration-Plants,* Part 129 (1990), No. 12,889.

45. "Tomār Kripāi," in *Bela Chale Jai,* No. 36.

46. Sri Chinmoy in no way suggests that the path of knowledge and insight, or *jñāna-yoga,* does not lead to full realization, but holds that it is more difficult for most than the path of love, as Sri Ramakrishna, among others, also says (*Gospel,* 170, 468, 482, 862). He points out that the path of knowledge itself also calls for love: "To enter into the world of wisdom we need constant love: love for truth, love for light" (*The Oneness of the Eastern Heart and the Western Mind,* Part 1, 147) and we have seen earlier in this chapter that "if we aspire for wisdom, then Love will come and inundate us."

47. *Songs of the Soul*, 39.

48. *Service-Trees,* Part 35 (2004), No. 34,166.

49. *Service-Trees,* Part 38 (2004), No. 37,628.

50. *Service-Trees,* Part 47 (2004), No. 46,044.

51. *Service-Trees,* Part 50 (2009), No. 49,636.

52. *Service-Trees,* Part 40 (2004), No. 39,764.

53. *Service-Trees,* Part 37 (2004), No. 36,700.

54. *Songs of the Soul*, 25.

55. *My Lord's Secrets Revealed* (New York: Herder and Herder, 1971), 13.

56. *Service-Boat,* Part 2, 7.

57. Ibid., 4. The word "psychic" here has the general sense of being related to the soul.

58. These may be fear and even hate. Sri Chinmoy comments significantly, "Hate is often an obverse form of love. You hate someone whom you really wish to love but whom you cannot love . . . . You can only hate someone that you have the capacity to love, because if you are really indifferent, you cannot even get up enough energy to hate him. Hatred is the frustration or blockage of normal, free-flowing love." *Earth's Cry Meets Heaven's Smile,* Part 3 (Santurce, Puerto Rico: Aum Press, 1978), 154.

59. *Service-Boat,* Part 2, 4.

60. *Fifty Freedom-Boats,* Part 3 (1974), 21–22.

61. *Yoga*, 21–22.

62. *Here and Now* (New York: Agni Press, 2001), 2.

63. *Service-Trees,* Part 46 (2006), No. 45,348.

64. *Food for the Soul*, 37.

65. *Service-Trees,* Part 36 (2004), No. 35,644.

66. *Service-Trees,* Part 37 (2004), No. 36,447.

67. *Surrender's Unlimited Power* (New York: Agni Press, 1974), 35.

68. *Eternity's Breath,* 12.

69. *Service-Trees,* Part 33 (2003), No. 32,529.

70. *Service-Trees,* Part 34 (2003), No. 33,221.

71. *The Oneness of the Eastern Heart and the Western Mind,* Part 2, 254.

72. *Service-Trees,* Part 35 (2004), No. 34,744.

73. *Service-Trees,* Part 37 (2004), No. 36,506.

74. *My Morning Soul-Body Prayers,* Part 4 (New York: Agni Press, 1999), 105.

75. *Eternity's Breath,* 11.

76. *My Lord's Lotus-Feet versus My Devotion-heart,* Part 1 (New York: Agni Press, 1998), 29–30.

77. *Service-Boat,* Part 2, 41–42.

78. *Our Path,* 2.

79. *Service-Trees* Part 36 (2004), No. 35,763; Part 41 (2004), No. 40,844, No. 40,877.

80. *The Oneness of the Eastern Heart and the Western Mind,* Part 1, 79.

81. *Commentaries,* 178.

82. *Sri Chinmoy Speaks*, 44–45.

83. *Eternity's Breath*, 4.

84. *Songs of the Soul*, 37.

85. *Commentaries*, 133.

86. *Ibid.*, 178–179.

87. *Surrender's Unlimited Power*, 13.

88. *Sri Chinmoy Answers*, vol. 2, 872.

89. *The Bhagavad Gītā*, Sargeant and Chapple, 725–726.

90. *Service-Trees*, Part 35 (2004), No. 34,502.

91. *Service-Trees*, Part 27 (2002), Nos. 627-29.

92. *Surrender's Unlimited Power*, 38.

93. Ibid., 42.

94. *Service-Trees*, Part 3 (1998), No. 2,934.

95. *Surrender's Unlimited Power*, 7.

96. Ibid., 29–20.

97. *Service-Trees*, Part 47 (2006), No. 46,716, No. 46,717.

98. *Service-Trees*, Part 40 (2004), No. 39,941.

99. *Everest-Aspiration*, 12–13.

100. *Death and Reincarnation*, 57.

101. *Eternity's Breath*, 14.

102. *Service-Trees*, Part 50 (2009), No. 49,076.

103. *Obedience: A Supreme Virtue* (New York: Agni Press, 1977), 19–20.

104. *Fifty Freedom-Boats*, Part 4 (1974), 45.

105. *Surrender's Unlimited Power*, 11–12.

106. Ibid., 32–33.

107. *Yoga*, 22.

108. *Service-Trees*, Part 47 (2006), No. 46,695.

109. *Chandelier*, No. 173.

110. *Service-Trees*, Part 1 (1998), No. 837.

111. *Yoga*, 21.

112. "Surrender-Life," in *Transcendence-Perfection* (New York: Agni Press, 2006 [1975]), No 283.

113. *Eternity's Breath*, 3.

114. *God's Hour*, 59.

115. *Flame-Waves*, Part 7 (New York: Agni Press, 1976), 27.

116. *Service-Trees*, Part 42 (2005), No. 41,006.

117. *Service-Trees*, Part 42 (2005), No.41,460 (2005); Part 6 (1998), No. 5,448.

118. *Aspiration-Plants*, Part 240 (1997), No. 23,970.

119. *The Oneness of the Eastern Heart and the Western Mind*, Part 3, 70.

120. Ibid., 23–24.

121. *My Race Prayers*, Part 1 (New York: Agni Press, 2004), No. 12.

122. *Service-Trees*, Part 24 (2002), No. 23,158.

123. *God's Hour*, 3.

Chapter 7

Acceptance and Transformation

THE CREATOR AND THE CREATION

God, Who is Love, has become the world. The One has become the Many and all that exists in the universe is a form of God: "The One is many in Its universal form. The Many are One in their transcendental form"[1] and "it is the same God / Who plays the role / Of God the Creator-Vision / And / God the creation-manifestation"[2] although all of creation is still only a particle of the total Being of the Supreme.[3] God's Love for God's creation is infinite. "God has become / His own Breath / To love the world / And / To care for the world."[4] The Love of God for all beings in creation, who are God's own many selves, is always increasing: "God loves not only human beings / But His entire Creation, every day, more and more."[5] Each soul is on a journey to become conscious of its oneness with the Source—to awaken to its true nature as a drop of the Ocean of Love that is God—and also to become conscious of its oneness with all other beings who, like one's own self, are drops of the Ocean of *Sat-Cit-Ānanda.*

Sri Chinmoy says, "God can never be separated from His creation. Creator and Creation are one, inseparable."[6] We thus cannot know the world as it really is without knowing its Origin and at the same time, because God is not other than the creation, we cannot attain knowledge of God by rejecting the world. They are ultimately indivisible and of equal significance: "God the creation / Is the Universal / Beloved Supreme,"[7] and "God the creation / Is as important / As God the Creator."[8] Therefore, "When I cry for God the Creator, / He comes to me as God the creation as well"[9] and, indeed, "God the creation / Satisfies / My God-hunger."[10]

As of knowledge, the same is true of love: we cannot love God the Creator without loving God the creation: "He who loves / God the Creator /

125

Must also love / God the Creation."[11] A person of aspiration loves the world in the conviction that "this world of ours is verily the aspiring Body of God, the glowing Dream of God and the fulfilling Reality of God."[12] As well, growing in self-giving love means that one "loves the world not for the sake of what the world can give us in return, but for the sake of love itself. Real love, selfless love, never ends, never fails. Love is its own immediate reward."[13] One eventually comes to see that one's "entire existence is in the very heart of the world."[14] The inseparability of God and the world means that "The more we can love / God the creation, / The nearer we shall feel / The Presence/ Of God the Satisfaction."[15] Sri Chinmoy says, "In vain I pray to God the Creator / And / In vain I meditate on God the Creator / If I do not love God the creation / And / If I do not serve God the creation."[16] As Swami Vivekānanda declares at the close of his poem *To a Friend*, "These are His manifold forms before thee, / Rejecting them, where seekest thou for God? / Who loves all beings, without distinction, / He indeed is worshipping best his God."[17]

ACCEPTANCE OF LIFE

Love for all of creation calls for radical world-acceptance, even of what might be difficult to see or feel as related to oneself. This inclusive and unconditional acceptance is the precondition of working for world-transformation. Sri Chinmoy powerfully states,

> My philosophy is the absolute acceptance of life. Life has to be accepted. In this life there is the living Breath of God. God is not only in Heaven, He is within us as well. God and His creation can never be separated. My message is this: If we really think of God, then we have to accept the world as real, just as God is real. First we have to accept the world as it is. If we do not accept the world, then what are we going to change? What are we going to transform?[18]

Our participation in the world's evolutionary progress makes necessary a loving embrace of all that exists, and excludes any sense of superiority on the part of those who may have positive attributes more abundantly. In a Bengali song Sri Chinmoy asks:

Sundara jadi kurupe nā bāse bhālo
Kuruper prāne kemane rājibe ālo
Dhruba tārā jadi adhruba pāne
Phire kabhu nāhi chāi
Mitthyā kemane labhibe mukti

Nāhi jāne keha hāi
Ātma tripti lakya moder noy
Rupāntari moder shreshta jai

If beauty does not love ugliness,
How can Light abide in ugliness-core?
If the pole-star does not look at falsehood with compassion-flood,
How can falsehood achieve liberation?
Alas, it is beyond, far beyond the imagination of all.
Self-satisfaction is not our goal;
Transformation-perfection is our victory's goal. [19]

Moreover, complete acceptance of the world, even of the repulsive, in humble self-abandonment, brings us into God's Presence: "To reach God's Height / I have discovered / A secret way," Sri Chinmoy says, "I just touch the lowest man's / Filthiest feet,"[20] but he adds, "God feels miserable / When I tell him / That I love / Even the undesirable / And unlovable human beings. / For Him, everybody is desirable / And lovable"[21] and "From God's point of view / No human being is disheartening / Or even discouraging."[22] Sarada Devi casts light on this oneness with all, saying, "In the fullness of one's spiritual realization one will find that He who resides in one's own heart, resides in the hearts of others as well—the oppressed, the persecuted, the untouchable, the outcast."[23] God has become the entire universe, and nothing in the world is without its own unique role and value; Sri Chinmoy affirms, "God not only loves / But also needs / Each and every creation of His / From the highest to the lowest."[24]

Oneness with the world also means identification with its pain and sorrows and taking action to relieve them, an ethics of compassion and beneficence. God-realization unites the realized person not only with the Bliss of the Source but also with the sufferings of the world: "Self-discovery makes you one / With the Joy of God the Creator / And with the sorrow of God the creation."[25] But at any stage of the spiritual journey, our love for the world must reach out with support and succor: "God expects / His worshippers / To heal this broken world."[26] This action comes from our deep identification: "God does not ask me to observe / The sorrow of the world, / But He asks me to become one / With all the sorrows of the world."[27] This oneness must be expressed in compassion that acts to help all beings. God says to the dedicated aspirant, "My child, I shall make you / My perfect emissary on earth, / To become inseparably one / With earth's excruciating pangs / And streaming tears / The way I have been doing / Throughout My entire Eternity"[28]—that is, to love the world more and more in the way that God loves it. The seeker prays, "My Lord, do give me the capacity / To wipe every tear / From every heart."[29]

SERVICE TO GOD THE CREATION

God loves us boundlessly. In gratitude and reciprocity, we are called to return
God's Love in self-offering service to God in the world: "God the Creator /
Loves you. / God the creation / Needs you. / To God the Creator / Give your
heart. / To God the creation / Give your life."[30] We take action because of
love: "We must serve / God the creation / Exactly the way we love / God the
Creator."[31] Sri Ramakrishna declares that we should serve all beings seeing
them as God: "*Siva jñāne jiver seva.*"[32] And the heart's innate capacity can
make this spontaneous: "The very nature of the heart / Is to love God the
Creator / And to serve God the creation."[33] In our outer life, service is directed
to making things better in concrete ways and as God's "emissaries" we take up
the task of fulfilling the world's needs: "Divine service / Means the acceptance
/ Of God's creation-responsibility/ As one's own, very own."[34] Shouldering
this responsibility can be costly but along with compassion, sacrifice arises
naturally from love, oneness and our longing for transformation. Sri Chinmoy
affirms, "If you are ready to suffer / For others' misery, / Then you are fiercely
thirsting / To disperse / The ignorance-clouds / Of humanity's cruelty."[35]
We have reflected above on his understanding that evil is not an ultimate or
absolute reality,[36] but he also holds that the existence of evil in this world is
of the utmost consequence as we make the commitment to transformation:
"You must immediately answer / The challenge of evil. / You must, / If you
want God-realisation / And / Life-perfection on earth." And moreover, "You
must unconditionally answer / The call of Light. / You must, / If you want
God-manifestation / And / God-satisfaction on earth."[37] In sum, "To love the
world / Is to make the world perfect."[38]

Love for the world, in radical acceptance and the consciousness of oneness,
is the basis of both ethics and spiritual practice, which are aspects of one
another and are indivisible. Sri Chinmoy says,

> When we start with one, we have to know that we are going to the Root, the
> Source, the Unity. But the Source needs manifestation; otherwise, it will remain
> unfulfilled. For manifestation we have to enter into the world of multiplicity.
> And finally we have to transform the world and bring Heaven's Perfection into
> the world. Only in this way can we have true satisfaction, and true satisfaction
> is God's Perfection-Love.

> In unity there must be the song of multiplicity. When we enter into the spiritual
> life, if we ignore the world around us, if we feel the world around us is dirty
> and undivine and can never be transformed, then we are mistaken. This attitude
> is unhealthy, abnormal. We have to accept the world around us as our very
> own, and inside the world we have to see and feel the living Breath and living
> Presence of God.

If we are real seekers of truth, like divine warriors we will face the world and brave the world here and now. . . . We have to feel that the members of society are like the limbs of our body. If even one part of our being is not transformed, then we are not perfect.[39]

This feeling of oneness must be actualized in everyday life for the good of others and for our own fulfillment. Sri Chinmoy says, "If we do not share with others what we have and what we are, we are bound to feel unsatisfied, no matter what we achieve and what we grow into." We must see others "as an extension of our own being" with "one source and one common goal. . . . Satisfaction and perfection lie only in self-giving."[40]

Service is a path to an ever-greater spiritual oneness and a deeper, wider love. As mentioned, Sri Chinmoy very often says that "self-giving is God-becoming." For the spiritual practitioner, "Devoted and soulful service / Means a vast expansion / Of our conscious oneness/ With God the Creation."[41] Giving one's self in service to others, in kindness and willing their good, transforms the individual through transcendence of the small sense of self into a vast and illumined sense of self, a larger self that knows it is one with all others and with God, their Source: "Self-giving / Is the expansion / Of the heart."[42] At the same time, when service effects positive concrete change, it is a means of transformation of the world at large. As well, the life of service of even one or a few people may inspire others to do likewise—to be engaged in action for their own transformation and at the same time for the betterment of the world as a whole.

INTEGRAL TRANSFORMATION
AND BEING IN THE WORLD

Because the purpose of the divine Play or Līlā is ever-increasing joy and fulfillment in God's evolving manifestation in the cosmos, to reject the external world is not only to reject an aspect of God's Reality but also to withdraw from participation in God's Plan for creation. A poem says: "Real aspiration can never be / The rejection of life. / Real aspiration is the beauty / Of life-acceptance / And the fragrance / Of life-transformation."[43] The spiritual life has to be practiced in the world while working for the welfare of the world. In a poem written in the last year of his life, Sri Chinmoy affirms, "World-renunciation is not for me. / World-acceptance, / And then world-transformation, / Is my Goal—my only Goal," and in another from the same time he says, "God will not be satisfied / Until He is fully manifested / Here on earth."[44] The path of love, acceptance and world-transformation is immensely challenging. Sri Chinmoy declares, "The denial of life is so easy.

/ The full acceptance of life / For the manifestation of God / Is a task more difficult / Than you can ever imagine."[45]

God-realization itself can be viewed as incomplete if it does not include all of life. In this perspective the attainment of spiritual "height" is not the final goal, but beyond it is "Oneness-Life," in which all of existence in its different aspects (the word "life" meaning this integral reality) is united with the Source. In the following passage, Sri Chinmoy uses the term "high" in two ways. The "highest Height" means the fullest integrality of God-realization, which is more complete than reaching the "highest pinnacle."

> A sincere seeker longs for God-realisation. For him, God-realisation means the transcendental Height, which is the height of Silence, the height of Light and Delight. One may reach the highest pinnacle of Truth, Light, Beauty and Delight, but that does not necessarily mean that one is near the highest Height. No! In order to achieve the highest, loftiest Height, one has to enter the oneness-life. If one neglects or rejects God's oneness-life, God's Universal Life, then no matter how many times he reaches the highest pinnacle, he cannot be closest or dearest to God, the Highest Absolute. The height has to be scaled, but we have to know that while climbing up the mountain, we are carrying within us the Universal Life, the life of multiplicity, which we are carrying to the Source, the transcendental Reality.[46]

The fullest realization thus includes the universal Life as well as the transcendent "pinnacle" of Silence, Light, and Delight. It is striking that in using the language of "upward" movement towards the Source, Sri Chinmoy says that we *are carrying within us the Universal Life*" (emphasis added). We might say that here the spiritual achievement is "horizontal" as well as "vertical." To say that this is a greater attainment may be related to his statement elsewhere that "It is easier to reach / The highest height / Than to plumb / The deepest depth."[47] In "The Seed," a poem written in India in his twenties, Sri Chinmoy articulates an experience of liberation united with different levels of cosmic manifestation while holding the depths of being within oneself: "I am the seed and root and boughs, / I am the aspiration-tree. / In me abides the deepest deep, / My goal I build; I am ever free."[48] We recall that in his description of *nirvikalpa samādhi*, he says that in this state one sees the universe *inside* one's spiritual heart. As well, the poem refers to identification with the dynamism of self-transcendence inherent in creation—the universe is called "the aspiration-tree."

Concerning individual spiritual attainment, another poem says simply, "God does not accept me / When I bring only my heart. / He accepts me / Only when I bring Him / My body, vital, mind and heart / Together."[49] In addition, not only in the spiritual or interior life of an individual person, but also in living in the outer world, there must be acceptance of all aspects of existence. Sri Chinmoy says,

> True spirituality tells us that we must not reject anything, we must not negate anything, we must not renounce anything. True spirituality tells us that we have to accept everything. We have to accept the world as such and then we have to transform our inner world and our outer world for God-realisation, God-revelation and God-manifestation. It is only in God-realisation, God-revelation and God-manifestation that we will find boundless Peace, boundless Light, boundless Delight.[50]

It is God's intention for any particular person that determines how that person should proceed in actual practice, as it is surrender to the divine Will that is most important in any given context. Sri Chinmoy explains: "I deny the things God wants me to deny. / I accept the things God wants me to accept. / Why? / Because my acceptance-light / And my denial-might / Contribute to my God's / Constant self-transcendence / In me."[51] The following poem similarly says: "Satisfaction I get / Not by renouncing, / Not by possessing, / But by becoming"[52]—"becoming" is none other than "God's constant self-transcendence in me." Withdrawal from the world as a solitary ascetic may surely be the time-honored vocation of a few, but for many others it may be inconsistent with integral becoming in the midst of life and community. A narrative poem tells us:

I lived a cave-life
  For meditation.
I shunned all my human friends
  To gain my only eternal
  And immortal Friend.

He came in and said:
  "Son, your cave will suffocate me.
I want to live in your palace-life.
It will give me what I admire—
  Oneness with the multitudes."[53]

In fact, whether we can consciously love and accept the world is an assessment of contemplative practice even in the early stages. Sri Chinmoy says, "if we can love the world even while seeing its teeming imperfections, then we know our meditation was good."[54] He elaborates:

> Acceptance and self-transcendence are the prerequisites of action and perfection. Action means acceptance of the world, no matter how weak or insufficient it is, for its present and future transformation. Perfection means constant

transcendence of today's achievement by means of self-giving. Self-giving is immediately followed by self-transcendence, and in self-transcendence only do we get the message of perfection.[55]

Self-giving is the direct expression of love and oneness. And Sri Chinmoy declares, "When the veil of illusion is torn" each of us will see that in the world of multiplicity we actually love "only one Person, God the Creator," and that we serve "only one Person, God the creation,"[56] one Person in and as countless persons.

THE VISION OF PEACE

To succinctly describe the overarching goal of the process of world-transformation, Sri Chinmoy most often uses the word "peace."[57] He says, "Peace does not mean the absence of war. . . . Peace means the presence of harmony, love, satisfaction and oneness. Peace means a flood of love in the world family. Peace means the unity of the universal heart and the oneness of the universal soul."[58] His vision of peace includes not only the inner serenity and silence of meditation, but also the end of conflict, violence, oppression and poverty, the establishment of harmony and friendship between people, and respect and care for the natural world—as mentioned, an ethics of loving, active beneficence founded in spiritual experience. Lasting peace or "world-oneness" and abundance of life for all can only be brought about by contemplative practice, self-giving service, acceptance of light and love for the world. "The secret / Of earth-transformation / Lies in the breath / Of lovers of God the creation"[59] and thus the spiritual aspiration of many people is an indispensable catalyst of this global process. Sri Chinmoy states that: "Peace is first / An individual achievement. / Then it grows into / A collective achievement. / Finally it becomes / A universal achievement."[60]

The intrinsic connection of peace in the world to love and oneness is of central importance. Conflict and the afflictive thoughts and emotions that cause it arise from a sense of separateness, functioning most potently in the mind, the "division-mind" with its desire for supremacy and domination, as already described. The power that can overcome this division is the "oneness-heart" which, as we have seen, is a faculty of knowledge as well as of feeling and is able to perceive the unity of existence. Spiritual life founded in the heart is a path to both inner and outer peace, healing and completeness. When the practice of yoga attains both the ontological knowledge and the affective experience of oneness, the successful outer manifestation of this inner illumination is love, harmony and peace.[61] The achievement of peace by individuals needs to be shared with the world at large through as many forms of expression as can be effectively put into practice, including personal communication, the arts, education, media, diverse issue-focused programs, advocacy, and policies for concrete change in different spheres of human life.

The word "peace" has connoted since ancient times not merely an end to conflict and turmoil but the most inclusive vision of human wellbeing in harmony with Nature and the universe. The Hebrew word for peace, *shalom*, also means wholeness and harmony, while a famous Sanskrit prayer, the Śānti Mantra of the Yajur Veda (36:17) invokes the blessings of peace on the whole cosmos and all its living beings: "To the heavens be peace, to the sky and the earth, / To the waters be peace, to plants and all trees, / To the Gods be peace, to Brahman be peace, / To all be peace, again and again, peace also to me!"[62] Peace in this fullest sense is well defined in the words of the Earth Charter, a global civil society declaration finalized in 2000: "Peace is the wholeness created by right relationships with oneself, other persons, other cultures, other life, Earth and the larger whole of which all are a part."[63] Sri Chinmoy affirms this all-embracing nature of the goal of peace, which is integral in the sense that it includes both the inner and outer dimensions of life. He sees "peace" not only as the goal but also as the beginning of the process of world-transformation and divinization: "When Peace is multiplied, Truth is multiplied. When Truth is multiplied, Love is multiplied. When Love is multiplied, God is multiplied."[64]

"Peace" comprehends the flourishing of human beings together with all beings in creation. How is peace related to the group of interconnected issues known as "the environment," and the relation between human beings and Nature? For Sri Chinmoy, "Nature," the whole manifested world or the cosmos, is the universal aspect of the Divine and thus Nature and "God the creation" are one and the same. Sri Chinmoy affirms: "In His transcendental aspect, / God is the Lord of Nature. / In His universal aspect / God is Nature itself."[65] Nature, unlike human beings, "obeys God implicitly"[66] and "God tells us / That we came into the world / Not to command Nature, / But to obey Nature."[67] But, alas! "Nature compassionately takes / Very little from us. / But we are always eager to devour / Not only everything from Nature / But also Nature itself."[68]

Sri Chinmoy identifies the causes of our "ruthless exploitation"[69] of Nature as fear and desire for power—the roots in ignorance of violence against the natural world and against other human beings are the same. He says,

Because we human beings see enemies all around us, because we are afraid someone will come and attack us, we use all our money and energy to make ourselves powerful. To make ourselves powerful enough to fight our enemies, we cut Mother Nature into pieces and take her resources [giving importance only to the technological advances that will bestow power]. As long as there is fear on earth, Mother Nature will never be able to fulfil her divinity. It is only when we no longer see others as enemies that we shall be able to keep Mother Nature intact.[70]

But no matter how extreme destruction may be, because Nature is God the creation, what has been destroyed can be healed, regenerated and restored by God the Creator. Human beings should not only prevent destruction in the first place, but also participate in restoration through our outer actions and also through our inner aspiration invoking God's help for the healing of Mother Earth.[71]

Sri Chinmoy gives great importance to the beauty of Nature as "God the visible:"[72] "Nature is / The revealed Beauty / Of God."[73] He explains, "God can be above in any form or formless, as infinite Light, infinite Peace, infinite Bliss. Again, He can be inside our hearts, where our real existence is. And if we open our eyes and look at Nature, at the mountains and rivers, that also is God."[74] Thus "An aspiring soul / Is apt to drink / The eternal beauty / Of Mother Nature,"[75] and indeed, the person who admires Nature's Beauty "is already accepted by God, the Mother, as Her chosen instrument."[76] "Nature's beauty helps us / To be as vast as possible, / As peaceful as possible / And as pure as possible."[77] Contemplative practice is, however, necessary to create receptivity and Sri Chinmoy encourages meditation on Nature's beauty[78] as a way to realize "God the Beauty."[79]

Sri Chinmoy states that "The essence of Nature's beauty is the Supreme Light or Supreme Delight in Nature,"[80] two immanent divine attributes which are also the two qualities of the soul that he mentions most often in his poetry. Beholding the beauty of Nature, the soul responds with a recognition of its own unity with what is beheld.[81] When we see divine beauty, Sri Chinmoy says, we will feel that we "are not only embracing the world, but also *becoming the world itself*" (emphasis added).[82] Thus Sri Chinmoy avers, "Reality is nothing but beauty in oneness, beauty of oneness and beauty for oneness."[83] He also says, "Divine love and divine beauty are inseparable"— to love and to see the beauty of the beloved are two aspects of one single experience.[84] Therefore the experience of the beauty of Nature is an essential part of love for the world as "God the creation."

GOD-MANIFESTATION AS EVER-TRANSCENDING PERFECTION

The ultimate goal of God-manifestation is the transformation of all aspects of life resulting in "perfect perfection," which gives the most complete fulfillment or "satisfaction:" "God wants Satisfaction / In His entire creation."[85] Realization, the "upward" movement of yoga to transcendence and conscious union with the Absolute, is followed by revelation disclosing what has been realized. Revelation in turn is followed by manifestation, both "downward" movements into the world to distribute the fruits of realization, compared to a mango brought down from a tree one has climbed; the mango is not merely shown to others but shared with them, eaten and assimilated. Thus "Realisation is not / The end of the road. / It is only a challenge / On the way to God's / Perfect Manifestation on earth."[86] At every stage of the journey, progress is impelled by aspiration: "Aspiration never ends. / Even after God-realisation / Aspiration is of paramount importance / For God-manifestation."[87]

Creation is "ever-continuing," "unfinished" and without end,[88] moving through an ever-transcending series of perfections through personal, collective and cosmic evolution. "Perfection grows. It has been doing so since the beginning of the creation's birth," Sri Chinmoy says.[89] In this transformation, the attributes of the transcendent Creator God such as Bliss, Light, Beauty and Power, are revealed and then received and assimilated by God's universal existence, the creation. This process is far vaster than the conscious spiritual aspiration of human beings, which is only its most recent phase and also is not its final one. Sri Chinmoy elaborates:

> The purpose of animal life is the quest for individuality and separativity. The purpose of human life is the quest for unity instead of the sense of separativity. The purpose of divine life is the quest for perfection—perfection in the inner world, perfection in the outer world, perfection in God's entire creation. The purpose of the Supreme's life is the quest for satisfaction, the satisfaction that nourishes the body-reality of His creation and the soul-reality of His ever-transcending Vision.[90]

At the human level of our present existence, we are participating in a cosmic progress.

> In the process of evolution each individual is making progress, and continuous progress ultimately leads to perfection itself. Perfection has to be the goal of each and every individual—perfection of the inner life and perfection of the outer life—for it is in perfection that satisfaction abides. . . . When we dive deep within, we clearly see that not only are individuals progressing, but God's creation as a whole is also progressing. Everything that exists is making progress. Even God the Infinite, God the Eternal and God the Immortal is progressing; He is constantly expanding His own Infinity, Eternity and Immortality. Continuous progress is the supreme Goal of His Transcendental Vision and His Universal Reality.[91]

Perfection is not a fixed state but is "ever-transcending," as is the divine Reality Itself: "today's goal, today's perfection, is tomorrow's starting point, and tomorrow's goal becomes the starting point for the day after tomorrow. Continuous progress is perfection. Self-transcendence is the song of constant inner progress and constant outer progress."[92] Ultimately "perfection" itself can be understood as progress, a progress that is always going beyond itself.

It is on earth, and not in other or higher worlds, that God-manifestation takes place. The cry, the hunger or the "inner mounting flame" of aspiration that impels evolution belongs to earth. In his poetry Sri Chinmoy develops this point. He says, "Heaven-smile / Knows / How to renew itself. / That is all. / Earth-cry / Knows / Not only how to renew itself, / But how to renew God, / The Beloved Supreme."[93] Similarly, he says that "Heaven-beauty lights / But cannot warm. / Indeed, it is earth-duty / That warms. / Heaven-smile awakens / But cannot liberate. / Indeed, it is earth-cry / That liberates."[94] Heaven's plenitude has to be expanded, and is, only by earth's aspiration. Sri Chinmoy puts this in one line in a song in Bengali and English: "*Swarga duār khulte habe martya chābi diye*—Heaven's door I must open with the earth-key."[95] On this core theme, a poem asks an ascending series of questions which all have the same answer:

Is your goal to love?
    Then here is the place.

Is your goal to love God in His own Way?
    Then here is the place.

Is your goal to become another God?
    Then here is the place.

Is your goal to transcend the previous God?
    Then here is the place.

Is your goal to transcend the present God?
    Then here is the place.

Is your goal, your only goal,
    To become the future God?
    Then here is the place.

Here is the place:
    Earth, Mother Earth.[96]

God-manifestation is the full divinization or God-becoming of the world—and Mother Earth is the venue of this transformation. "The transformation / Of our consciousness / Shall take numberless years,"[97] Sri Chinmoy advises, but joy is in progress itself and not in reaching a preconceived goal at a predicted time. Our limited consciousness cannot foresee, let alone prescribe, what may take place or when. In any case, in the divine Play God can always change God's Plan, as he at times points out. Our mission is to love and serve the world in oneness with the God's cosmic and universal Will, without expecting specific results according to our own ideas. Let us recall that when asked to state his philosophy in a single line, Sri Chinmoy said: "Our philosophy is the acceptance of life for the transformation of life and also for the manifestation of God's Light here on earth at God's choice Hour in God's own Way."[98]

LOVE AND TRANSFORMATION

Sri Chinmoy powerfully affirms, "If you really care for the world, / Then love the world, / Serve the world, / Become the world, / And do not think of / Your personal salvation."[99] This consecration to the good of all brings to mind the Bodhisattva in Mahāyana Buddhism, who vows to attain Buddhahood, or full enlightenment, but not for one's own sake—rather to forgo Nirvana while constantly engaging in compassionate action for the benefit and liberation of all sentient beings.[100] A Bengali song says, "*Sabār mukti jāchi āmi āmi sabār / Sabāi āmār chirantaner bishwa /*—I long for the liberation of all souls; I belong to all and all belong to me. We comprise Eternity's universe."[101] Another says, "*Sabār sāthe jukta haya mukti bhikkha magi*—United with all I must beg for liberation."[102] Sri Chinmoy says that God requests us to bring the world with us when we come to God,[103] and the aspirant promises to God, "*Eklā āmi tomār kacche jabonā mā, jabonā; / Sabār sāthe tomāi pābo, ei shudhu mor sādhanā*—Alone I shall not go to You, Mother, I shall not go. / With all I shall get You: / This is my life's only aspiration, only meditation, only Goal."[104]

When Sri Chinmoy says, "love the world, serve the world, become the world," what does he mean by "become the world"? To "become the world" is a longing of the heart and the soul, which wants "to become inseparably one / With the world," and "to become the world itself."[105] One "becomes the world" through love: "My heart / Knows how to love the world / And become the world."[106] Sri Chinmoy explains, "Do not expect anything from the world; only love the world and offer your capacity, your inner wealth, your joy. Everything that you have, give to the world unconditionally."[107] This unreserved love is learned from God through the heart and soul:

"God the Compassion teaches us / Sleeplessly / How to love the world / Unconditionally,"[108] and teaches in the depths of meditation as well as in the outer life: "Silence teaches me / How to love the world / And become the world."[109]

Sri Chinmoy also says, "With love / I see the world. / With devotion / I feel the world. / With surrender / I become the world."[110] Love, devotion and surrender are three phases on the continuum of love, and complete surrender is total self-offering in consciousness of identity; as mentioned above, one eventually comes to see that one's "entire existence is in the very heart of the world."[111] Through self-offering we awaken to the unity of existence, coming to know the non-separateness of the many beings in the universe and to love them as ourselves: "Love is the eye that the soul uses / To see the world. / Oneness is the heart that the soul uses / To feel and become the world."[112] This love and this self-offering are the very purpose of our existence. "What is your heart for, / If it is not solely meant / To love God the Creator?" "What is your life for, / If it is not solely meant / To serve God the creation?"[113]

In this poem Sri Chinmoy reaffirms the essence of the path of acceptance, love, and self-giving service: "My Lord tells me / That if I want to be His champion, / Then I must not renounce the world. / I must accept the world, / Love the world / And become the world, / For its ultimate transformation."[114] What is this "ultimate transformation"? Love is the way of transformation: "The love of the heart / Is the way / To world-transformation."[115] Love is also the Goal. As the Infinite is always surpassing Itself, even the "ultimate transformation" will forever arrive at Love, for God is eternally Love—"Love divine is the destination of the ever-transcending Beyond."[116]

NOTES

1. *The Oneness of the Eastern Heart and the Western Mind,* Part 2, 40.

2. *Here and Now,* 42.

3. See Chapter 3, 47.

4. *Service-Trees,* Part 40 (2004), No. 39,800.

5. *Enthusiasm,* Part 10 (New York: Agni Press, 2006) Song for Dec. 6.

6. *The Oneness of the Eastern Heart and the Western Mind,* Part 1, 304.

7. *Service-Trees,* Part 5, (1998), No. 4,897.

8. *Service-Trees,* Part 12 (1999), No. 11,218.

9. *Philosopher-Thinkers: The Power-Towers of the Mind and Poet-Seers: The Fragrance-Hours of the Heart in the West* (1998), 142.

10. *Service-Trees,* Part 14 (1999), No. 13,303.

11. *Service-Trees,* Part 27 (2002), No. 26,930.

12. *United Nations Works,* Vol. 1, 53.

13. Ibid., 7.

14. Ibid., 122.

15. *Service-Trees*, Part 9 (1998), No. 8,596.

16. *My Morning Soul-Body Prayers*, Part 2 (1999), 97.

17. Swami Vivekananda, *In Search of God and Other Poems* (Kolkata: Advaita Ashrama, 2003 [1947], 41. Also in *Collected Works*, 11th ed. (Calcutta: Advaita Ashrama, 1978), Vol. 4, 493–496.

18. *Realisation-Soul and Manifestation-Goal* (New York: Agni Press, 1974), 55.

19. *The Garden of Love-Light*, Part 3, Songbook (New York: Agni Press, 1975), No. 34.

20. "A Secret Way," in *Flower-Flames*, Part 1 (1979), No. 78. In Indian tradition, touching a person's feet is a gesture of respect or reverence. Its mention in this poem also recalls the Christian practice of foot-washing, done on Holy Thursday remembering that Jesus washed the feet of his disciples during the Last Supper. This is related in the Gospel of John, where Jesus says, "So if I, your Lord and Teacher, have washed your feet, you also ought to wash one another's feet" (John 13.14); in the ancient world washing the feet of a guest would normally be done by a servant. Swami Vivekananda referred to this event in the life of Jesus a few days before his own passing (Swami Nikhilananda, *Vivekananda: A Biography.* New York: Ramakrishna-Vivekananda Center, 1964 [1953]), 177. Bible references are to the New Revised Standard Version (New York: Oxford University Press, 1989).

21. *Service-Trees*, Part 9 (1998), No. 8,422.

22. *Service Trees*, Part 2 (1998), No. 1,877.

23. *The Gospel of the Holy Mother Sri Sarada Devi*, Recorded by Her Devotee-Children (Madras: Sri Ramakrishna Math, 1984), 59–60.

24. *Service-Trees*, Part 31 (2003), No. 30,689.

25. *Service-Trees*, Part 5 (1998), No. 4,102.

26. *Service-Trees*, Part 30 (2002), No. 29,056.

27. *Service-Trees*, Part 26 (2002), No. 25,818.

28. *Flower-Flames*, Part 62 (1983), No. 6,180.

29. *Service-Trees*, Part 1 (1998), No. 765

30. *Aspiration-Plants*, Part 232 (1984), No. 23,181.

31. *Service-Trees*, Part 14 (1999), No. 13,810.

32. Pravrajika Vraprana, "Bridging the Gap between the Sacred and the Secular: *Seva* as Ascetic Practice." Paper given at the Annual Conference of the Dharma Academy of North America (DANAM), November 2007, 4. See also Swami Saradānanda, *Sri Ramakrishna the Great Master*, tr. Swami Jagadānanda, 6th ed. (Chennai: Sri Ramakrishna Math, 2008 [1952]), 1163.

33. *Service-Trees*, Part 27 (2002), No. 26,291.

34. *Service-Trees*, Part 26 (2002), No. 25,539.

35. "If You Are Ready to Suffer," in *Flower-Flames*, Part 65 (1983), No. 6,496.

36. Chapter 4, 74–76.

37. "You Must Answer," in *Europe-Blossoms*, No. 975.

38. *Service-Trees*, Part 30 (2002), No. 29, 655.

39. *United Nations Works*, Vol. 1, 138–140.

40. Ibid., 130, 128.

41. *Aspiration-Plants,* Part 16 (1983), No. 1,576.

42. *Service-Trees,* Part 33 (2003), No. 23,354.

43. *Service-Trees,* Part 4 (1998), No. 3,815.

44. *Service-Trees,* Part 50 (2009), No. 49,378, No. 49,774.

45. *Aspiration-Plants,* Part 172 (1992), No. 17,153.

46. *United Nations Works,* Vol. 1, 145.

47. *Service-Trees,* Part 31 (2003), No. 30, 661.

48. In *My First Friendship with the Muse* (New York: Sri Chinmoy Lighthouse, 1973), 3.

49. *Service-Trees,* Part 27 (2002), No 26,804.

50. *United Nations Works,* Vol. 1, 174.

51. "Denial and Acceptance," in *The Golden Boat,* Part 18 (New York: Agni Press, 1974) No. 21.

52. *Service-Trees,* Part 33 (2003), No. 32,305.

53. "The Cave-life," in *The Wings of Light,* Part 5 (1974), No. 32.

54. *Beyond Within* (New York: Aum Publications, 1974), 276.

55. *United Nations Works,* Vol. 1, 125.

56. "When the Veil of Illusion Is Torn," in *Flower-Flames,* Part 74 (1983), No. 7,393.

57. In this section I draw on my essays "Sri Chinmoy's Vision of Peace," in *Beacons of Dharma: Spiritual Exemplars for the Modern Age,* edited by Christopher Patrick Miller, Michael Reading and Jeffery D. Long (New York: Lexington Books, 2020), 235–250, and "Sri Chinmoy's Philosophy of Nature," *Journal of Dharma Studies,* Special Issue on Ecotheology edited by Christopher Fici and Kenneth Valpey, 4, no 1 (April 2021).

58. *United Nations Works,* Vol. 1, 123.

59. *Aspiration-Plants,* Part 223, (1995), No. 22,233.

60. *Service-Trees,* Part 4 (1998), No. 3,491.

61. It may once have seemed naïve to say that "outer peace depends on inner peace," but today this idea is widely acknowledged as a basic operating principle in a time when change is widely understood to depend on values and attitudes, and "political will" is seen as a necessary part of solutions to complex problems.

62. In Raimundo Panikkar, *The Vedic Experience: Mantramañjarī, An Anthology of the Vedas for Modern Man and Contemporary Celebration* (Delhi: Motilal Banarsidass, 1977), 306, slightly revised.

63. Available at http://earthcharter.org/invent/images/uploads/echarter_english.pdf.

64. *God's Hour,* 73.

65. "Two Aspects of God," in *Flower-Flames,* Part 88 (1983), No. 8,725.

66. *My Morning Begins* (1996), 58.

67. *Service-Trees,* Part 7 (1998), No. 6,745.

68. *Aspiration-Plants,* Part 191 (1993), No. 19,050.

69. *Aspiration-Plants,* Part 175 (1992), No. 17,452.

70. *Sri Chinmoy Answers,* Vol. 1, 278.

71. Ibid., 279.

72. *My Golden Children* (New York: Agni Press, 2013), 59.

73. *Service-Trees*, Part 47 (2007), No. 46,874.

74. *Nineteen American Mothers and Nineteen American Sons with Sri Chinmoy* (New York: Agni Press, 1976), 14.

75. *Service-Trees,* Part 14 (1999), No. 13,929.

76. *God's Hour*, 65.

77. *Aspiration-Plants*, Part 169 (1992), No. 16,806.

78. *Sri Chinmoy Answers,* Vol. 1, 385.

79. "To Study Nature's Beauty," in *Flower-Flames,* Part 88 (1983), No. 8,777.

80. A *Galaxy of Beauty's Stars* (New York: Agni Press, 1974), 38.

81. Speaking of the philosophy of Plotinus, Margaret R. Miles says that "we see something as *beautiful* when it matches the beautiful form that is ourselves, that is, soul. We detect beauty by kinship." *Plotinus on Body and Beauty* (Malden, MA: Blackwell Publishers, 1999), 39.

82. *Galaxy*, 6.

83. *Galaxy*, 3.

84. *Galaxy*, 15.

85. "The Outer Man Wants Success," in *Flower-Flames,* Part 87 (1983), No. 8,680.

86. *Aspiration-Plants,* Part 18 (1983), No. 1800.

87. *Service-Trees*, Part 31 (2003), No. 30,660.

88. On "ever-continuing," *The Unreal Heights of Real Absurdities* (1991), 1; on God's creation as "unfinished," *Aspiration-Plants,* Part 63 (1984) No. 6,384; *Service-Trees*, Part 33 (2003), No. 32,017; and "God does not, cannot and will not ever accept any end to His creation. For creation is His progress, His own movement and God wants endless progress in infinite ways." *Realisation-Soul,* 48.

89. *Commentaries*, 204.

90. *Everest-Aspiration*, 145.

91. *World-Destruction: Never! Impossible!* Part 1 (New York: Agni Press, 1994), 7–8.

92. *Perfection-World* (New York: Agni Press, 1974), 34–35.

93. "Renewal," in *Europe-Blossoms*, No. 617.

94. "Earth-cry Liberates," in ibid., No. 451.

95. *Four Hundred Song-Birds,* Part 1, (1986), No. 46.

96. "Here Is the Place," *The Dance of Life,* Part 9 (1973), No. 31.

97. *Service-Trees*, Part 33 (2003), No. 32,532.

98. See above, Chapter 1, 15.

99. *Service-Trees*, Part 38 (2004), No. 37,829.

100. The Bodhisattva's vow occurs beginning with the earliest Mahāyāna scripture, *The Perfection of Wisdom in Eight Thousand Verses (Aṣṭasāhasrikā-prajñāpāramitā)* through many major texts and reaches a culminating expression in Śāntideva's *Bodhicaryāvatāra*. See Har Dayal, *The Bodhisattva Doctrine in Buddhist Sanskrit Literature* (Delhi: Motilal Banarsidass, 1970 [1932]), 19 and Ch. 3; also Nancy R. Lethcoe, "The Bodhisattva Ideal in the Aṣṭa and Pañca Prajñāpāramitā Sūtras," in *Prajñāpāramitā and Related Systems: Studies in Honor of Edward Conze,*

ed. Lewis Lancaster, Berkeley Buddhist Studies Series 1 (Berkeley, CA: Center for South and Southeast Asia Studies at the University of California and The Institute for Buddhist Studies, 1977), 263–280; and Śāntideva, *The Bodhicaryāvatāra,* tr. Kate Crosby and Andrew Skilton, Oxford World Classics Series (New York: Oxford University Press, 1998). I bracket technical questions of how the Bodhisattava vow differs and develops from text to text and in different strata of the same text.

101. *Supreme, I Sing Only for You* (New York: Agni Press, 1974), 37.

102. *Four Hundred Song-birds,* 4.41.

103. "Ever and Never," in *My Flute,* 18.

104. *The Garden of Love-Light,* Part 2, 25.

105. *Service-Trees,* Part 30 (2002), No. 29,243, and Part 16 (1999), No. 15,560.

106. *Service-Trees,* Part 41 (2004), No. 40,843.

107. *Realisation-Soul,* 9.

108. *Service-Trees,* Part 6 (1998), No. 5,027.

109. *Service-Trees,* Part 7 (1998), No. 34,342.

110. *Aspiration-Plants,* Part 30 (1984), No. 2,992.

111. Above, 126.

112. *Two God-Amusement Rivals,* Part 2, No. 290.

113. *Service-Trees,* Part 5 (1998), Nos. 4,172-73.

114. *Service-Trees,* Part 9 (1998), No. 8,227.

115. *Service-Trees,* Part 48 (2007), No. 47,982.

116. *Colour-Kingdom* (New York: Agni Press, 1974), 15.

Bibliography

BOOKS BY SRI CHINMOY

Note: Sri Chinmoy is the author of over 1,500 published works and only those cited in this book are listed here. With a few exceptions, references have been made to the original editions (if not cited, the date of the earliest edition is given in square brackets). The most complete and readily available collection of Sri Chinmoy's works is found at the website www.srichinmoylibrary.com. The Collected Works of Sri Chinmoy from Ganapati Press, located in Oxford and Lyon, is now under way in preparation for Sri Chinmoy's birth centenary in 2031. A number of volumes have been published non-sequentially. For information on this undertaking, see www.ganapatipress.org

Chandelier. Pondicherry: Sri Aurobindo Ashram, 1959.
Our Path. New York: Sri Chinmoy Lighthouse, 1970.
My Lord's Secrets Revealed. New York: Herder and Herder, 1971.
Songs of the Soul. New York: Herder and Herder, 1971.
Arise, Awake! Thoughts of a Yogi. New York: Frederick Fell, 1972.
My Ivy league Leaves. New York: Sri Chinmoy Lighthouse, 1972.
Astrology, The Supernatural and the Beyond. New York: Aum Publications, 1973.
The Dance of Life, Parts 1–20. Santurce, Puerto Rico: Aum Press, 1973.
Death and Reincarnation: Eternity's Voyage. New York: Aum Publications, 1973.
Europe-Blossoms. Santurce, Puerto Rico: Aum Press, 1973.
The Garden of Love-Light, Part 1. Santurce, Puerto Rico: Aum Press, 1973.
God's Hour. New York: Sky Publishers, 1973.
Kundalini: The Mother-Power. Santurce, Puerto Rico: Aum Press, 1973.
Promised Light from the Beyond. New York: Aum Publications, 1973.
Art's Life and the Soul's Light. New York: Agni Press, 1974.
Beyond Within: A Collection of Writings 1964-1974 by Sri Chinmoy. New York: Agni Press, 1974.

Canada Aspires, Canada Receives, Canada Achieves, Part 2. New York: Agni Press, 1974.

Colour-Kingdom. New York: Agni Press, 1974.

Earth's Cry Meets Heaven's Smile, Books 1-2. Santurce, Puerto Rico: Aum Press, 1974.

Eternity's Soul-Bird, Part 1. New York: Agni Press, 1974.

Fifty Freedom-Boats to One Golden Shore, Part 2. New York: Agni Press, 1974.

Fifty Freedom-Boats to One Golden Shore, Part 3. New York: Agni Press, 1974.

Fifty Freedom-Boats to One Golden Shore, Part 4. New York: Agni Press, 1974.

A Galaxy of Beauty's Stars. New York: Agni Press, 1974.

The Goal Is Won. New York: Agni Press, 1974.

God, Avatars and Yogis. New York: Agni Press, 1974.

God-Life: Is It a Far Cry? New York: Agni Press, 1974.

A God-Lover's Earth-Heaven Life, Part 1. New York: Agni Press, 1974.

The Golden Boat, Parts 1-20. New York: Sri Chinmoy Lighthouse, 1974.

The Hunger of Darkness and the Feast of Light, Part 1. New York: Agni Press, 1974.

I am Telling You a Great Secret: You Are a Fantastic Dream of God: Children's Questions on God. New York: Agni Press, 1974.

The Illumination of Life-Clouds, Parts 1–2. New York: Agni Press, 1974.

The Journey of Silver Dreams. New York: Agni Press, 1974.

Life-tree Leaves. New York: Agni Press, 1974.

Mind-Confusion and Heart-Illumination, Part 1–2. New York: Agni Press, 1974.

My Maple Tree. Ottawa: Bhakti Press, 1974.

Perfection-World. New York: Agni Press, 1974.

Problems! Problems! Are They Really Problems? Part 1. New York: Agni Press, 1974.

Realisation-Soul and Manifestation Goal. New York: Agni Press, 1974.

Service-Boat and Love-Boatman, Parts 1–2. New York: Agni Press, 1974.

Supreme, I Sing Only for You. New York: Agni Press, 1974.

Surrender's Unlimited Power. New York: Agni Press, 1974.

Why the Masters Don't Mix. New York: Agni Press, 1974.

The Wings of Light, Parts 1–20. New York: Agni Press, 1974.

The Vision of God's Dawn. New York: Agni Press, 1974.

Earth-bound Journey and Heaven-bound Journey. New York: Agni Press, 1975.

Eternity's Breath: Aphorisms and Essays. New York: Agni Press, 1975.

Fifty Freedom-Boats to One Golden Shore, Part 6. New York: Agni Press, 1975.

God-Journey's Perfection-Return. New York: Agni Press, 1975.

The Garden of Love-Light, Part 3. New York: Agni Press, 1975.

Pole-Star Promise-Light, Part 2. New York: Agni Press, 1975.

Supreme, Teach Me How to Surrender. New York: Agni Press, 1975.

Transcendence-Perfection. New York: Agni Press, 1975.

Flame-Waves: Questions Answered at the United Nations, Part 7. New York: Agni Press, 1976.

God the Supreme Musician. Revised 2nd edition. New York: Agni Press, 1976.

The Inner Hunger. New York: Agni Press, 1976.

Nineteen American Mothers and Nineteen American Sons with Sri Chinmoy. New York: Agni Press, 1976.

Soulful Questions and Fruitful Answers. New York: Agni Press, 1976.

Aspiration-Glow and Dedication-Flow, Part 1. New York: Agni Press, 1977.

Conversations with the Master. New York: Agni Press, 1977.

The Doubt-World. New York: Agni Press, 1977.

Ego and Self-Complacency. New York: Agni Press, 1977.

God and the Cosmic Game. New York: Agni Press, 1977.

Inspiration-Garden and Aspiration-Leaves. New York: Agni Press, 1977.

The Meditation-World. New York: Agni Press, 1977.

Miracles, Emanations and Dreams. New York: Agni Press, 1977.

Obedience: A Supreme Virtue. New York: Agni Press, 1977.

Soul-education for the Family-World. New York: Agni Press, 1977.

A Soulful Cry versus a Fruitful Smile. New York: Agni Press, 1977.

Everest-Aspiration. New York: Agni Press, 1978.

Flame-Waves: Questions Answered at the United Nations, Part 12. New York: Agni Press, 1978.

Ten Thousand Flower-Flames, Parts 1–100. New York: Agni Press, 1979–1983.

Wisdom-Waves in New York, Part 1. New York: Agni Press, 1979.

A Peace-collecting Pilgrim-Soul. New York: Agni Press, 1980.

Sound and Silence, Part 1. New York: Agni Press, 1982.

Tomorrow's Dawn. New York: Agni Press, 1982.

Twenty-Seven Thousand Aspiration-Plants, Parts 1–270. New York: Agni Press, 1983–1998.

Khama Karo. New York: Agni Press, 1987.

Meditation: Man-Perfection in God-Satisfaction. New York: Agni Press, 1989 [1978].

My Silver Jubilee Rainbow-Heart-Whispers. New York: Agni Press, 1989.

My Father Shashi Kumar Ghosh: Affection-Life, Compassion-Heart, Illumination-Mind, by Madal. New York: Agni Press, 1992.

The Unreal Heights of Real Absurdities. New York: Agni Press, 1992.

My Heart-Melody. New York: Agni Press, 1994.

To the Streaming Tears of My Mother's Heart and to the Brimming Smiles of My Mother's Soul, by Madal. New York: Agni Press, 1994.

World-Destruction: Never, Impossible! Part 1. New York: Agni Press, 1994.

Commentaries on the Vedas, Upanishads and Bhagavad Gita: The Three Branches of India's Life-Tree. New York: Aum Publications, 1996.

Four Hundred Song-Birds: Blue, Green, White, Red, Parts 1–4. New York: Agni Press, 1996.

My Consulate Years. New York: Agni Press, 1996.

My Morning Begins. New York: Agni Press, 1996.

Two God-Amusement-Rivals: My Heart-Song-Beauty and my Life-Dance-Fragrance, Parts 1–13. New York: Agni Press, 1996.

Yoga and the Spiritual Life. New York: Aum Publications, 1996 [1970].

Professor-Children: God's Reality-Fruits. New York: Agni Press, 1997.

Blessingful Invitations from the University-World. New York: Agni Press, 1998.

My Brother Chitta, by Madal. New York: Agni Press, 1998.

My Flute. New York: Aum Publications, 1998 [1972].

My Lord's Lotus-Feet versus My Devotion-heart, Part 1. New York: Agni Press, 1998.

Philosopher-Thinkers: The Power-Towers of the Mind and Poet-Seers: The Fragrance-Hours of the Heart in the West. New York: Agni Press, 1998.

Seventy-Seven Thousand Service-Trees, Parts 1–50. New York: Agni Press, 1998-2009.

My Morning Soul-Body Prayers, Parts 1–11. New York: Agni Press, 1999.

My Christmas-New Year-Vacation-Aspiration–Prayers, Part 1–61. New York: Agni Press, 2000–2008.

Here and Now. New York: Agni Press, 2001.

Sail, My Heart-boat, Sail, Part 1. New York: Agni Press, 2001.

The Oneness of the Eastern Heart and the Western Mind, Part 1. New York: Agni Press, 2003.

A Service-Sun, a service-flame, by Chinmoy, 3rd printing. New York: Agni Press, 2003 [1974]).

My Race Prayers, Part 1. New York: Agni Press, 2004.

The Oneness of the Eastern Heart and the Western Mind, Parts 2–3. New York: Agni Press, 2004.

Enthusiasm, Part 10. New York: Agni Press, 2006.

Bela Chale Jai. New York: Agni Press, 2010 [1979].

A Peace-collecting Pilgrim-Soul. New York: Agni Press. 2010.

I Wanted to Be a Seeker of the Infinite. New York: Agni Press, 2012.

My Golden Children. New York: Agni Press, 2013.

Sri Chinmoy Oneness-Home Peace Run: An Ever-Blossoming Dream. New York: Sri Chinmoy Oneness-Home Peace Run, 2014.

Sri Chinmoy Answers, Volume 1, 2nd ed. Oxford and Lyon: Ganapati Press, 2015.

Sri Chinmoy Answers, Volume 2, 2nd ed. Oxford and Lyon: Ganapati Press, 2015.

Sri Chinmoy Speaks. Oxford and Lyon: Ganapati Press, 2015.

United Nations Works, Vol. 1. Oxford and Lyon: Ganapati Press, 2020.

OTHER WORKS

Affeich, Andrée and Maya Azzam. "Sufi Terms and Their Translation from Arabic to English: Diwân al-Hallâž as a Case Study." *Terminalia* 19 (2019): 28–38; DOI: 10.2436/20.2503.01.131.

Alfassa, Mother Mirra. *Collected Works of the Mother,* 17 vols. Pondicherry: Sri Aurobindo Ashram, 2003.

Amrith, Sunil S. *Crossing the Bay of Bengal.* Cambridge, MA: Harvard University Press, 2013.

Aṣṭasāhasrikā-prajnāpāramitā: The Perfection of Wisdom in Eight Thousand Ślokas, translated by Edward Conze. Calcutta: The Asiatic Society, 1970 [1958].

Aurobindo, Sri. *Sri Aurobindo Birth Centenary Library*, 30 vols. Pondicherry: Sri Aurobindo Ashram Publications Department, 1971–1973.

———. *The Life Divine*, 10th ed. Pondicherry: Sri Aurobindo Ashram Trust, 1977.

———. *Collected Works of Sri Aurobindo*; available at http://www.collectedworks ofsriaurobindo.com.

Bādarāyana. *The Vedānta Sutras of Bādarāyana with the commentary by Śaṅkara*, translated by George Thibaut, Part 1 (*Sacred Books of the East*), edited by F. Max Müller, Vol. XXXIV. New York: Dover Publications, 1962.

Banerji, Debashish. "Traditional Roots of Sri Aurobindo's Integral Yoga." *Integral Review* 9, no. 3 (2013): 94–106.

———. ed. *Integral Yoga Psychology: Metaphysics and Transformation as Taught by Sri Aurobindo.* Twin Lakes, Wisconsin: Lotus Press, 2020.

Beckerlegge, Gwilym. *The Ramakrishna Mission: The Making of a Modern Hindu Movement.* Delhi: Oxford University Press, 2006.

Bennett, Vidagdha. *Simplicity and Power: The Poetry of Sri Chinmoy 1971-1981.* New York: Aum Publications, 1991.

———. *Madal the Child.* Mandurah, West Australia: Equilibrium Books, 2010.

———. *A Shakpura Village Boy.* Mandurah, West Australia: Equilibrium Books, 2011.

———. *Under a Blue Pondicherry Sky.* Mandurah, West Australia: Equilibrium Books, 2012.

———. *Reverie.* Mandurah, West Australia: Equilibrium Books, 2013.

Bhagavad Gītā, translated by Winthrop Sargeant, Revised Edition edited by Christopher Chapple, Foreword by Christopher Chapple. Albany, NY: State University of New York Press, 1994.

Biernacki, Loriliai and Philip Clayton, eds. *Panentheism across the World's Traditions.* New York: Oxford University Press, 2014.

Bosch, F. D. K. *The Golden Germ: An Introduction to Indian Symbolism.* New Delhi: Munshiram Manoharlal Publishers, 1994 [1960].

Brown, C. MacKenzie. *Hindu Perspectives on Evolution: Darwin, Dharma and Design.* London: Routledge, 2013.

Chapple, Christopher Key. *Yoga and the Luminous.* Albany: State University of New York Press, 2008.

Chaudhuri, Sukomal. *Contemporary Buddhism in Bangladesh*, 2nd ed. Calcutta: Atisha Memorial Publishing Society, 1987.

Clarke, Mrinali C. with a Foreword by Purushottama Bilimoria. *The Ever-Transcending Quest: A Literary Analysis of the Poetry of Sri Chinmoy.* New Delhi: D. K. Printworld, 2015.

Clayton, Philip. "Panentheisms East and West." *Sophia* 49, no. 2 (2010): 183–191.

Clayton, Philip and Arthur Peacocke, eds., *In Whom We Live and Move and Have Our Being: Panentheistic Reflections on God's Presence in a Scientific World.* Grand Rapids, MI: William B. Eerdman's Publishing Company, 2004.

Dayal, Har. *The Bodhisattva Doctrine in Buddhist Sanskrit Literature.* Delhi: Motilal Banarsidass, 1970 [1932].

Ethnologue: Languages of the World. https://www.ethnologue.com/language/crg.

Flood, Gavin. *The Ascetic Self: Subjectivity, Memory and Tradition.* Cambridge: Cambridge University Press, 2004.

Frese, Pamela R. and S. J. M. Gray, "Trees." In *The Encyclopedia of Religion*, Editor in Chief Mircea Eliade, vol. 15. New York: MacMillan Publishing Company, 1987, 26–33.

Gavrilyuk, Paul and Sarah Coakley, eds. *The Spiritual Senses: Perceiving God in Western Christianity.* Cambridge, UK: Cambridge University Press, 2012.

Gerety, Finnian McKean Moore. *This Whole World Is Om: Song, Soteriology, and the Emergence of the Sacred Syllable,* PhD diss. Harvard University 2015. https://dash.harvard.edu/handle/1/17467527.

Ghosh, Mantu. *Mantu's Heart-Songs.* New York: Agni Press, 2000.

Gordon, Leonard A. *Bengal: The Nationalist Movement 1876-1940.* New York: Columbia University Press, 1974.

———. *Brothers against the Raj: A Biography of Indian Nationalists Sarat and Subhas Chandra Bose.* New York: Columbia University Press, 1990.

The Gospel of the Holy Mother Sri Sarada Devi, Recorded by Her Devotee-Children. Madras: Sri Ramakrishna Math, 1984.

Green, Arthur. *Seek My Face, Speak My Name.* Northvale, NJ: Jacob Aronson Inc., 1992.

Greenough, Paul R. *Prosperity and Misery in Modern Bengal: The Famine of 1943-1944.* Oxford: Oxford University Press, 1982.

Hadot, Pierre, edited with an Introduction by Arnold I. Davidson, translated by Michael Chase. *Philosophy as a Way of Life: Spiritual Exercises from Socrates to Foucault.* Malden, MA: Blackwell Publishing, 1995.

Hartshorne, Charles and William L. Reese, eds. *Philosophers Speak of God*, 2nd ed. Amherst, MA: Humanity Books, 2000 [1953].

Haught, John F. *The New Cosmic Story: Inside Our Awakening Universe.* New Haven: Yale University Press, 2017.

Heehs, Peter. *The Bomb in Bengal: The Rise of Revolutionary Terrorism in India 1900-1910.* Oxford: Oxford University Press, 1993.

———. *The Lives of Sri Aurobindo.* New York: Columbia University Press, 2008.

———. "The Kabbalah, the Philosophie Cosmique and the Integral Yoga: A Study in Cross-Cultural Influence." *Aries* 2, no. 2 (2011): 219–247.

———. ed. *Situating Sri Aurobindo: A Reader.* Oxford: Oxford University Press, 2013.

Holy Bible. New Revised Standard Version with Apocrypha. New York: Oxford University Press, 1989.

Huchzermeyer, Wilfried. *Sri Aurobindo and European Philosophy.* Auroville: Prisma, 2016.

Inden, Ronald B. *Marriage and Rank in Bengali Culture.* Berkeley: University of California Press, 1976.

Jain, Shamini, Jennifer Daubenmier, David Muehsem, Lopsang Rapgay and Deepak Chopra. "Indo-Tibetan Philosophical and Medical Systems: Perspectives on the

Biofield." *Global Advances in Health and Medicine* 4, suppl (2015): 16–24; DOI: 10.7453/gahmj.2015.026.suppl.

Jaini, Padmanabh S. *The Jaina Path of Purification.* Berkeley: University of California Press, 1979.

Jordens, J. T. F. *Dayananda Saraswati: His Life and Ideas.* Delhi: Oxford University Press, 1997.

Kaelber, Walter O. "Asceticism." In *The Encyclopedia of Religion,* Editor in Chief Mircea Eliade, vol. 1. New York: MacMillan Publishing Company, 1987, 441–445.

Kavi, Lallū Lal, *Prema-Sāgara or Ocean of Love, Being a Literal Translation of the Hindi Text of Lallū Lāl Kavi* as Edited by the Late Professor Eastwick, Fully annotated and explained Grammatically, Idiomatically and Exegetically by Frederic Pincott. Westminster, UK: Archibald Constable, 1897.

Kopf, David. *British Orientalism and the Bengal Renaissance: The Dynamics of Indian Modernization* 1773-1835. Berkeley: University of California Press, 1969.

———. *The Brahmo Samaj and the Shaping of the Modern Indian Mind.* Princeton: Princeton University Press, 1979.

Lethcoe, Nancy R. "The Bodhisattva Ideal in the Aṣṭa and Pañca Prajñāpāramitā Sūtras." In *Prajñāpāramitā and Related Systems: Studies in Honor of Edward Conze,* edited by Lewis Lancaster. Berkeley, CA: Center for South and Southeast Asian Studies at the University of California and The Institute for Buddhist Studies, 1977, 263–280.

Levine, Michael P *Pantheism: A Non-theistic Concept of Deity.* New York: Routledge, 1994.

Lipner, Julius. *The Face of Truth: A Study of Meaning and Metaphysics in the Vedāntic Theology of Rāmānuja.* Albany, NY: State University of New York Press, 1986.

Long, Jeffery D. *Jainism: An Introduction.* New York: I. B. Tauris, 2009.

———. "Religious Experience, Hindu Pluralism, and Hope: *Anubhava* in the Tradition of Sri Ramakrishna." *Religions* 10, no. 3 (2019): 210; DOI:10:10.3390/rel10030210.

———. *Historical Dictionary of Hinduism,* 2nd ed. Lanham, MD: Rowman & Littlefield, 2020.

McDermott, Robert A., ed. *Six Pillars: Introductions to the Major Works of Sri Aurobindo.* Chambersburg, PA: Wilson Books, 1974.

———, ed. *The Essential Aurobindo.* Great Barrington, MA: Lindisfarne Press, 1987.

Maitra, S. K. *The Meeting of the East and the West in Sri Aurobindo's Philosophy.* Pondicherry: Sri Aurobindo Ashram Trust, 1968 [1956].

Miles, Margaret R. *Plotinus on Body and Beauty.* Malden, MA: Blackwell Publishers, 1999.

Newall, Venetia. "Egg." In *Encyclopedia of Religion,* Editor in Chief Mircea Eliade, vol. 5. New York: MacMillan Publishing Company, 1987, 36–37.

Nikhilananda, Swami, translated. *The Gospel of Sri Ramakrishna,* 7th Printing. New York: Ramakrishna-Vivekananda Center, 1984 [1942].

Nikhilananda, Swami, *Vivekananda: A Biography*. New York: Ramakrishna-Vivekananda Center, 1964 [1953].

Olivelle, Patrick. *Upaniṣads*. New York: Oxford University Press, 1996.

———. "Heart in the Upaniṣads." *Rivista di Studi Sudasiatici* 1 (2006): 51–67.

Panikkar, Raimundo. *The Vedic Experience: Mantra Mañjari, An Anthology of the Vedas for Modern Man and Contemporary Celebration*. Delhi: Motilal Banarsidass, 1977.

Pedersen, Kusumita P. "The Hindu Renaissance in Bengal." *World Faiths Insight* New Series 21 (February 1989): 35–46.

———. "The Nature of God in the Philosophy of Sri Chinmoy." *ARC, The Journal of the Faculty of Religious Studies, McGill University* 34 (2006): 159–180.

———. "The Creativity of Sri Chinmoy." Paper given at the Convening of the Parliament of the World's Religions, Barcelona, July 2004.

———. "Sri Chinmoy's Work at the United Nations: Spirituality and the Power of Silence." *CrossCurrents* 60, no. 3 (September 2010): 339–351. Special Issue on Religion and the United Nations edited by Azza Karam and Matthew Weiner.

———. "Sri Chinmoy's Contributions to Interreligious Harmony." In *Unity in Diversity,* edited by Tapan Camillus de Rozario, Eva Sadia Saad and M. Tazuddin, publication of the 2nd International Conference on Interreligious and Intercultural Dialogue, Centre for Interreligious and Intercultural Dialogue (CIID), University of Dhaka, November 2010, 53–63.

———. "Sri Ramakrishna and Sri Chinmoy." *Prabuddha Bharata or Awakened India* 116, no. 1 (January 2011): 109–114.

———. "The Poetry of Sri Chinmoy: A Philosopher in the Heart." In *Antonio T. de Nicolás: Poet of Eternal Return,* edited by Christopher Key Chapple. Ahmedabad: Sriyogi Publications & Nalanda International, 2014, 299–310.

———. "Uniting Sports and Spirituality." *Hinduism Today,* April/ May/ June 2018, 56–63. https://www.hinduismtoday.com/modules/smartsection/item.php?itemid =5854.

———. "Sri Chinmoy's Vision of Peace." In *Beacons of Dharma*, edited by Christopher Patrick Miller, Michael Reading, and Jeffery D. Long. New York: Lexington Books, 2019, 235–250.

———. "This *Prema* Dwells in the Heart of Them All: Swami Vivekananda on Love and Compassion." In *Vivekananda: His Life, Legacy and Liberative Ethics,* edited by Rita D. Sherma. New York: Lexington Books, 2020, 103–124.

———. "Sri Chinmoy on the Nature and Goals of Contemplative Practice." In *Contemplative Studies and Hinduism: Meditation, Devotion, Prayer, and Worship*, edited by Rita D. Sherma and Purushottama Bilimoria. New York: Routledge, 2021, 67–84.

———. "Sri Chinmoy's Philosophy of Nature." *Journal of Dharma Studies* 4, no. 1 (April 2021). Special Issue on Ecotheology edited by Christopher Fici and Kenneth Valpey.

Qanungo, Suniti Bushan. *A History of Chittagong,* vol. 2. Chittagong: Dipankar Qanungo, 2010.

Radhakrishnan, Sarvepalli. *The Principal Upaniṣads*, translated and with an Introduction. New York: Humanities Press, 1953.

Rāmānuja, *Brahma Sūtras Śrī-Bhāsya,* translated by Swami Vireśwarānanda and Swami Ādidevānanda, Kolkata: Advaita Aśrama, 2012.

Rawal, Sanjay. "3100: Run and Become." New York: Illumine: Social Change thru Media, 2018. Length 1:30:00. https://3100film.com.

The Rigveda; The Earliest Religious Poetry of India, vol. 3, translated by Stephanie W. Jamison and Joel P. Brereton. New York: Oxford University Press, 2014.

Rollosson, Natabara and Sanjay Rawal. "Challenging Impossibility." New York: Illumine: Social Change thru Media, 2011. Length 27:54. http://www.challenging impossibility.com.

Samuel, Geoffrey and Jay Johnston, eds. *Religion and the Subtle Body in Asia and the West.* New York: Routledge, 2013.

Śāntideva, *The Bodhicaryāvatāra*, translated by Kate Crosby and Andrew Skilton. New York: Oxford University Press, 1998.

Saradananda, Swami. *Sri Ramakrishna the Great Master*, tr. Swami Jagadananda, 6th ed. Chennai: Sri Ramakrishna Math, 2008 [1952].

Scholem, Gershom G., *Major Trends in Jewish Mysticism*. New York: Schocken Books, 1961 [reprinted from the 3rd revised edition, 1954].

Siegrist, Saudamini. "The Writing of Devotion: Teresa of Avila, Richard Crashaw, Julian of Norwich, 'Cloud of Unknowing', John Donne, Thérèse of Lisieux, Emily Dickinson, Sri Chinmoy Kumar Ghose." PhD diss. New York University 1999. *Dissertation Abstracts International,* Section A: The Humanities and Social Sciences 60, no. 5 (1999): 1545.

Singhvi, L. M. "The Jain Declaration on Nature." In *Jainism and Ecology: Nonviolence in the Web of Life,* edited by Christopher Key Chapple. Cambridge, MA: Harvard University Press, 2002, 217–224.

Tilak, Shrinivas. *Understanding Karma: In Light of Paul Ricoeur's Philosophical Anthropology and Hermeneutics.* Nagpur: International Centre for Cultural Studies India, 2006.

Učida, Norihiko, *Der Bengali-Dialekt von Chittagong: Grammatik, Texte, Wörterbuch.* Wiesbade, Germany: Otto Harrassowitz Verlag, 1970.

Van Schendel, Willem. *A History of Bangladesh.* Cambridge: Cambridge University Press, 2009.

Vireswarananda, Swami. *Teachings of Sri Sarada Devi, The Holy Mother.* Chennai: Sri Ramakrishna Math, 1983.

Vivekananda, Swami. *Collected Works*, 11th ed. Calcutta: Advaita Ashama, 1978.

———. *In Search of God and Other Poems.* Kolkata: Advaita Ashrama, 2003 [1947].

Vrajaprana, Pravrajika. "Bridging the Gap between the Sacred and the Secular: Seva as Ascetic Practice." Paper given at the Annual Conference of the Dharma Academy of North America (DANAM), November 2007.

Wimbush, Vincent L. and Richard Valantasis, eds. *Asceticism.* New York: Oxford University Press, 1995.

Index

Absolute. *See Sat-Cit-Ānanda*
acceptance of the world, 5, 73;
    condition for transformation, 126–31;
    as "our philosophy," 15
Alfassa, Mirra (The Mother), 5–7, 42n,
    68, 73, 87
Ārya Samaj, 4
asceticism, 102n26
aspiration: defined, 54; in the heart, 49;
    in human life, 68
ātman, 65, 71, 79; *antarātman*, 96; in
    the heart, 71
AUM or Om, 49
Aurobindo, Sri, 4–7, 57, 62n55, 73, 80;
    influences, 18n29; Integral Yoga of,
    6–7; life, 6; major works, 6
avatāra, 37

Banerji, Debashish, 18n29
Bengal Famine, 6
Bhagavad Gītā, 7, 47, 79, 104, 104n74,
    115
bhakti. See devotion
Bhattacharya, Pranab Kumar, 8
Bishwas, Ambika Charan, 4
Bishwas, Yogamaya, 1–6
Bliss. *See* Delight
Bodhisattva, 137
Brahman, 25, 46–47, 49, 54, 58–59, 96;
    as Seed, 47, 54; self-transcendence

of, 29; used when referring to
    Sanskrit texts, 23
Brahmo Samaj, 4
breath, 72
Brereton, Joel, 103n65
Bṛhadāraṇyaka Upaniṣad, 97
Buddha, 37

chakras: *ajñā* chakra or "third eye," 94;
    heart chakra. *See* heart; as portals to
    macrocosmic, 71
Chāndogya Upaniṣad, 34, 46, 53
Chinmoy, Sri (Chinmoy Kumar Ghose):
    art works, Jharna-Kala and Soul-
    Birds, 12–13; birth and childhood,
    1–5; Divine Enterprises (small
    businesses), 14; early spiritual
    life, 5, 7; Indian Consulate, work
    at, 9; interfaith movement in, 12;
    journey to America, 9; life on Sri
    Aurobindo Ashram, 5–9; music and
    composition, 11; Peace Run, 14;
    running, 14; Sri Chinmoy Centre,
    9–10; Sri Chinmoy Marathon Team,
    14; Thant, U, 11; United Nations,
    11–12; U Thant Peace Award, 11;
    weightlifting, 13; writings, 10–11
Chittagong, city and region, 1–3
Chittagong Armory Raid, 4
Christianity, 53, 97, 139n20

153

About the Author

Kusumita P. Pedersen is professor emerita of Religious Studies at St. Francis College and received her doctorate in Buddhist Studies from Columbia University. She is Chair of the Interfaith Center of New York and a Trustee and member of the Climate Action Task Force of the Parliament of the World's Religions, as well as a member of the Climate Working Group of the Committee of Religious NGOs at the United Nations. She is co-author of *Faith for Earth: A Call for Action* (UN Environment Programme and Parliament of the World's Religions, 2020) and co-author of *Global Ethics in Practice: Historical Backgrounds, Current Issues and Future Prospects* (Edinburgh University Press, 2016) and has written a number of articles and book chapters on environmental ethics, human rights, and the interfaith movement. She has compiled and edited librettos for two works by Philip Glass: *Symphony No. 5: Bardo, Requiem and Nirmāṇakāya* (1999) and *The Passion of Ramakrishna* (2006). A student of Sri Chinmoy (1931–2007) since 1971, she has published a number of essays on his philosophy and poetry.